ABOUT THE AUTHOR

SHEILA MARGARET OTTLEY, the daughter of a master printer, was born at Hoyland in 1923, in an old house at which she still resides, of two families both deeply rooted in South Yorkshire.

She was educated at Ecclesfield Grammar School and St Hugh's College, Oxford, where at the age of 20, during the Second World War, she took an Honours Degree in English Language and Literature.

After spending some years as a schoolteacher and as a civil servant in the London area, for the major part of her working life she ran the library and information service at a United Steel Companies (later British Steel Corporation) research centre in Sheffield.

Her first published work took the form of short stories and poems on the children's page of the *Yorkshire Weekly Post* during the early 'thirties. As Margaret Ottley she has contributed letters and articles to *The Dalesman*, the *Yorkshire Ridings Magazine* and other regional periodicals. For many years she contributed regularly to the correspondence column of the Yorkshire Post. Her first book-length work is *While Martha Told the Hours*.

Her interests include walking, railway history, reading biographies and travel books, cooking, listening to classical music and, as light relief, watching the occasional 'whodunnit', frame of snooker or wildlife programme on television.

WHILE MARTHA TOLD THE HOURS

WHILE MARTHA TOLD THE HOURS

A South Yorkshire Tapestry

by

Sheila Margaret Ottley

Illustrated by Lynda Lawrence

With a Foreword by W.R. Mitchell
former Editor of 'The Dalesman'

BRIDGE PUBLICATIONS

PENISTONE · ENGLAND

Bridge Publications
2 Bridge Street, Penistone
Sheffield S30 6AJ

Copyright © Sheila Margaret Ottley 1988

Illustrations copyright © Lynda Lawrence 1988

First Published 1988

All rights Reserved. No part of this publication
may be reproduced, stored in a retrieval system
or transmitted, in any form or by any means,
electronic, mechanical, photocopying,
recording, or otherwise, without the prior permission
of the Copyright owner

British Library Cataloguing in Publication Data

Ottley, Sheila Margaret
 While Martha told the hours : a South York-
shire tapestry
 1. (Metropolitan County) South Yorkshire.
Hoyland. Social life, history
 I. Title

 ISBN 0-947934-18-9
 ISBN 0-947934-17-0 Pbk

Printed and Bound in Great Britain by
Whitstable Litho Printers Ltd., Whitstable, Kent

In memory of my father, Cecil Ottley,
who once said,
'If you don't write these things down,
they will be forgotten.'

Contents

Preface
Foreword
Area Map
Location Map
Town Map

1	The U.D.C. and Local Services	1
2	Shopping and Shopkeepers	32
3	Pubs and Clubs	69
4	Trade and Industry	79
5	Road and Rail	105
6	Education	125
7	Church and Chapel	144
8	Sport and Entertainment	167
9	Medicine and Health	194
10	Streets and Home Life	218

Index

Preface

A true Cockney is said to be someone who was born within sound of Bow bells. If a true Hoylander is someone born within sound of 'Old Martha', I can claim to be one, having been born and lived for many years a hundred yards or so from the Town Hall. Hence the viewpoint of this book is Hoyland town centre, and references to Hoyland Common and Elsecar consequently tend to be peripheral.

The memories the book contains are mine and my parents'. I should like, however, to express my thanks to those personal friends and to members of the staff of Barnsley Central Library who have helped to verify certain details.

September 1988

Netherfield House
Hoyland

Foreword

MARGARET OTTLEY's amazing ability to recall incidents from her life in South Yorkshire was evident in the many letters she sent me for publication during the years I edited *The Dalesman*. She has the enviable gift of almost total recall and writes succinctly, in great detail, about the incidents, characters, customs and events of her South Yorkshire community.

Letters sent by Miss Ottley to *The Dalesman* and to many other periodicals are usually short. We in Yorkshire value brevity. I was delighted to learn that she has put all her 'little bits' about the life and times of Hoyland into a coherent, ever-interesting and historically most valuable review of the community as it was within living memory. I commend her as a local historian and also as the author of *While Martha Told the Hours*.

The oldest among us have lived through many profound social changes. Margaret Ottley informs and entertains. She tells us in an early chapter not only about the establishment of the Urban District Council but also that when printing the Socialists' election posters the author's father used a quality red ink, which did not fade to yellow in strong sunlight! In the twenty years up to 1940, acres of farmland vanished under council and private estates built of brick. Margaret Ottley presents the fact and tells us some corners had been 'cut' in the construction of the Council property, and the kitchen walls were of bare brick. Every statistic has a homely lining.

A dalesman I was questioning said: 'What's ta want to go pokin' about in t' deeard past for?' It is a dull person who is not interested in what has gone before. Now that children seem more interested in watching television than listening to one of the old 'uns telling tales about the family, it is vital for perceptive folk like Margaret Ottley to jot down local facts, figures and yarns for the edification of generations yet unborn.

Throughout the book, the bare facts are illuminated by many illustrations drawn from the author's experience, such as mother's insistence, when Margaret was due to see the school doctor, that she must breathe through her nose, 'or they'll say you've got to have your tonsils out.'

I must confess that I have not yet set foot in Hoyland. When I go there, I will feel at home, having read Margaret Ottley's warm-hearted record of this Yorkshire community. I commend the book without reservation, not only for what it is but because I know it represents a lifetime of diligent research by a native.

1988 W.R. MITCHELL

AREA MAP

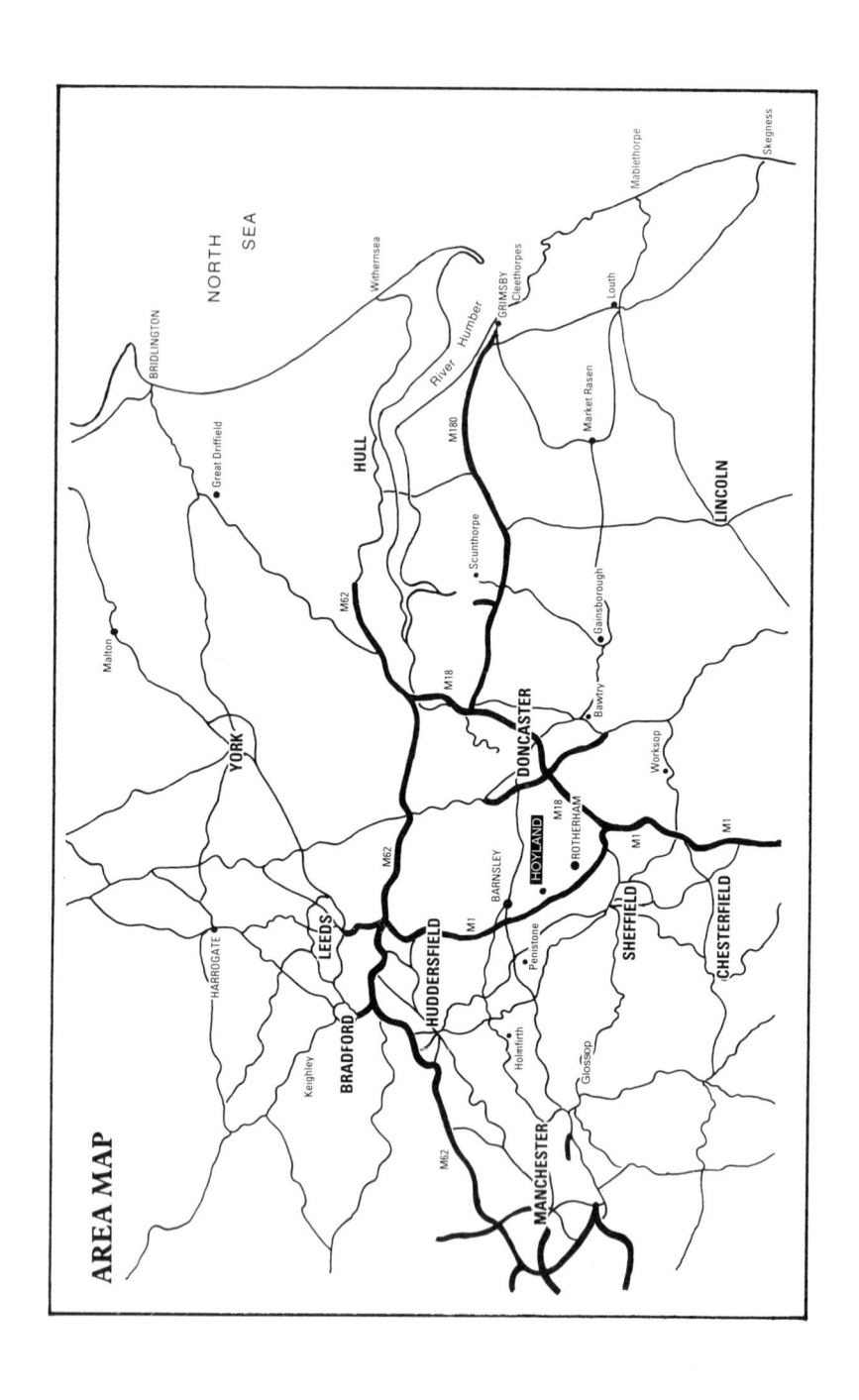

LOCATION MAP

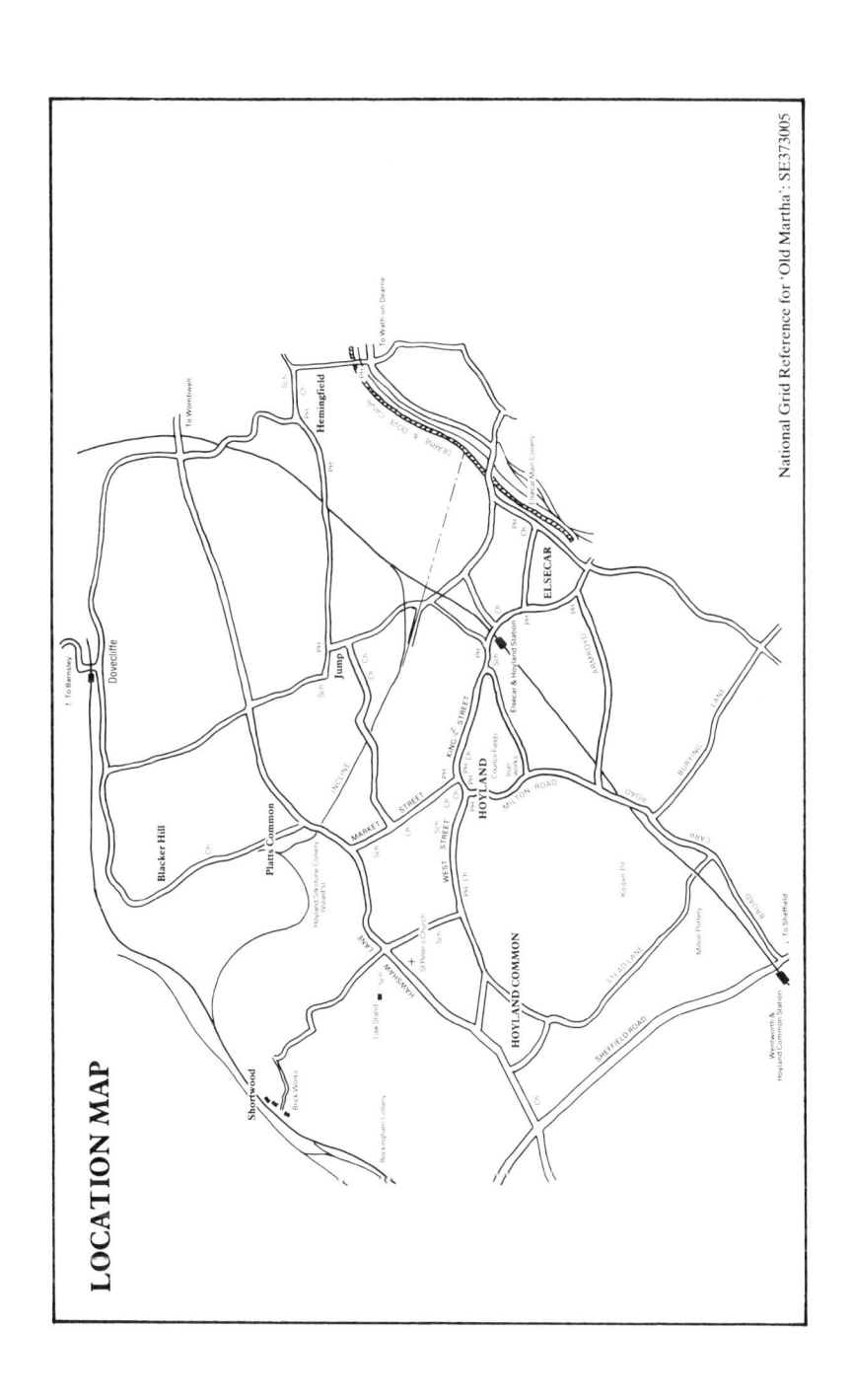

National Grid Reference for 'Old Martha': SE373005

TOWN MAP

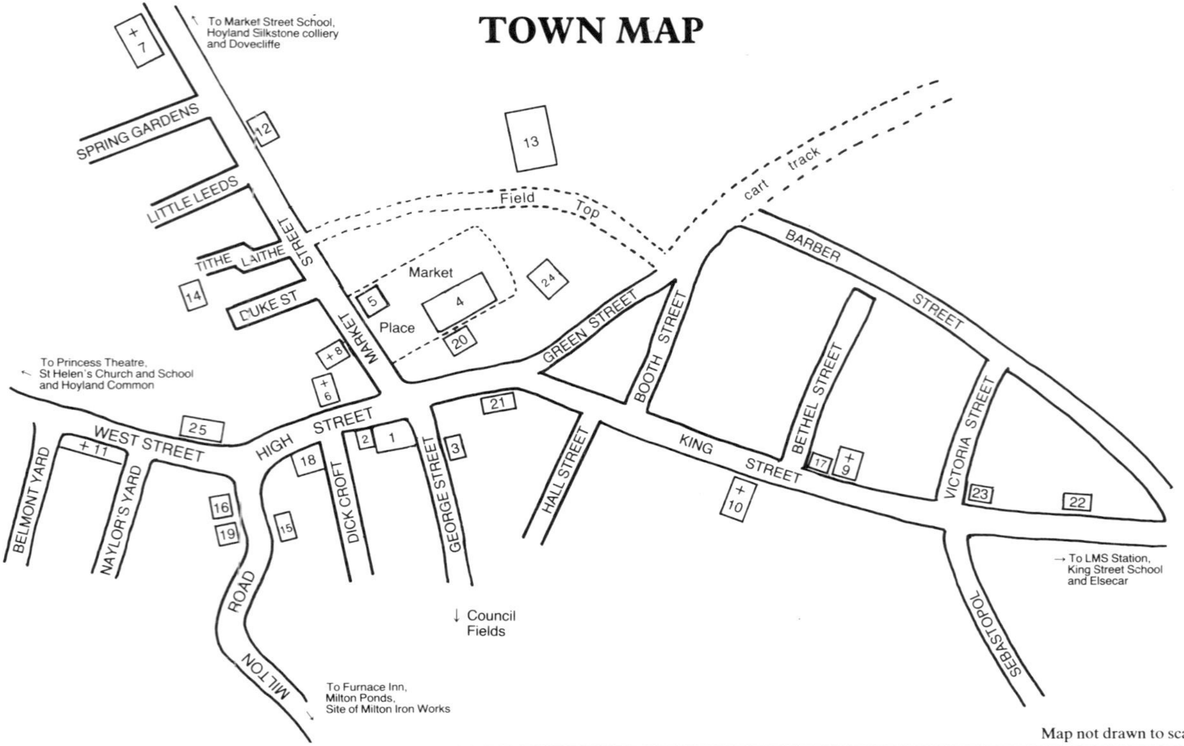

Map not drawn to scale

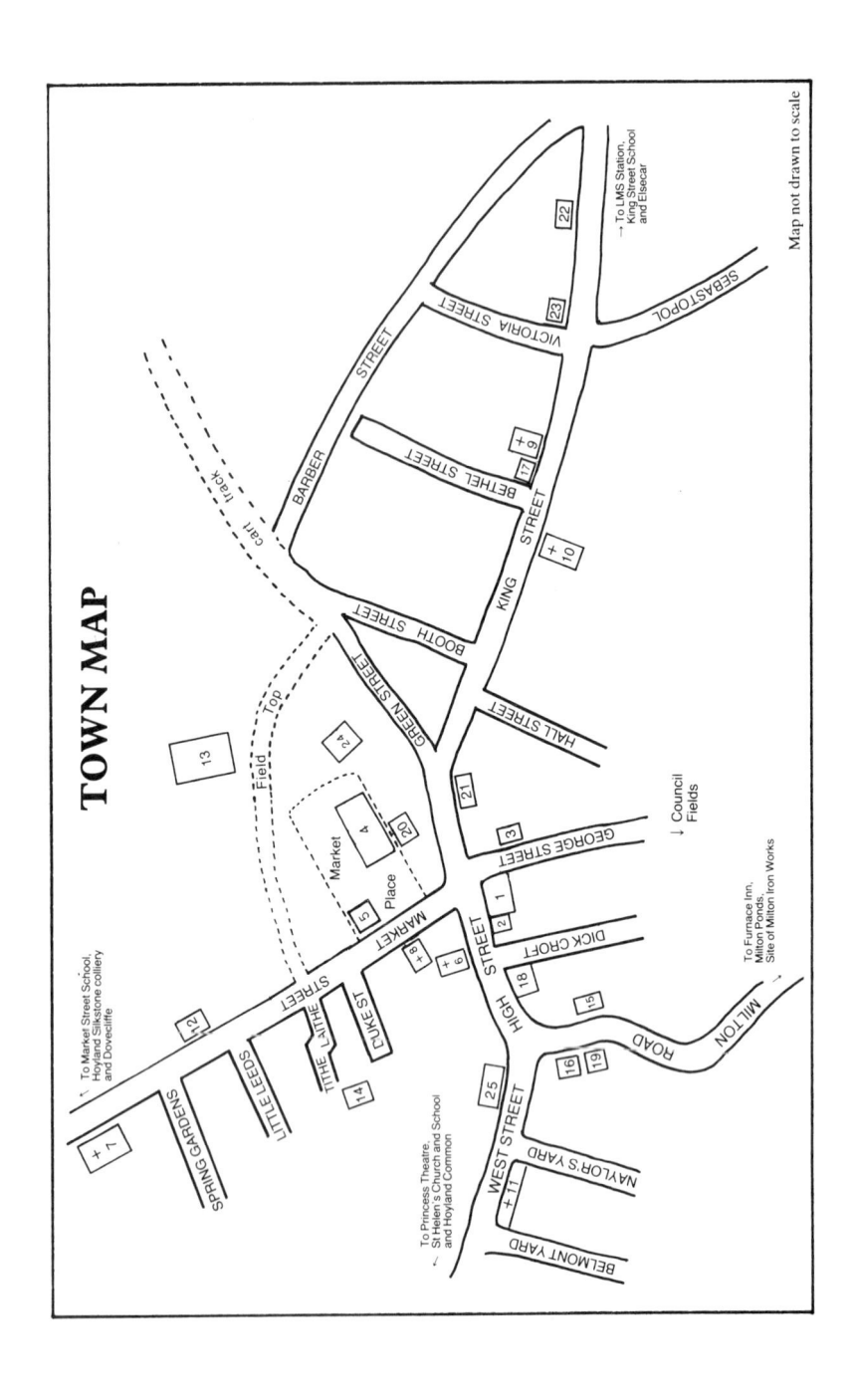

Key to Town Map

1 Town Hall
2 Fire Station
3 Police Station
4 Cinema
5 Little Infants' School
6 John Knowles Church
7 St Andrew's Church
8 Wesleyan Chapel
9 Bethel New Connexion Chapel

10 Mount Tabor Primitive Methodist Chapel
11 Bethany Mission
12 Post Office
13 Manor Farm
14 Tithe Barn
15 Smithy
16 Ball Inn
17 Five Alls
18 Gardeners' Arms

19 Gate Inn
20 Strafford Arms
21 Turf Tavern
22 Rock Inn
23 Queen's Head
24 Greenfield House
25 Gas Showroom

CHAPTER ONE

The U.D.C.
and Local Services

Origins

'HOILAND' is first mentioned in the Domesday Book. Its name is thought to be derived either from the Danish 'hoi', meaning 'hill-land', or from the Old Norse 'haugr', meaning a hill. (Pre-Conquest Yorkshire was a Viking area.) Though either describes its location, the former seems the likelier of the two. (Repetition of the kind found in 'hill-land land' occurs in various other English place names.) It is shown on a map dated 1086 in which year, according to the Domesday Survey, it comprised one manor and two carucates of land (a carucate being a piece of ground sufficient to provide work for one plough). Medieval Hoyland's history was undistinguished, though some surviving records link it to important events and issues of those days. In 1310 Robert de Newmarch is said to have led a band of Hoyland men to Berwick-on-Tweed, to fight the Scottish followers of Robert the Bruce. In 1379, during Richard II's reign, a time of high taxation and great unrest, a poll tax was levied on the fifty-eight people of Hoyland who were then over the age of sixteen, to finance the wars against Scotland and France.

It is important, however, when dealing with this early period, not to confuse references to this Hoyland with those to High Hoyland on the far side of Barnsley, in those days known simply as 'Hoyland' too. (The Vicar of Hoyland who was taken to court for stealing a chalice and cope from Cawthorne church certainly came from High Hoyland, since Hoyland Nether, which was for centuries in the parish of Wath-upon-Dearne, had not even a chapel-of-ease within its boundaries until the early eighteenth century.) It was no doubt to distinguish them from each other, as well as from the hamlet of Upper or, as it was sometimes called, Over Hoyland, that the adjectives 'Nether' and 'High' were later appended.

During the Middle Ages the dense forest covering this part of South Yorkshire, and mentioned in the first chapter of *Ivanhoe*, was gradually cleared to make way for farming and slowly, both then and in Tudor, Stuart and Hanoverian times, the population of the township grew. By 1801 the number of people in Hoyland Nether had risen to 823. In his *Topographical Directory of England*, which was published in 1848, Samuel Lewis records their number as having risen to 2,597, adding that 'the chapelry' ('Hoyland Chapel' being the name by which St Peter's Church was in its early days known) 'comprises 2,008 acres of which 806 acres are arable, 955 grassland, 117 wood, 95 in homesteads and orchards, and 34 canal.' He also states that the Lord of the Manor is Earl Fitzwilliam, and that the district abounds in iron and coal.

It was thanks to the exploitation of these two minerals that Hoyland's population had further risen to 12,464 by 1901. In the

THE U.D.C. AND LOCAL SERVICES 3

eighteenth and early nineteenth centuries the Fitzwilliams had built adjacent Elsecar, to house their colliery workers. Platts Common had grown in late Victorian times to house Hoyland Silkstone's mining families. Hoyland Common, with its gridiron of streets, likewise owed its Victorian development to mining, men who worked at the Lidgett and iron-stone pits living there, as well as some employed at Rockingham.

Hoyland Town Hall and 'Old Martha'

The story of modern Hoyland can be dated from 1891, during which year a Local Board was formed to run the affairs of this growing centre of population. The Board had its headquarters in the Town Hall, a structure neither new nor purpose-built. A gaunt, two-storey edifice of stone on the corner of High Street and George Street, with oblong windows and tall chimney stacks, it had been built fifty years previously, in 1840, at a cost of £1,100, to serve as a Mechanics' Institute where working men could attend classes and lectures meant to 'improve' their minds. Then in 1876 the town had bought it, for considerably less than it cost to build, using money raised in 1858 by selling some common lands to Earl Fitzwilliam.

In the same year that the Board was formed, however, the building's appearance was much enhanced by the addition of a graceful clock tower built of Derbyshire stone, 'for the perpetual use and benefit of the people of Hoyland', at the expense of Mrs Martha Knowles whose grocery business, just across the square, was owned in later years by Rowland Cross. Several local names were associated with its construction. The architect was Walter John Sykes of West Bank House, the builder Francis Guest Robinson of Birdwell. The job of altering the Town Hall front, building the centre of it out to support the tower, went to a Hoyland builder named John Hague. The opening ceremony, performed by Mrs Knowles, was followed by a day of public feasting.

Six years later, in 1897, perhaps encouraged by the gratitude with which her gift of a town clock was received, Mrs Knowles also gave the clock in St Peter's tower, 'as a thank-offering to God on the completion of the sixtieth year of the long and happy reign of our beloved Queen Victoria.' In 1902, 'two birds were killed with one stone' when, to commemorate the Queen's long and prosperous reign and the Coronation of her son Edward VII, an unusual grey granite horse trough, with a smaller trough for dogs to drink from below, was placed at the roadside in front of the main Town Hall doors, which faced across the street below the clock tower.

In the next quarter of a century, the Town Hall's exterior underwent no further alterations. By the mid-twenties it had acquired that air of changelessness typical of Victorian civic buildings. The clock tower in the intervening years had become a symbol of the town itself, its distinctive outline, seen against the sky, welcoming home rail travellers approaching Elsecar and Hoyland Station from the south. The clock, affectionately dubbed 'Old Martha', had no chimes but, winter and summer, rain or shine, duly and sonorously struck the hours. (I remember lying in bed on New Year's Eve a few years later as a teenager and, because New Year's Day was my birthday, shuddering slightly on hearing it strike twelve, consigning both another calendar year and another year of my life into oblivion.)

Nevertheless, despite appearances, changes were imminent. The inaccurately-labelled Town Hall Square (not so much a square as a wide confluence of roads) had become so unaccustomedly busy with traffic that a policeman was placed on duty there, directing the increasing number of vans, lorries and motor-cars. Moreover, buses had appeared on the scene, and the main stop for those going towards Barnsley was directly in front of the Town Hall façade. About the end of the 'twenties, therefore, the horse trough was removed, partly because it now formed an obstruction to traffic and partly because draught horses of the kind which once pulled brewery drays and delivery vans were becoming a thing of the past. At the same time, to widen the pavement and make room for people to queue for buses, the steps leading up to the main Town Hall doors were removed and a small side entrance

THE U.D.C. AND LOCAL SERVICES

with a single door was constructed round the corner, facing West Street.

About this time, a gentlemen's convenience was opened in the centre of the town. It was underground, in the angle of the Town Hall at its George Street end, discreetly screened by boards on which were posted notices of poll, posters issued by the Ministry of Health urging people to have their children immunized, and similar items of instruction and exhortation. The ladies' convenience, at the other end, was inside the Town Hall itself, on the ground floor next to the Rating Office.

A less obvious change, which took place in the 'thirties, was the replacement of 'Martha's' weight-and-chain system with an electric movement, an innovation which, though it saved work, rendered her boom less impressive and also meant that, during a power cut, she was immobilized like any kitchen wall clock.

No further structural changes then took place until under a town centre re-development programme the Town Hall, which had seemed indestructible, was closed during June 1973 and was immediately demolished. The clock tower, about whose removal there had been a considerable outcry, was taken down carefully, stone by stone, with the vague promise that one day it might be re-built if some suitable site could be found. (Elsecar Park and the John Knowles Memorial Church were two places suggested, but neither of these ideas was followed up.) The stones, each bearing a number, were taken to the council yard in West Street. The clock itself was entrusted to the care of Wm. Potts & Sons of Leeds, the firm of clock-makers which had installed it.

The Urban District Council

Under the terms of the Local Government Act of 1894 the Local Board, still only three years old, was replaced by an Urban District Council, which itself was to come to an end eighty years on when, as part of the sweeping local government changes of 1974 Hoyland, like Wombwell, Worsbrough, Dodworth and other previously independent places round about, was absorbed into the Metropolitan Borough of Barnsley.

The Council had twelve members, three to each ward, the four wards being named Hoyland, Hoyland Common, Elsecar and St Peter's. (St Peter's Ward comprised Platts Common and most of the area between Hawshaw Lane and West Street.) Of the councillors representing each ward, one came up for re-election every year, each time for a further three-year period.

Most of the earliest councillors to serve were local businessmen. Among them was Councillor William Ottley, my father's uncle, a King Street draper and Princess Theatre impresario. Never a person to be trifled with, he took public health as a pillar of his platform, fulminating in one election address about the town's refuse collection system and alleging that 'night soil' (from earth closets) was left to await collection near ratepayers' doors and (through a printer's error or slip of the pen) that in the main streets fish-heads could be found 'petrifying' in the sun.

On one occasion during his term of office a circus or menagerie came to town, giving its shows in the old Market Place. Someone with a macabre sense of humour had posters printed telling people that, at a certain time on a certain day, Councillor Ottley would enter the lion's cage, with Councillor Nightingale standing by. (A twist was given to this statement by the fact that Councillor Nightingale was an undertaker, who had his premises down Milton Road.) Determined to have the last laugh, Councillor Ottley did in fact spend some seconds in the cage before the assembled crowd at the stated time. People who knew him have suggested that the lion was perhaps more afraid than he was.

By the inter-war period the Labour Party, whose first M.P. was elected in 1900, was gaining ground in local politics, Hoyland Council in those days including both Independents and Socialists. The former had their election posters printed in neutral black, the latter in bright red. (My father used a quality red ink which did not fade to yellow as quickly as others.) Hoyland Ward was the one most consistent in returning Independents. Elsecar, possibly conditioned by Fitzwilliam paternalism, also elected a number. Perhaps owing to its links with Hoyland Silkstone, and the bitterness when that colliery closed, St Peter's always had Socialist

THE U.D.C. AND LOCAL SERVICES

leanings. Hoyland Common went still further, and at one time was known as 'Little Moscow'.

Two 'characters' serving the Hoyland Ward for many years as Independents were Councillors William Frederick Crabb and Nathaniel Mell. Councillor Crabb, a small, grey-moustached man with a loud, hearty laugh, who was first returned in 1921, was the Elsecar Gas Company's meter reader, and lived in King Street in the end-terrace house immediately above the Wesleyan Manse before moving after his wife's death to West Street with his daughter, Mrs Grace Burdin, and her husband.

The Crabbs, who had quite a large family, suffered a strange tragedy when one of their sons, a bachelor living and working in London, left his lodgings to come home for the Christmas break and, despite a police message broadcast on the 'wireless', was never seen or heard of again.

It was while Mr Crabb was Chairman of the Council, in 1924, that a businessman, Mr Herbert Edwin Key, presented the town with a Chairman's chain of office. Some years later, using the proceeds of a fête, a medallion for the Chairman's wife was purchased. It was a pointed oval and, to symbolize Hoyland's dual rôle as a centre of both mining and agriculture, depicted a miner's lamp and crossed pickaxes, under which was a plough. (This design could until recently be seen on the roadside boards marking the approaches to the former Urban District.) At first the medallion was worn on a ribbon. Then a chain on which to hang it was donated by the two Kenworthy brothers, who were Hoyland Common motor coach proprietors.

Tall, stooping, white-moustached Councillor Mell was an undertaker and joiner whose West Street workshop stood where the back of the Health Centre has been built. He also kept a furniture shop, No. 1 West Street (which is now Taylor's Electrical), from which my parents in their early married years purchased a number of useful household objects including two oblong stools of different sizes, the wooden-railed cot to which I was transferred when I outgrew my frilly 'Treasure' cot, and my toddler-sized wooden rocking chair.

Mr Mell was for many years a magistrate and, as its then longest-serving member, eventually came to be called 'The Father of the Council'. A memorial to him, his two wives and other members of his family, in the form of a grey granite pillar with gold lettering, can be seen to the right of the pathway leading from the upper gateway of St Peter's Churchyard.

Mr Mell's elder son, Percy Wilfrid, took over the undertaking business from him. His younger son, Maurice, a solicitor, who closely resembled his father in looks, became Clerk of the Council at Solihull, where his work for that town was commemorated in the naming of Maurice Mell Avenue. (At his own request Maurice Mell was given an unusual funeral, his cremation ashes being buried at sea at the spot where his wife, who died while on board ship, had been buried earlier.) Councillor Mell's elder daughter, Gladys, married Herbert Evans of Elsecar, a brother of Mrs Amanda Hinton whose husband was for years the landlord of the Strafford Arms. His younger daughter, Dorothy, married the Rev. Eric Kenworthy, a Methodist minister.

Another Hoyland man who served on the Council as an Independent, though he did not always represent the same ward, was Mr William Allen, equally well-known as an architect. Mr Allen, a large, bluff bachelor, left a lasting mark on Hoyland by designing such distinctive features as the John Knowles Church, the Miners' Welfare and the houses on the Longfields Crescent estate. At one time his office was in the small Market Street house, at the corner of Spring Gardens, that is now a dental surgery. During his later years his home was the red-tiled bungalow in West Street which stands opposite the top of Valley Way, and his office a small building in the garden. There he kept a grey parrot which one of his sisters, Mrs Marlowe, brought home from Australia. It had a colourful vocabulary, especially when its beak was being trimmed, an operation needed frequently. It was being more than usually eloquent on one occasion when Mr Makinson, the minister at Hill Street Congregational Chapel, called. Tactfully, the clergyman assured his host that he 'could not quite make out what the bird said.' (Its profane career ended abruptly when

THE U.D.C. AND LOCAL SERVICES 9

some years later, by a bizarre mischance, it fell from its perch and – I suspect it was a New Zealand kea – was fatally impaled on its own beak.)

An Independent councillor for Hoyland Common until his death, which occurred in the 'thirties, was Edwin Cook, a joiner and undertaker in Stead Lane. He was the father of the late Harry Cook (not to be confused with Mr Harry Cook of Tankersley Lane) and the grandfather of Graham Cook, who now runs the same funeral-directing business. There was also, for a brief period, an Independent Hoyland Common councillor named Fred Ireton.

They were, however, greatly outnumbered by the Labour members who at various times represented that ward. Further down Stead Lane, in an end-terrace house not far from the corner of Chapel Street, lived Labour Councillor Frank Burkinshaw (nicknamed 'Staggy' because, I was once told, of the athletic way in which he strode about during his youth), who was in charge of Shortwood Sewage Works. He had also at one time been employed at the old picture house in Central Street, a former Primitive Methodist mission hall, which was named in consequence 'Staggy's Alhambra'.

His wife, Councillor Mary Burkinshaw, a plump, homely-looking woman with spectacles, also served as a Labour member for a time. She was among those sitting on the platform at my first Ecclesfield Grammar School Speech Day, which was held in Ecclesfield Cinema because the school hall was too small for it, and was a distant relative of mine, she and my Great-Grandmother Sarah Ottley both being members of a Silkstone farming family named Mosley.

Other Labour members to serve Hoyland Common over the years included Councillor Albert Laister, a fervent campaigner for miners' rights, and the two Moxon brothers, Herbert Clarence and Claude, the first of whom was also for a time a county councillor.

Three men elected as Independents at Elsecar during the inter-war period were all Elsecar Main officials. One was the manager, tall, heavily-built Reginald Edward Horrox, who lived in an old stone-built house in Armroyd, facing the 'Crab Field', with clematis growing round its front door. Another was Richard J. Polden ('Timey Dick'), the colliery time-keeper, who lived three doors above the Horroxes and whose term of office was abruptly ended by his untimely death. The third Independent was Leonard Butterworth, who lived in one of four semi-detached Armroyd houses built for senior members of the 'New Yard' staff, and who like Mr Polden died prematurely.

Independents at Elsecar came and went. Labour councillors tended to stay in office as long as they remained willing to serve. One such member, who gave many years of service, was Councillor Albert Edward Wilkinson, a tall, thin-faced Elsecar Main checkweighman who lived in his own house in Cobcar Street, facing the Midland Club. (His son Winston Wilkinson became well-known too, being in business as a coal leader.)

Another Labour member for Elsecar was Councillor Thomas ('Tommy') Tomlinson, who occupied the first end-terrace house to the left as one walks or drives down Fitzwilliam Street, owned the Crown Garage (formerly a smithy) and played a leading part in the running of the Wesleyan Reform Chapel. He was elected a county councillor and, while Chairman of the West Riding County Council, received a knighthood and became Sir Thomas. In his capacity as the County Council Chairman, he attended the Queen's Coronation Service at Westminster Abbey in June 1953.

Two long-serving Labour members for St Peter's were Councillors Vincent James Houlton and John Leo Joyce. They were both Roman Catholics. Councillor Houlton, originally returned as an Independent, was the Headmaster of St Helen's School. Councillor Joyce was the landlord of a pub at Platts Common, the Pheasant Inn. Another Labour member at Platts Common, who served the township for a number of years, was Councillor George Clark.

An Independent councillor for St Peter's for a short period was Mr William Simister Coulson, an insurance agent. Mr Coulson, a stocky man who wore spectacles and seldom went out without a

THE U.D.C. AND LOCAL SERVICES 11

rolled umbrella, lived at High Cottages in King Street, opposite the top of Noble Street. He was the father of the two Coulson brothers who in the middle decades of the century ran a Hoyland painting and decorating business.

The Clerk of the Council was a solicitor, monocled Colonel William Elmsley Raley, head of the firm of Raley and Sons (now Raley and Pratt) of Regent Street in Barnsley, a Freeman of Barnsley in honour of whom the Raley School (later re-styled Honeywell) was originally named. The Colonel, who had held this office since the formation of the Hoyland Local Board, was assisted by his son, swarthy, foreign-looking Mr Sidney Raley (referred to by his father as 'Mr Sid') who, when war broke out in 1939, became Hoyland's Food Officer, with Councillor John Leo Joyce as his assistant. (The Food Office, from which ration books were issued, was set up at No. 3 King Street, in what had been Fred Thompson's butcher's shop, and was also staffed by several women clerks including tall Miss Edith Lodge of Gill Street and Miss Margaret Saunders, a policeman's daughter from the top of Royston Hill.)

Council meetings, which were attended by either the Colonel or his son, were held on Tuesday evenings in the Council Chamber on the first floor at the back of the Town Hall. Since the Colonel himself was getting on in years, at the time I recall it was Mr Sidney Raley who, soon after nine in the evening on the day (at that time always a Saturday in March) when the Urban District Council elections were held, stepped forward when the big doors facing the square were flung open and, to a chorus of cheers, jeers and catcalls, announced the votes each candidate had polled and duly declared the winners to have been elected.

In March 1939 the successful candidate for Hoyland Ward, who had managed to defeat Councillor Crabb, was a young newcomer, Dennis Eaden, whose father, John Eaden of Barber Street, was already on the Council. The younger Councillor Eaden was destined to be both a town and a county councillor, and to be decorated by the Queen for thirty years' service to the people of

Hoyland, after which he continued in office for another thirteen years.

One election day evening, soon after the Second World War, counting the votes took much longer than usual, the waiting crowd growing restless and indulging in wild speculations to explain the delay. When at last the doors were opened it transpired that there had been a dead heat at Elsecar, the Independent, Herbert Hague, proving on several recounts to have polled exactly the same number of votes as his Labour opponent, Mrs Marples. The candidates had been told by the Clerk that, provided they agreed, the matter could legally be decided by drawing lots instead of putting the town to the expense of a further election. They had agreed, and slips of paper bearing their names had been placed in Police Sergeant Moran's helmet. The name the Sergeant had drawn out was Mr Hague's, causing him to be credited with an extra vote and so to be declared duly elected.

Council Departments and Officials

Besides the Council Chamber itself, the Town Hall included a warren of smaller rooms, all occupied by various local government officials.

The Sanitary Inspector's office was approached through a side door in George Street. (This dignitary, in more outspoken days designated bluntly the Nuisance Inspector, today enjoys the more euphonious name, 'Environmental Health Officer'.) The Sanitary Inspector in the late 'twenties was Mr Skitt, who lived at No. 2 Vernon Cottages, opposite King Street School, and had a daughter about my age called Beryl. He was succeeded by Mr Swift, a small man who stayed only a short time and was followed by John Yates, a tall Londoner who had a dark moustache. (When ordering printing at my father's office, Mr Yates often talked about London, his conversation sprinkled with such names as Piccadilly, Birdcage Walk and The Mall. In those days, when few Hoyland people ventured 'down south', they sounded almost as foreign and far-away as places on the surface of the moon.)

The Sanitary Inspector when war broke out in 1939 was his

THE U.D.C. AND LOCAL SERVICES 13

successor, William George Danks, a thick-set man, also with a moustache, who lived in Wilkinson Road and was for a time a warden at Holy Trinity, Elsecar, where his wife played the organ. Mr Danks died suddenly in hospital after an operation in the early 'sixties. His successor was Mr Horace Smith, who still lives in Hoyland but is now employed by the Metropolitan Borough Council in Barnsley.

Assistant Sanitary Inspectors between the Wars included Mr Wilfred Ramsden (whose brother Leonard became the Chief Wages Clerk at Elsecar Main), Mr John Joyce (the only son of Councillor John Leo Joyce), and Mr George Millar of Wakefield (a tall, tweedy young man with a penchant for broad humour, who left Hoyland to take up a post at Royston).

Some of the Sanitary Inspectors' time was spent taking samples of milk, produced locally and sold straight from the can, to check whether it complied with government standards regarding constituents and cleanliness. Some was spent inspecting meat killed locally, to make sure that the carcases were not diseased. Some was spent visiting and fumigating verminous dwelling-houses. A great deal was spent putting pressure on private landlords to make life more hygienic for their tenants by providing a separate lavatory for each house, instead of two or more families sharing one, and to replace 'Duckets' with water closets.

The 'Ducket', named after its patenter and known technically as a waste-water closet, was an ingenious device whereby human waste products, collecting in a pivoted iron box fixed into the ground beneath the pedestal, were flushed away not by mains water from an overhead cistern with a chain but by water draining from the kitchen sink. Less than fully hygienic it may have been, but it had the twin virtues of neither freezing in frosty winters nor aggravating the water shortage in summer droughts. The Sanitary Department in the 'thirties, nevertheless, waged ceaseless war on it, and 'converting' Duckets was so often talked of that, as a child, I took 'Have you been converted?' to refer to the state of one's plumbing, not to that of one's soul.

The council's refuse collection vehicles were dark green, with sliding lids like those on a fish-and-chip range. On their sides was posted the optimistic injunction to 'Burn more refuse and reduce your rates.' The refuse was tipped on the 'Cinder Hills' or 'Ash Mounts', which have now been levelled and grassed over as playing fields, between Millhouses Street and the LMS railway, and was used for filling in the 'Cat and Dog Pond'. Beside the pond stood a refuse destructor, like a huge brick garage at one end of which rose a factory-sized chimney. The dull, sour smell from this sometimes hung heavily over the town.

All the Sanitary Department's activities, including some which were vaguely classified as 'miscellaneous sanitary visits', were faithfully recorded year by year in the Medical Officer of Health's Report, a booklet my father printed, copies of which are preserved at Barnsley Central Library. It also contained a morbidly-fascinating table showing how many Hoyland citizens had died during the previous year, and what the causes of their deaths had been. (Some fatal illnesses whose names occurred, including puerperal pyrexia or childbed fever, are fortunately seldom heard of now.)

On the ground floor at the other end of the Town Hall building, with a small vestibule opening off High Street, was the Rating Department. The Rating Officer was Charles (usually referred to as 'Charlie') Jones, a small man with straight dark hair, a round face and a distinctively staccato way of speaking. He was a member of a local family and had married Miss Ellen Hunter, an Elsecar girl whose parents moved from Church Street to Armroyd Lane, where they lived next to the Horroxes. The Joneses had two sons, born in the 'twenties, and lived in a house at the bottom of Clough Road.

Mr Jones's was not the most enviable of jobs. Grumbling about being charged rates is nothing new. The Urban District Council was sometimes accused of indulging in profligate spending, and the cynical remark was often heard that 'ratepayers' money is worth twopence a bucketful.' When war broke out in 1939, besides carrying out his existing duties he became National Registration Officer, dealing with any matters which concerned the identity cards of local residents or of strangers visiting the area.

THE U.D.C. AND LOCAL SERVICES 15

A popular assistant of Mr Jones's, Mr Tommy Butterworth, who left the Town Hall to become a butcher, died recently in June 1988.

Entered by the main door was the Accounts Department. Here, too, there were some local people employed. One was Norman Chappell of Hoyland Common, the lay reader who ran St Peter's Mission Church. Another was Eric Shaw of Elsecar who, after serving in the RAF during the Second World War, went into business as a newsagent at the lower corner of Church Street and Hill Street and later moved to Scarborough, where he ran a tobacco and sweet shop part-way between the Railway Station and the Valley Bridge.

The Council's Surveyor was Mr John R. Shephard, a tall, austere-looking man with a small moustache, who lived in the detached house at the corner of Hawshaw Lane and Upper Hoyland Road, and whose wife was one of the people who supplied the altar flowers at St Peter's. It was under Mr Shephard's supervision that about the early 'thirties Milton Road, no longer required to form a gentle curve that horse-drawn traffic could negotiate, was made shorter, steeper and straighter and a new road, by-passing the long curve past the gates of Skiers Spring Lodge, was driven through Spring Wood from Footrill Cottages to the bottom of Stead Lane.

Mr Shephard was assisted by his son, who was usually referred to as Jack Shephard, and by Dennis Edmund Chadwick, a member of a well-known Hoyland Catholic family. Mr Chadwick, whose career was sadly cut short by his death at the age of forty-four, designed houses and old people's bungalows for several of the Council's housing estates, including those at Royston Hill and Hill Crest.

The Housing Manager, another Hoyland man, was Mr Albert Dewsbury, whose own home was a council property, one of the pair on the corner of West Street and Longfields Crescent, facing the War Memorial.

The Fire Service

The Fire Station, just large enough to house one appliance and with its glass-paned doors painted bright red, was sandwiched between the west end of the Town Hall and Mr D.P. Beattie's clothing shop.

The Brigade was made up of part-time volunteers, most of them Urban District Council employees. In the 'thirties, to summon them in case of need, a siren was fixed on the Town Hall roof, worked by a button in a 'break-glass' case on the front wall of the building just below and to one side of the large central doorway. (When war broke out not long afterwards, it was used as the town's air-raid siren, whose undulating wail was supplemented by short, staccato blasts on colliery buzzers.)

Sometimes the assembled volunteers did not include a man able to drive the fire engine. On at least one occasion Mr Harry Cooper had to leave Storey and Cooper's shop across the street to act as emergency driver. (Fortunately the slight delay caused no loss of life, the reason for the call being a smouldering hearth rug.)

On the whole, however, in pre-war years trivial calls and false alarms were few in number. Though some people risked setting their chimneys alight to avoid paying a shilling to the sweep, the brigade was seldom called to chimney fires. Not only were its services charged for; the police could and did prosecute householders for allowing fires in their chimneys to start. (This zealousness was a relic of the days when, with wooden buildings huddled close together, a chimney fire could set a town ablaze.) Consequently, when 'Wailing Willie' roused people from sleep, it was a cause for wakeful consternation, everyone anxiously wondering whether the fire was at the home of a relative or friend.

The fire I recall most clearly from my childhood broke out on a peaceful Sunday afternoon in the late 'twenties at Bott's pork butcher's shop on the upper corner of Booth Street and King Street. Standing with my father and mother across the way, on the pavement outside the Co-op pharmacy, I watched with fascinated horror as the side door of the room behind Bott's shop burst

THE U.D.C. AND LOCAL SERVICES

open and, accompanied by a cloud of dark grey smoke, a child's large, multi-coloured rubber ball was violently expelled into the gutter. (My mother, afraid that the whole street might go up in flames, was clutching a large handbag into which she had hurriedly pushed her marriage lines and other family papers.) Luckily the outbreak was soon contained and nobody was hurt, the butcher having gone fishing for the afternoon and his wife having taken the children to tea at her mother's.

A more serious conflagration occurred one night, soon after the fire buzzer was installed, when some pigsties near St Helen's Church caught fire and the hapless animals were burnt to death, the blaze having taken so strong a hold before being seen that by the time the fire brigade arrived it was impossible to rescue them.

Another occasion on which the town was roused from sleep, during the late 'thirties, was when Jump Working Men's Club caught fire. It was gutted and was afterwards replaced with the present brick building in Wentworth Road.

Gas and Electricity Services

Few Hoyland people before the Second World War used electricity. The Yorkshire Electric Power Company supplied those who did, charging fourpence-halfpenny a unit (about two pence in decimal currency, but considered expensive at a time when £3 was an average weekly wage). When a house was built at Hoyland Common in the 'thirties without chimneys and with provision for no other fuel, it was looked upon as a phenomenon and promptly dubbed 'The All-Electric House' with a mixture of mockery and envy.

The vast majority of Hoyland homes, even those erected since the First World War either by the Council or by private owners, were heated by open fires and lit by gas. The incandescent mantles used on the gas jets, looking like tiny beehives of white gauze and crumbling at the slightest careless touch, were obtainable from Rawlin's or Firth's in King Street, who also sold patterned or plain glass shades, often elegantly fluted, to cover them.

The Elsecar, Hoyland and Wentworth Gas Company, founded

in 1857, supplied coal or 'town' gas from its Wath Road works at the end of the 'Ash Gates' and across the street from the entrance to the Elsecar goods station. The main gas-holder was at the works itself. There was a smaller one in the back garden of the double-fronted house opposite, at which lived Edwin Stenton, the gas-works manager and local historian. For a few pence a bucket the Company also sold tar for treating hen-houses and garden fences.

The gas fitters whom I remember from my youth, usually to be seen walking in pairs with meters slung over their shoulders, included William Bowden (a tall brother-in-law of Wilfred Rawlin, the plumber and painter), tall, red-haired John Pinder (who moved to High Street when his former home in High Croft was pulled down during the 'seventies) and a character always known as 'Little Walter'.

About 1934 the works was taken over by the larger Sheffield Gas Company which, under its Hoyland manager, Mr Edmund R. Hartley, opened an office and showroom at No. 1 West Street, formerly Councillor Mell's furniture shop. An assistant in the office for some years was a girl from further up the street, Miss Sadie Hawley. There bills could be paid and gas appliances bought, though not many consumers in those days received quarterly bills, most rented houses having penny slot meters. (There was often a shortage of pennies in the town when meters were due to be emptied.) A useful household object then on sale, but nowadays no longer obtainable, was the gas iron, which looked similar to its electric counterpart and was heated by lighting an adjustable gas jet inside it − a vast improvement on the flat irons and even more dangerous box irons used by previous generations.

The streets of Hoyland, too, were lit by gas, as they had been since the early eighteen-nineties. The light was housed in a four-paned glass case, tapering slightly towards the base like some sweet cartons, topped by an ornamental metal lid and fitted on to a fluted iron lamp post. (When gas gave place to electric sodium lighting there was a rush to buy these lamp standards

THE U.D.C. AND LOCAL SERVICES

some of which, now fitted with electric bulbs, can be seen lovingly preserved in private gardens.)

During my childhood a familiar sight, before automatic time switches replaced him, was the lamp-lighter sprinting along at dusk, pausing briefly at each post to raise a long wooden pole and tip the little bar which brought gas in contact with the flickering pilot light, just like his counterpart the 'leery man' in Stevenson's *Child's Garden of Verses*. He was always in a hurry; hence, no doubt, the expression 'going like a lamp-lighter'. The only lamp-lighter whose name I knew was Mr George Worthy, a tall, thin, pallid, worried-looking man who lived with his wife, his daughters Beatrice and Alison and his son Harold (a contemporary of mine at King Street School) at No. 3 Green Street, the middle one of three small cottages, with no back doors and one room to each floor, which were demolished a few years ago.

In the 'thirties, the Yorkshire Electric Power Company made an abortive bid to seize a share of the Hoyland heating and lighting market, opening a showroom in a little shop below the Mount Tabor Chapel in King Street. (It was one of three single-storey shops formerly run as a draper's and outfitter's by the Ramsey family, one of whose members, Harold Ramsey, was the organist at St Peter's Church before leaving the district to settle in Bristol.) The Gas Company immediately struck back, coming to my father to have handbills printed, for distribution to each householder, laying stress upon the versatility and comparative cheapness of its own product. The rival showroom closed soon afterwards, and it was not until after the Second World War that electricity finally managed to gain a secure foothold in the area.

The Water Supply

The Dearne Valley Water Board supplied Hoyland's piped water from about 1890 until some years after the Second World War, when this function was taken over first by Sheffield Corporation, then by the Yorkshire Water Authority. The water, said to come from old colliery workings, was pumped up a shaft at Broomhill, between Wombwell and Darfield. One day, when I was about nine years old, I went down with my mother on the bus to deliver some printing ordered by the Board to its Broomhill office at the pumping station. The man in charge took me to view the shaft, descending into darkness and criss-crossed by gleaming metal ladders. For weeks afterwards I had nightmares about it, just as I had a few years earlier about the 'folly' in Wentworth Castle grounds, with its hint of racks and dungeons, after going there to see the rhododendrons one Whitsuntide.

Hoyland's water was pumped to the storage reservoir at the town's highest point, near the Law Stand (a building the Dearne Valley Water Board owned for a time), a fact which was to lead to trouble when, in 1947, the feed pipe crossing the canal at Broomhill burst and for most of a sticky, sweltering week, Hoyland people had to rely for their water on emergency tankers on loan from Sheffield, where they had been used after the air raids of December 1940. During the early 'twenties similar problems though of shorter duration had occurred when, owing to subsidence caused by Hoyland Silkstone, the mains in Hoyland streets burst frequently and supplies were cut, often for several hours, after due warning given by an old man who plodded from door to door announcing glumly, 'The water will be turn-id orf.'

Dearne Valley water was always crystal clear and refreshingly cold (unlike that at an aunt of mine's house near Rawmarsh, upland surface water stained brown with peat and with a flavour much like that of walnuts). On the debit side, it was hard and full of lime, which made it difficult to work up a lather when washing clothes or shampooing one's hair, left a dark, greasy 'tidemark' round the bath and coated the insides of kettles with scaly white 'fur'. Even in the driest summer, however, it never failed. Hence, as a small child, I was unaware of the problems drought can cause until one summer, visiting Thornton Dale while staying at Scarborough, a young cousin and I pounced gleefully on a street pump (something we knew only from picture books) and started working its handle vigorously, whereupon a terrifying-looking woman in mob-cap and wrap-round overall ran from her house and across

THE U.D.C. AND LOCAL SERVICES

a white plank bridge over the beck, shouting, 'Don't you know that there's a water shortage?'

Even so, not everyone appreciated the benefits of good, clean tap water. My father often told the story of how an uncle of his who lived at Hoyland Common had a well in his back garden protected only by a swivelling iron lid level with the ground. The Sanitary Inspector, a Mr Ramsbottom, frequently called to take samples of water from it, partly to ensure that it was not polluted by seepage from the household's earth closet ten yards or so away. The uncle bitterly resented this, saying that piped water caused lead poisoning and that neither he nor his wife nor his daughter was going to be 'leaded'.

The Board's Inspector for the Hoyland area was Herbert Kay, who was for obvious reasons nicknamed 'Tappy'. He lived at No. 103 King Street with his wife, their son Jeffrey and their daughter Kathleen. (As Mrs Magson, 'Kitty' Kay was for many years the headmistress of West Street Infants' School, and was much in demand for opening fêtes, church sales of work and similar functions.) Another member of the household was Mrs Kay's sister, Miss Linda Hall, a skilled dressmaker and Spirella corsetière.

Besides doing his job for the Water Board, for which he wore leather leggings or high boots and carried a long iron stop-tap key, Mr Kay was a member of the fire brigade. His official tasks included chasing up water-rate cheats, evaders and defaulters. The rate for an average household in those days came to only two or three old pence a week. An extra ten shillings a year was charged for a house equipped with a fixed bath. One quite comfortably-off aunt of my father's, who prided herself upon being genteel, refused stubbornly to have a bath fitted, despite the pleadings of her relatives, and made do with a portable zinc one instead, determined not to pay this extra levy.

The Police Service

The West Riding Constabulary's Police Station occupied a conveniently central site at the top end of George Street, being the first building on the left-hand side beyond the Globe Tea Company's premises. Built in 1889 two years before the Local Board was formed, at a time when Hoyland was growing in size and importance, it was a stolid, double-fronted, red-brick structure with the royal arms in stone over its front door, and served also as the sergeant's residence.

In the 'twenties this official was Sergeant Marsh, whose punctilious enforcement of discipline made him unpopular with some underlings. He was followed by tall, military-looking Sergeant Dales whose widow, Mrs Mary Jane Dales, now in her nineties, is still a resident of Elsecar. Sergeant Dales' successor, fresh-complexioned Sergeant Alfred Lessons, died suddenly in 1941 while in his mid-forties and was buried in Kirk Balk Cemetery, where his simple memorial can be seen beside the path parallel to the railings. After her husband's death, Mrs Lessons became the manageress of Elstone's sweet and tobacco shop in High Street (formerly George Wilkinson's and now Walker's garden and card shop). The Lessons' daughter Phyllis, during the war, enjoyed a brief vogue as a teen-age singer, being heard several times on the radio.

'Bobbies' during my childhood were much better known to the people they worked among than are their successors. They lived locally, and some stayed for a number of years. Consequently their personal idiosyncrasies were noted and remarked on.

Genial PC Woodall lived in Cherry Tree Street. He was a tall, broad-shouldered man with a black moustache who had married his widowed landlady, Mrs Tipler, mother of the coach proprietor of that name. It was PC Woodall who dispelled any fears that as a toddler I might have experienced of meeting a policeman in uniform, by producing sweets from his helmet when he came to bring various official printing orders. (Some of these were for notices concerning missing or wanted persons. There was also a regular order for posters each year for the ever-popular 'Bobbies' Dance' which used to take place at the Milton Hall.) My mother sensibly reinforced this good impression by saying 'Remember that a policeman is your friend' instead of, like some parents, making him a bogy-man by threatening to 'fetch t' bobby' when I was guilty of some childish misdemeanour.

PC Sparling, who lived in Headlands Road, was a tall, thin-faced, red-haired young man nicknamed 'Lofty', whose daughter Jean inherited his looks. His attitude towards life and the policeman's lot was sardonically detached. Once, told that two men were fighting in the street, he dismissed the matter with the succinct remark, 'They buy their own clothes, don't they?' Seeing a poster displayed in my father's office advertising a knur-and-spell contest at Platts Common and naming the man who was to hold the stakes, whose probity he appears to have held in doubt, he smiled and asked, 'And who's going to hold the stake-holder?'

Police houses, seldom in those days purpose-built, were distinguished by the black-and-white badge-shaped plaques displayed on their façades. One was at Elsecar, at the top end of the former lodging house or 'Bun and Milk Club'. Another, now a private residence, was at the bottom end of Milton Road, facing its junction with Millhouses Street. Its occupant for a time in the early 'thirties was stocky, middle-aged PC Marvin, a dog-lover who, when he in turn brought printing orders, made a friend of our Labrador retriever, Chant. In his off-duty time he went fishing. One summer Sunday my parents and I were invited to tea at the Marvins' house, where their son played the piano for us and Mrs Marvin confided that she would never dare to live in a house damaged by subsidence. In the kitchen I gazed fascinatedly at a large piece of wasp cake, full of fat white grubs meant for use as fishing bait and with, at intervals, an adult wasp emerging menacingly.

When PC Marvin left Hoyland he was succeeded by PC Whittaker, a young man with a small daughter named Sylvia. The new constable's hobby was photography, in which he took a keen interest, often consulting my father and my Uncle Fred, both of whom produced exhibition prints, about its finer details.

In retrospect, Hoyland during the 'twenties and 'thirties seems to have been monotonously law-abiding. Despite the boredom and frustration of unemployment or of only being allowed to work part-time, smashed shop windows, graffiti and other forms of vandalism were virtually unknown. The work of the police was mainly routine: conducting traffic in the Town Hall Square; chasing dog licence defaulters (whose pups, when six months old, were liable to develop 'licence fever' and be put down before the law could catch up with their owners); prosecuting people whose chimneys caught fire or whose motor-bikes had faulty silencers; and patrolling the streets at night trying the doors of lock-up premises.

There was, however, one notable exception. During the early 'thirties, a succession of mysterious burglaries took place, mostly at detached houses occupied by trades or professional people. (When in 1932, at Whitsuntide, my parents and I spent ten days down in Devonshire at Paignton – the furthest we had ever ventured from home – my mother anxiously debated whether she ought to leave the window shutters closed, a course which, though it would help to keep him out, might also alert the burglar to the fact that the property was temporarily empty.)

Not long afterwards, the fatal mistake was made that occurs in all the best detective fiction. One victim, Percy Haines of Armroyd Lane, reported that the items stolen from him included a five-shilling piece on which his wife had scratched some kind of mark to identify it. (Although still legal tender, five-shilling pieces were no longer minted and were on the way to being collectors' items.) The police now had a chance to prove themselves. Painstakingly, just like their counterparts in some 'whodunnit' shown on television, they went round from shop to shop and pub to pub, asking if such a coin had recently been spent there. Walter Sylvester of the Ball Inn distinctly called to mind not only the coin but also the man he had received it from. It was found at Whitworth's Brewery in Wath, whose traveller had collected it with other takings only the previous day, and the net closed inexorably around the suspect.

He proved to be an unemployed bachelor who had left his home in the depressed north-east to join an uncle and aunt who lived in Hoyland, in a council house near the War Memorial. When his room, which he always kept locked, was searched it

THE U.D.C. AND LOCAL SERVICES

was said to contain a number of stolen objects. (His relations, whose honesty was not called in doubt, had been given the impression that he had found a job which entailed going out to work each evening.)

In 1971, having served the town for over eighty years, the old, stoutly-built Police Station was closed, as was its newer Birdwell counterpart. A flat-roofed, single-storey building took their place on a site once occupied by a small farmhouse near the bus stop at Hoyland Lane End. To make way for town centre re-development, the Police Station in George Street was pulled down; its site forms part of the car park at the rear of Willis's supermarket. Birdwell's handsome stone building survives intact, but serves a very different purpose as the headquarters of the Aetherius Society, a community of spiritual healers.

The Postal Service

Hoyland has had a Post Office since 1830 and it is known that in 1838, the year after Queen Victoria's accession, a postal service ran three days a week between the Gate Inn and Barnsley, which at that time was on the mail coach route between Leeds and London.

There is still a Victorian postbox in a wall opposite the west end of Millhouses Street, and the bow-fronted Old Post Office Buildings on the corner of West Street and Milton Road were standing until fairly recently, but already, when I first knew it in the 'twenties, the Post Office itself had moved elsewhere.

At that time, the premises on Market Street that have now been converted into a café comprised two shops. On the left, as one looked towards them from the street, was the ladies' outfitter's run by the Fishers (who also sold sweets and tobacco in the cottage-like building on the corner of Duke Street). On the right was the Hoyland Post Office — dark, narrow and cramped and run by Mrs Marshall, a small, grey-haired widow with a mournful voice who, although it was not customary then to employ postmistresses, had been kept on in that capacity after her postmaster husband died in harness.

Mrs Marshall was assisted by her two daughters: tall, dark, curly-haired Margaret (always called 'Maggie'), who in the 'thirties married and, as Mrs Evans, went to live at Alnwick in Northumberland, and smaller, quiet-spoken Mary with her cloud of thick, lighter brown hair. Mrs Marshall's son Harry, tall and dark like his sister Margaret, was a friend of my father's and frequently came to our house, where my early attempts to pronounce his name resulted in 'Ali Marsule'. He and my father were keen photographers and, laden with tripods and other gear and sometimes accompanied by my Uncle Fred, went on outings to such local beauty spots as Wentworth Park, Stainborough and Rockley. Later in my childhood Harry moved to Nottingham, where he worked in the Post Office for some years before being promoted and becoming the Postmaster at Peterborough. Another member of the Marshall household was a grey parrot in a large round cage, but whether it was a talking bird or not I cannot say.

Deep consternation was felt in Hoyland when, about the end of the 'twenties, the Post Office moved to its present site in Ryecroft Place, in slightly more commodious premises next door to Wilfred Thompson's antique shop and across the road from George Hirst Allen, the grocer. Householders from the Milton and King Street areas resented the extra distance they had to walk. People with town centre shops and offices complained of the additional time it now took to post their business mail.

Predictably, it was Mr D.P. Beattie, the High Street outfitter and organizer of annual excursions and other events, who came to their assistance by persuading the GPO to install an additional postbox in the heart of the town. The forerunner of the present free-standing box near the kiosk on the corner of High Croft, it was built into the end wall of his house which faced towards the side door of the Town Hall, and soon came to be known as 'Beattie's box'. Also, mainly to enable business people to post letters written when they had closed their shops, by which time the last local collection of mail had been made, he arranged for a small postbox to be carried on the 9.10 p.m. Circular Route bus to Barnsley.

THE U.D.C. AND LOCAL SERVICES 27

Painted red and embossed with the Post Office cipher, this was roughly the size of a deed box and was padlocked to the vertical rail at the top of the steps of the single-decker bus, causing something of a melée when some people were trying to board, some to descend from the bus and some to reach the box, all at one time. (This facility proved very popular on Thursdays with people who had waited until the last possible minute to fill in and send off their pools coupons.) A favourite ploy with nosey queue members, curious to know what a friend or neighbour was posting, was to say, 'Don't wait. If you give it to me I'll put it in with mine,' an offer it seemed churlish to refuse, especially if the evening was cold or rainy.

There were no postwomen. The mail was brought round by a team of men who wore smart navy uniforms trimmed with red, and peaked caps with brass badges. Their pay was low, but the job was secure — something which counted for a lot in those days. The postman on our round for many years was called McQuillen and lived in a house on the opposite corner of Rock Mount to Goddard's (now Hague's) butcher's. Two other postmen were called Hodgson and Doughty. There were two deliveries of mail each weekday (within my parents' memory there had been more) and, both then and for many years after the Second World War, Sunday collections and Christmas morning deliveries were taken for granted. Though Market Street was only a sub-office, mail was sorted there in an outbuilding which on dark mornings was a brightly-lit hive of activity.

Throughout the inter-war time of price stability, a letter in a sealed envelope cost three-halfpence (less than the decimal penny of today). Until 1936 its dark brown stamp bore the bearded face of King George V in an intricate border. An unsealed letter or greetings card cost only a halfpenny. The colour of the halfpenny stamp was dark green.

The Telephone and Telegraph Service

Relatively few Hoyland residents in the 'twenties and 'thirties were on the telephone. Most of those were professional or trades people who needed the 'phone for business purposes. (As early as 1911, Herbert Garner the ironmonger put in his advertisements: 'National Telephone — No. 6 Hoyland'.) Till the first small automatic exchange was built on the site of the old Maltkiln Terrace in West Street, nearer the road than its modern counterpart, all calls were channelled through the operator, who resided and worked at 'Telephone House', the double-fronted house in Milton Road next door to the Ball Inn. Receivers at the beginning of this period were still of the upright 'daffodil' design. The first Town Hall call-box I remember was a pale stone colour with red window-frames.

To convey urgent messages to 'phone-less households, the Post Office telegraph service was still widely used. Messages were despatched between offices in Morse code (fluency in which was a pre-requisite to being appointed a sub-postmaster), and each office employed a telegraph boy (the 'telegraph boy with his nose turned up' of the comic song) who, in navy uniform and stiff round cap, took round telegrams in their buff envelopes on a light motor-cycle.

For a while after he left St Peter's School, before being apprenticed to the printing trade, my father worked as a telegraph boy at Hoyland Common, where he was supplied with an ordinary push-bike. A great many telegrams had to be delivered to Bell Ground House off the old turnpike road where, long before England became multi-racial, the door was opened by a black manservant who accepted the envelopes with grave courtesy.

Since sometimes these buff envelopes contained news of a relative's illness or death, the sight of a telegraph boy walking up to the door was usually greeted with trepidation. Not all telegrams, however, contained bad news. One of the happier variety was sent by a young man called Jordan to his parents in Hoyland when he had passed an important examination. With the succinctness needed in a message where nine words were allowed for the basic shilling fee, he quoted the line from 'Art thou weary, art thou languid?', a hymn heard more frequently then than now, 'Sorrow vanquished, labour ended, Jordan passed'.

THE U.D.C. AND LOCAL SERVICES

Banking Services

Hoyland's largest bank, the National Provincial (which a few years ago merged with the Westminster, becoming the National Westminster), was originally housed in the Town Hall, inside the large doors facing towards the square. It was to these temporary premises that my mother was sent, when she was a senior pupil at Elsecar Girls' School in the first decade of the present century, to deposit her fellow-pupils' weekly savings.

By the 'twenties, however, the National Provincial had moved into No. 2 Market Street, a property previously occupied by Bellamy's Corner Boot Store. Until it was rebuilt during the 'thirties, this Hoyland 'Nat Pro' was a gloomy place of dark green paint and ugly metal grilles, even more cramped than before its recent expansion, the Market Street end of the premises forming a separate shop. In earlier years this little shop had been Colville's tobacco and grocery store. Later, before being incorporated into the bank, it was occupied by a boot repairer named Ernest Welburn, who lived in an old house on Hoyland Road where Alexander's dental surgery now stands.

The Bank had a part-time Hoyland Common branch, in a shop between Allott's Corner and the Prince of Wales, and one at Elsecar in the shop next door to Linley's greengrocer's in Fitzwilliam Street, between the old Post Office and Wentworth Road. The house on the corner of Foundry Street and Hill Street was another property owned by the Bank. Consequently it was always called 'The Bank House'.

The bank manager until 1939 was John Linn, who resided at Elsecar. He was small and elderly, with a grey moustache, and had a slight impediment in his speech which prevented him from pronouncing 'th', and made him call his place of work 've bank'. Shortly before the Second World War broke out the Linns retired to Scarborough, just in time to face the traumatic experience of having evacuees billeted in their new home.

Mr Linn's successor, taciturn Norman Sherwell, came north from Aylesbury and, with his wife and two schoolboy sons, lived at South Grove, the large stone residence between the Cloughs and Broad Street previously owned by Mr Hugh Buxton, the retired Headmaster of King Street School. Mr Sherwell was a devout Methodist and a firm believer in old-fashioned values, deploring the way in which using fountain pens had spoilt children's handwriting and doubting the wisdom of opening students current accounts which, he believed, allowed them to lose track of their expenditure. (Dying a few years after he retired to Worthing, he did not live to see the proliferation of cheap ball-points and plastic credit cards.) He also deplored the grammatical lapses heard in certain wireless programmes. Some customers, to Mr Sherwell's annoyance, called him 'Mr Shinwell', confusing his name with that of 'Manny' Shinwell who, during the years immediately after the War, became the Minister of Fuel and Power in Clement Attlee's Labour Government.

When the bank was rebuilt, the first floor was converted into a flat to house the caretaker. This for many years was Mr George Skorrow, a member of a well-known Hoyland family.

Barclay's Bank, two doors away, was even smaller, occupying the far half of the premises, now Selway and Co.'s Estate Office, between the National Provincial and the old Wesleyan Chapel. It was merely a subsidiary of Wombwell and was managed by suave, dark-moustached Mr Totty, who lived in Barnsley. My father always called it 'The Butchers' Bank', but whether the reason was that most Hoyland butchers did business there or that the little shop next door to it was occupied by Taylors the butchers I was never quite sure.

Hoyland also had a third bank, the Yorkshire Penny (which, to dispel any 'cloth cap' association or the implication that it dealt exclusively with trivial amounts, a few years since shed the 'Penny' and became the less evocatively named Yorkshire). Its Hoyland agent (there was no branch in the town) was Mr Herbert Edwin Key, a Market Street estate and insurance agent. Although his banking hours were limited to one evening a week, a number of small savers chose to go there, happier dealing with a local man in a rather less formal atmosphere, and perhaps thinking a bank

THE U.D.C. AND LOCAL SERVICES 31

rooted in Yorkshire a safer place to entrust their money to than one with its headquarters in distant London.

Unless they were well enough off to be able to save, few working people in the 'twenties and 'thirties had dealings with a bank of any kind. The custom of paying weekly wages direct into banks, for employees themselves to draw them out, did not become widespread until the 'sixties, when it was adopted to foil 'wages snatches' — the ambushing of wages clerks returning with large sums to count into wage envelopes. (Before that it was a Thursday morning ritual for a chauffeur-driven car to pull up at the National Provincial, bringing a wages clerk from the 'New Yard' — re-named by the Coal Board the Central Workshops — to collect the Elsecar Main miners' pay, which even in those days must have amounted to a sizeable sum.)

Except for some women who had been recruited during the First World War, when men were called into the Services, and when peace came had as a favour been kept on (among them was my father's elder sister, Aunt Elsie, who worked in Barnsley at the Midland on Market Hill), bank clerks during the years between the Wars were exclusively male. In those days of unemployment and low wages a bank job, like a teaching post, was deemed a plum, offering security and a reasonable salary and being pensionable. Hence the banks could pick and choose when recruiting staff, and impose conditions that no individual or his union would tolerate today. Clerks were not only asked to dress soberly and to deport themselves with dignity; they were not allowed to marry until they reached the point on their salary scale at which they were judged to be earning sufficient to set up house and support a family without being lured into embezzlement. (Should a young man have to marry earlier for reasons of 'social necessity', two courses only were then open to him. Either he must quit his job, or his people must pay over a large sum as a bond guaranteeing his future good conduct.)

CHAPTER TWO

Shopping and Shopkeepers

INTER-WAR HOYLAND was a town of little shops, mostly privately-owned, which between them supplied anything from an ice-cream to a made-to-measure suit. They started at the lower end of West Street and continued as far as the end of Victoria Street, and also on Market Street for a short distance. Their number and how they managed to thrive at first seems odd, in view of the Depression and of the fact that Hoyland was much smaller then than now. The explanation is possibly that, at a time when few people owned motor-cars and the return bus fare to Barnsley was ten old pence out of a £3 average weekly wage, there was more incentive to shop locally than there has been during more recent years.

Grocers' Shops

Buying groceries during the 'twenties and 'thirties was very different from buying them today. There were no supermarkets or self-service stores. Goods were bought over the counter, either from the proprietor himself or, if the shop was big enough to merit his employing them, from one of his assistants.

Bacon was sliced from the flitch on a machine to a thickness chosen by the customer. The sole varieties of cheese in stock were usually Cheshire and Cheddar. Huge barrel-shaped cheeses were sliced with a wire into wedge-shaped pieces of the size required. Butter came either in blocks or in tubs. Most of those wives who could afford the price chose Danish to put on their families' bread, thinking New Zealand (sometimes known as 'Empire') suitable only for cooking purposes. To use margarine was suggestive of poverty.

There were few pre-packaged dry goods. Sugar was weighed out with a metal scoop into rough dark blue bags, the tops of which were then skilfully tucked in. Currants were weighed into clover-pink bags and sultanas into saffron-yellow ones. Sometimes this was done while the customer stood and watched. Sometimes the assistants were made to do weighing-up to keep them busy during slack periods. Till the late 'thirties there was no 'instant' coffee. Either coffee was ground or it took the form of bottled coffee essence.

Most shops made deliveries to customers' homes, either by van or on errand boys' bicycles.

The doyen of Hoyland grocers' shops was undoubtedly that of Rowland Cross and Son, which stood at the corner of King Street and Market Street and had been owned during Victorian times by the Knowles family, being run during the late nineteenth century by Mrs Martha Knowles and her son John, after whom the John Knowles Church was later named.

A low, dark shop with a window on each side of its recessed doorway, that on the left filled with dishes of dry goods such as prunes, currants, rice and butter beans, that on the right with bacon, ham and cheese, Cross's was run by Mr Rowland Cross and his son William Barber. Adjoining it at the Market Street end was a small, double-fronted, stone-built house where Mr Barber Cross lived with his wife, son Rowland and daughter Vera. Over the back door of the house was a stone, obviously dating from the Knowles's time, inscribed 'WK 1852'. The Crosses employed several women assistants and also stocky, black–moustached Mr 'Tommy' Turner, who went out collecting and delivering orders as far afield as Jump and Hemingfield.

When motor-cars first became popular, Crosses had a petrol pump installed in the space formed by the angle of the dwelling-house and shop. Later they built a glass-fronted extension there for selling hardware. Outside this there usually hung a string of the disk-shaped tin bottles, known as 'Dudleys', in which miners in those days took their tea to work.

Like local 'institutions' everywhere, Cross's became the butt of jokes and canards. A notice was said to have once been displayed in its right-hand window saying 'Choice Miners' Bacon. We could almost Eat it Ourselves'. In actual fact, as what would nowadays be called a 'special offer', Rowland Cross at least once bought a crate of Egyptian eggs, labelled 'Little Gems', which he sold very cheaply. It was rumoured that a customer had hatched some, producing tiny snakes and crocodiles. Because there was a butcher further down King Street named Henry Vincent Hastie, schoolboys used to call to each other when they met, 'Why was Rowland Cross?' to which the answer was, 'Because he saw Vincent Hastie.'

Facing Cross's, on the corner of King Street and George Street, were the premises of the Globe Tea Company, usually known simply as 'The Globe', a long, narrow shop with a window on to each street and a glass-paned door up two steps across the corner. It was managed by dapper Mr 'Billy' Benson, who wore the traditional white-fringed grocer's apron, lived in a council house up Hawshaw Lane, and once told my father that on summer evenings he liked nothing better than to visit the Rockingham Arms at Wentworth for 'a game of bowls and a jar'. In the early 'twenties, one of Mr Benson's assistants was the young son of Mr Albert Garnett, the verger at St Peter's.

Despite its name, The Globe sold not only tea but groceries of all kinds. It had a number of specialities, the most popular of which, in my parents' youth, was its 'new season's' fig-and-rhubarb jam (disparagingly known as 'fig-and-string'), of whose arrival housewives were apprised through handbills brought round by the errand boy. No record of its price seems to have survived. That of the Globe Tea Company's flour, however, is known to have been 1s.1d. a stone – roughly five pence in today's currency.

Before moving to No. 1 King Street, The Globe had occupied one of the two larger of the three shops owned by Mr Albert Woolley, a baker, in West Street. By the early 'thirties this was being kept by Mr Wilton Brooke, a Hoyland Common man who, before becoming a grocer, had been at different times a postman and a colliery deputy at Wath-upon-Dearne.

The premises were inconvenient and cramped, especially the living accommodation. Therefore, during the 'thirties, Mr Brooke built himself the house and shop on the corner of West Street and Valley Way. There he and his wife, formerly Miss Florence Lang, who acted as his assistant at busy times, counted many business and professional people among their customers, building up a reputation for supplying the leading brands of tinned and packaged goods. They specialized in coffee 'ground while you wait', and also pioneered the sale in Hoyland of Mapleton's Health Foods.

A staunch Socialist, perhaps through having worked down a coal mine, florid-faced Mr Brooke would often pause, bacon knife in his hand, to deliver an indignant tirade on something that struck him as a social injustice or political blunder, a habit which prompted one customer to send him a picture postcard from Bournemouth addressed to 'Mr W. Brooke, Grocer and Whittler'. (He thought the Fitzwilliams tyrannical oppressors of the poor and thoroughly distrusted Winston Churchill, whom he suspected of 'warmongering'.)

During the Second World War, grocery prices were fixed by the Ministry of Food, with the result that sometimes a customer's bill included an odd farthing. Most shopkeepers rounded this up to the nearest halfpenny. Meticulous in all things, Mr Brooke got a bag of farthings from the bank so that he could always give the correct change.

In their spare time, on Wednesday afternoons and Sundays, the Brookes often went walking, exploring the Thurgoland and Stainborough areas and calling for tea at the Eastfield Arms, sometimes alone, sometimes with their close friends Mr and Mrs Barnet Trinder of Broad Carr Road.

Both the Brookes' children were school-teachers, Miss Edith Brooke teaching Standard 3 at King Street, though she later married and lived elsewhere, Ralph Brooke becoming the headmaster of a school on the outskirts of Sheffield.

An older-established private grocer in inter-war Hoyland was Mr George Hirst Allen (the brother of William Allen, the architect,and a member of a local farming family), who kept the shop, now a boutique, on the corner of Market Street and Little Leeds. It was a fascinating place for a child to visit, being warmed in winter by a large slow-combustion stove, called a 'tortoise' because of the tortoise embossed on its lid, such as can sometimes be seen in village churches.

Like Mr Brooke, Mr Allen specialized in catering for the discriminating housewife. He sold expensive and mouth-watering biscuits. His coffee was ground in a hand-powered mill with a brass funnel, into which the beans were poured, and a large green-enamelled wheel like that of an old-fashioned wringer. On a shelf behind the coffee mill there stood a row of red-black-and-gold lacquered tins in which sugar, rice and other dry goods were stored.

Shopping at Allen's was always a leisurely business. A large man with a round rosy face and a white moustache, Mr Allen moved slowly and ponderously between shelf and counter, flour room and shop and loved talking, especially about ways of cooking food, an art of which he was a connoisseur. Shopping there was also a convenient way to keep informed of interesting local happenings.

Between the Wars, in spite of the Depression, three new 'chain' grocery stores were opened in Hoyland: Brough's (a firm based in Newcastle-upon-Tyne, whose shop next door to Mr Brooke's is now a do-it-yourself centre); Gallon's (in premises which have since been demolished, next door to Taylor's electrical shop); and Melia's (now Wray's butcher's in High Street). In keeping with the architectural trends of the time, the two latter had walls hygienically tiled in white, some of the tiles displaying floral motifs.

The shop most noted for its decoration, however, was the Maypole Dairy Company's at No. 28 King Street, one white-tiled wall of which incorporated a large reproduction of the Company's emblem, a group of figures dancing round a maypole. The shop frontage was equally ornate, encrusted with elaborately carved woodwork painted bottle green, picked out in gleaming gold. (As a child, whenever I heard my mother sing, 'Come lasses and lads, get leave of your dads and away to the maypole hie,' I thought it was this provision store that they were being urged to visit.)

From the day The Maypole opened this Hoyland shop, about two years before the First World War, until he retired to Skegness some time after the Second, its manager was thin-faced, cheerful Mr Albert Reynolds. Sensibly, because the unheated shop with its tiled walls and marble floor was chilly even at the height of summer, he always worked wearing a flat cloth cap. He and his wife Ethel lived at Royston Cottages, near the junction of Longfields Crescent and Royston Hill, and worshipped at St Andrew's, where Mrs Reynolds proved a great organizer of whist drives, harvest suppers and funeral teas.

The Maypole did not sell bacon, ham or cooked meats, but specialized as its name implies in dairy produce, marketing its own brands of margarine: 'Mayday' at fourpence a pound, 'Mayco' at sixpence, 'Mayfair' at eightpence and, heading the list,

'May Queen' (said to contain butter, though the proportion was not specified) at tenpence. The premises resounded to the slapping of lumps of margarine into pound-sized blocks on water-cooled slabs spaced along the counters, using wooden 'Scotch hands' (a heavy 'beater' held in the left hand and a thinner, lighter 'slicer' in the right). If a pat was going to be placed in the window, it was embossed either with an acorn or with a cow.

People of my parents' generation remembered how during the First World War, before the introduction of rationing made equal shares available to all, shoppers from both Hoyland and Elsecar queued for hours when it was rumoured that The Maypole had received a delivery of margarine or lard. (Until wartime shortages forced them to buy it the former, commonly known as 'Maggie Anne', had been regarded by many with suspicion.)

The Maypole also supplied tea, preserves and eggs, its most popular brand of tea being 'Mikado'. (Many a Hoyland rabbit hutch was constructed from a shilling egg crate which had been bought there.) Another speciality was fruit tinned by S.E. Booth and Co. of America. A large tin of Booth's pineapple chunks cost fourpence-halfpenny, cheap even by the standards of those days, and predictably leading to the rumour that the contents were cubes of fruit-flavoured turnip; in the same spirit 'butter-slapping' was often alleged to blend water into the margarine to make it weigh more.

With the possible exception of Broughs, however, the largest grocery premises in Hoyland were those of the Barnsley British Co-operative Society's Branch No. 11, situated opposite the top of Booth Street and bounding the view southward from our yard gate, their stone façade and round-topped window casings suggestive of J.B. Priestley's 'Bruddersford'.

Between the Wars this branch was managed first by a Mr Birkhead (of whom I remember little except that he was a thin-faced man who wore glasses and that once, when I was suffering from a 'chesty' cold, his wife when talking to my mother in the street recommended her to try Vick Vapour Rub), then by tall, brisk Mr Harold Copley, who attended the Wesleyan Chapel on

Market Street, where he was always the first to arrive for the early Communion service on Easter morning. Like most Barnsley British grocery managers they lived in a narrow house next to the shop, its front room opening straight on to the pavement. This was later incorporated into the store and the Copleys moved to No. 190 King Street, formerly the Co-op drapery manager's residence.

The large windows flanking the Co-op grocery's double doors, which were opened with a lop-sided brass 'sneck', were never dressed very interestingly. They usually held a few pots of jam and packets of breakfast cereal or washing powder. There was no need to lure customers in. What attracted the wives of the unemployed and lower–paid workers from the neighbouring streets was the half-yearly dividend or 'divvy', sometimes as much as half-a-crown in the pound, paid on their purchases. Many a child owed its new pair of boots or shoes, its pretty Anniversary dress or some other treat to the fact that its mother's 'divvy', being her 'perk', was less likely than other spare cash in the house to be diverted for the purchase of beer or 'bacca'.

The shop was always full of customers, many of them shabby, some of them wearing shawls. Behind the counters, men in warehouse coats busily got together people's purchases. They included tall, pallid-looking Tom Meynell or Mennell, little Harry Denton with his black curly hair and Wilf Skorrow, of whom it was jokingly said he was so tall that when he went outside he bumped his chin against the guttering. In the 'twenties there was also a plump young woman called Mary, who had been recruited in the First World War and, like many women given 'men's' jobs then, had been allowed to stay on when peace came.

When a customer's order was complete, the assistant would recite the ritual chant, 'Any lard, cheese, eggs or bacon?' Then he would add the bill aloud at lightning speed, invariably repeating each price three times, like an exceptionally fluent auctioneer. The customer was then given a ticket or 'check' stating her Co-op registered number, the date and the sum of money she had spent, a carbon copy being kept for the Barnsley office, where her dividend would be worked out from it. The colour of the checks changed each half-year, but was always white or some other pale shade.

There was no orderly queuing at the counters. The customers served first were usually those who pushed or insinuated their way to the front, managed to catch and hold an assistant's eye, or simply shouted loudest. If as a child I was sent to the Co-op for two-pennyworth of yeast or some other small item (a hated errand), I was jostled and lost sight of in the crowd. A favourite ruse for getting served out of turn was to ask wheedlingly for 'just a quarter of tea', brazenly adding a list of other items when this had been produced. There was often at least one woman present, too, who claimed to be in a desperate rush because she had 'left t' bread i' t' ooven.'

There was a newer grocery branch at West Bank (now a painter and decorator's store), facing towards the War Memorial and serving the Longfields Crescent and Kirk Balk areas. It was managed by Mr W. Shevill, who was at one time a warden at St Peter's Church. (The Shevills made their mark on the district in other ways, one son becoming the headmaster of a school at Brampton, another an insurance broker with offices at Hoyland Common and Doncaster.) There were other branches at Hoyland Common, Blacker Hill, Jump and Church Street, Elsecar. The latter was managed by a Mr Johnson one of whose daughters, Mrs Doris Hague, was the Headmistress of Elsecar Infants' School whilst the other, Mrs Irene Stenton, was the wife of Mr Edwin Stenton, the manager of the Elsecar Gas Works.

Butchers' Shops

In inter-war Hoyland, as in its larger neighbour Barnsley and other centres of heavy industry, there was a great demand for butcher's meat.

It was widely held that a man needed good red meat, even if he was not doing a heavy job. During the Depression, when money was in short supply, the wife of one unemployed Hoyland man was said, when she made a meat-and-potato pie, to place what meat she could afford at one end and mark the pastry over it with

SHOPPING AND SHOPKEEPERS

a cross, ensuring that the man of the family got it all, whilst she and her small daughter ate potato and onion.

Most butchers bought their beasts still 'on the hoof' and killed them in their own slaughter-houses which, although discreetly hidden behind the scenes, could in warm weather make their presence felt when the hides and skins lorry was due to call. Half-carcases of beef, yellow and dark red, hung round each shop on gleaming metal rails. To absorb the drops of blood which fell from them, the floors were strewn with sawdust. Until refrigerators became electric-powered, a common sight outside a butcher's was a dripping lorry delivering ice blocks for the 'fridge'.

The cheapest and most popular meat was beef. My mother cooked a rib on Sunday and served it hot with Yorkshire pudding and two vegetables. What was left she served cold the following day, and made into hash or 'tatie pie' on Tuesday. It cost about two shillings.

Mutton and lamb, being more expensive than beef, were bought mainly by the better-off until, when war broke out in 1939, housewives were asked to take mutton three weeks in four, leaving the country's beef for its servicemen. (Shoppers also learned a new vocabulary, the names given to cuts in Ministry of Food price lists often differing from those in common use. What in Hoyland had been known as 'lift', for instance, was now officially called silverside.)

Pigs, like cows, were usually killed locally. The next day one could purchase a 'pig's fry' consisting of a pork chop and a slice each of liver, kidney and sweetbread. Since poultry in those days cost more than meat, some families had loin of pork for their Christmas dinner. Those who had poultry usually bought a locally-reared chicken, probably still needing to be plucked and drawn. Frozen 'oven-ready' birds were unheard of. When my father won a turkey in a Christmas draw organized by one of his customers, it was an unexpected luxury. Neither we nor anyone else in the 'thirties dreamed that one day turkeys would be commonplace and available in supermarket freezers.

Before Christmas, most butchers liked to attend the annual Smithfield Show, buying a prize beast and displaying its red, yellow or blue rosette in the middle of the shop window accompanied by a specially-printed, fancy-bordered card. Another common sight in a butcher's window in December was that of a pig's head, scalded, cleaned and holding an orange in its mouth. (The story is told that a visitor from London once called at a Hoyland Common butcher's shop, curious to know what kind of meat this was. 'It's a pig's head,' the butcher informed her. 'Yes, I know that,' the visitor answered impatiently. 'What I meant was, is it beef or is it mutton?')

To satisfy its demand for meat, inter-war Hoyland possessed a large number of butchers' shops, outnumbering even those of its grocers.

On the corner of High Street there was Mrs Guest (the great-grandmother of Mr Christopher Guest). She was a matronly-looking widow who dressed in black and, when weighing meat, held her hands over it as if in blessing.

On Market Street was Mr James Taylor, whose shop is now Selway and Co.'s office in Hoyland. As a child I was always fascinated by a huge pair of horns on the wall behind its counter. A tea-time speciality of Taylors' was 'penny ducks with veils' — faggots each wrapped in a suet—like skin, with hot gravy poured over them from a jug. Further on was Mr Thomas Frederick Guest whose shop and slaughter-house, now both demolished, adjoined what was in 1951 to become the Festival of Britain Garden. (It was in this slaughter-house that, during the War, Hoyland's weekly allocation of butcher's meat, no longer killed locally and averaging some 19,000 lb. of beef and lamb from abroad and 2,000 lb. of home-produced beef, mutton and veal, was shared out among local retailers.) Mr Guest also had a shop at Platts Common. Leonard Whorton's wooden lock-up shop was half-way between Guest's property and 'The Board School'.

At No. 3 King Street, next to The Globe, was Mr Fred Thompson, who had a club foot and whose shop was noted for selling delicious home-made potted meat. Further down, opposite the Maypole Dairy Company, was Henry Vincent Hastie, whose name was linked jokingly with that of Rowland Cross. He died in

SHOPPING AND SHOPKEEPERS 43

November 1932 and was followed in the business by his son Reginald. William Hague's shop, on the other side, was a few yards below Victoria Street (next to John Guest and Sons, the pawnbrokers) and formed part of a short terrace called 'Netherfield'. Edwin Goddard, a brisk little man who was succeeded by his tall son Harry, had the shop on the corner of King Street and Rock Mount that is now owned by Mr David Hague. (During the War, Mr Goddard was Chairman of Hoyland's Retail Butchers' Committee.) When I passed on my way to and from King Street School, I often paused to glance admiringly at the aproned plaster piglets in Goddard's window. The Goddards also had a Hoyland Common shop on Hoyland Road, one of those at the corner of Princess Street.

The Co-op had a butcher's shop at No. 24 King Street, two doors above The Maypole. For a time during the inter-war period its manager was Mr Percy Turner, who left to found the family business at Jump now noted for its pies and other meat products. Below Booth Street a Sheffield firm called Sayer had a shop which specialized in frozen meat, nicknamed 'frozo', a commodity then widely looked down upon and bought by some people for use as pet food. (My parents bought frozen liver, which was placed on a dish in the cellar to thaw out, as a treat for our black Labrador retriever, Chant.) One of Sayer's assistants was Miss Bessie Maltby, who was later better known as a greengrocer.

In the 'twenties Hoyland also had two pork butchers. One, Charles Smith, kept a little shop facing the top of Green Street. He moved to Thorne, where he became a councillor, and the shop was for a time run as a draper's by Miss Dorcas Hall (who is now Mrs Charlesworth). The other pork butcher, whose name was Bott, was at the corner of Booth Street in a shop which had been occupied some years before by William Ebblethwaite, a pawnbroker. Mr Bott left after the shop was gutted by fire one Sunday afternoon towards the end of the decade.

In the 'thirties Mr Frederick Daniel Bean, who was already in business at Platts Common, opened a pork butcher's at No. 30 King Street, sharing its entrance with the Maypole Dairy Company. In the Second World War it often had a lengthy queue for pies, black pudding and other unrationed pork products. (In earlier years this shop had been run by a ladies' and gentlemen's tailor named Jones.)

Greengrocers' Shops

Over the past fifty years, greengrocers' shops have changed considerably less outwardly than those of grocers and butchers. There are, however, some minor differences between shopping for fruit and vegetables then and now. Apples, oranges and other common fruits were available in fewer varieties, whilst such exotic items as kiwi fruit, avocado pears and peppers of various shades were quite unheard of by most Hoyland people. Peaches came in their season, but not nectarines. Strawberries (perhaps they were cheaper then) were sold not only in punnets but in seven-pound baskets. My mother always bought several each year and, adding gooseberries to combat the excessive sweetness, made jam to last us till the following summer.

The seasons for some kinds of produce were shorter, too. English—grown celery, with black earth adhering to it, was an autumn and winter vegetable, its sharp scent a harbinger of the 'back-end'. There was no clean, green, tasteless foreign celery, hygienically sealed in plastic packs. The sources of imported produce were fewer. No box or wrapping paper bore the name 'Israel' (a state which in those days did not exist) and, until Britain joined the Common Market, nobody here associated apples with France.

A sight no longer seen on greengrocers' counters, though in pre-war days it was commonplace, is that of a large block of cooking dates placed on a metal tray with a fork beside it for prizing off the quantity required.

Till the myxomatosis outbreak of the 'fifties made them out of favour and in short supply rabbits, a cheap source of tasty meat, were likewise associated with greengrocery. Before the War one often saw a bunch of them, stiff-legged and glassy-eyed, hanging from the back of a greengrocer's dray, ready for skinning on a blood-stained board while the customer stood waiting.

SHOPPING AND SHOPKEEPERS 45

Already, by the beginning of the 'twenties, the family most closely associated with the sale of greengrocery in Hoyland was the Halls, whose John Knowles magazine advertisement showed a basket of fruit and told readers, 'We Better Serve Ourselves by Serving Others Best.'

The founder of this firm was Mr George Hall, who started out as a potato merchant, going to Lincolnshire and buying whole fields of them. He and his wife, Kate, had eight sons and eight daughters, several of whom became greengrocers themselves on reaching adult life.

The Halls' shop in King Street, No. 35, now standing empty at the corner of Southgate, was run after her husband's death by Mrs Hall, assisted by her two youngest daughters, Edna and Doreen. Tall, slim Edna, who reminded me as a child of the nineteen-thirties fashion model Evelyn Spilsbury, married a Sheffield man. Fair-haired Doreen married Jack Garner, who worked for Fords at their Dagenham plant and was the youngest son of Herbert Garner, the ironmonger.

Mrs Hall died in 1939, but various members of her family, ending with her granddaughter Mrs Kate Marsden, kept the shop on until the 'seventies. At one time Mrs Marsden's father, Frank Hall, whose grandsons John and Frank are well-known in Hoyland, kept a greengrocer's shop next to the Futurist.

Higher up King Street on the other side, next door to Cross's, was a small, low shop with '1834' carved over its doorway. The living accommodation attached to it had old-fashioned sideways-sliding 'Yorkshire' windows. This was run as a fruit and vegetable shop till about the late 'twenties by the Halls' eldest son Henry and his wife, the parents of Miss Dorcas Hall who at one time kept the small drapery shop that had been Smith's pork butcher's. I particularly remember them because, each Saturday when I was very young, my mother and I called to buy a 'Toblerone'.

When this family left, the shop was taken over by the Halls' eldest daughter and her husband, Mr and Mrs Weadon Maltby. When her husband died in 1936, Mrs Alice Ann Maltby kept the business on, establishing a reputation as both a high-class fruiterer and the town's leading florist. She herself died in 1972. Her son and daughter, Victor and Bessie, stayed in business until 1985, though the quaint old shop had by then been pulled down and replaced with the modern glass-fronted one now occupied by Eadens. Miss Maltby died soon after their retirement.

On the corner of King Street and Bethel Street was a dark little greengrocer's shop kept by Mr Frank Clarkson, who was tall, thin-faced, stooping and elderly and whose sister married Mr Jesse Parr, a partner in the firm of John Parr and Sons, the builders. At Christmas time Clarkson's was a joy for a child to visit, because it sold not only Christmas trees but, for a penny or a halfpenny each, fascinating baubles or 'wessly bobs' to trim them. Imported, I was told, from Germany, they included brightly-coloured churches with gleaming spires, thatched cottages with turkeys by their doors, fir cones, bunches of bloom-encrusted grapes and other realistic-looking glass fruits.

The shop, which in earlier years had been run by a costumier named Hudson, was after Mr Clarkson's retirement kept on as a grocery store by his daughter, Mrs Fogg. It is now the 'Vanity Box' hairdressing salon.

A newcomer to Hoyland in the early 'thirties was a Rotherham greengrocer, Mr Rowland Watson, who took the King Street shop next door to Hastie's that had been Ernest Joll's china shop, Mr Joll having retired prematurely when his business suffered during the Depression. After staying there for only a short time, Mr Watson moved to a small wooden shop at the top end of Green Street, which he gave the imposing name 'Covent Garden' and which customers called the 'convent stall', 'Rotherham stall' or 'wooden hut'. He opened only on Fridays and Saturdays, and always sold his produce slightly cheaper than other greengrocers in the area. (When war broke out and fruit became very scarce, the queue at 'Covent Garden' often stretched two abreast down to the wall at the end of old Green Street.)

The little shop, which was painted dark green and had two large unglazed windows closed with shutters, stood outside the impressive gates of Greenfield House (the home of Rowland Cross, the grocer) where the back road to Hoyland market now branches off. It had been erected there by Mr Cross and for a short time in the 'twenties had been run by one of his daughters, Gladys, and her first husband, a young man from Harley named Uttley. The Uttleys were followed by Mr and Mrs Thomas Doyle, who later kept the Gardeners' Arms in High Street.

During the inter-war years there were also several hawkers in the town with horse-drawn drays who brought fruit and vegetables from door to door, calling on their regular customers. One of them, stout, genial Thomas Doyle, who for a time also kept the wooden shop in Green Street, was a devout Roman Catholic and helped to marshal the annual May and Corpus Christi processions. Mr Doyle's visits always called for vigilance since, while he was assembling my mother's order, his horse displayed an irresistible urge to eat our privet hedge.

Another itinerant greengrocer was Herbert Ibbotson, whose wife kept a small shop at the top of Gill Street. He was an equally loyal Wesleyan and, when he came to our house on Tuesdays and Fridays, was often singing an aria from *Elijah* or some other sacred oratorio.

There was also Albert Miles whose father, elderly, white-moustached Mr Fred Miles, kept a small lock-up fruit shop at the end of Belmont Yard in West Street.

Fish Shops and Fish Friers

During the 'twenties and 'thirties, as today, greengrocers sold the more common kinds of fish — mainly cod, kippers and finnan haddock, the latter always known in Hoyland as 'finny'. One of my earliest recollections is of being sent to Doyle's shop at the top of Green Street for a bloater — which I always pronounced 'floater' — for my tea.

The customer wanting a wider choice could patronize Mr Richard Harry Cochrane, who began by coming round with a small van and then moved into a shop, No. 4 West Street, which formed part of the Old Post Office Buildings. The items regularly to be seen on his slab included fresh salmon, crabs, lobsters (still plentiful then) and scallops, which my mother never bought but which fascinated me by their likeness to egg yolks. (I was also slightly puzzled by their name, the traditional meaning of 'scallops' in Hoyland being thick slices of potato, deep-fried in batter.)

Mr Cochrane was followed after the Second World War by Mr Ben Sorby, who stayed in business there till a few months before this shop and neighbouring ones were pulled down in 1981.

Another fishmonger was Mr Fred Crabtree, a thin, shabby-looking man with a drooping moustache who lived in a four-roomed house on Elizabeth Street and brought his wares round on a cart. His arrival in a street was heralded by the cry, 'Fresh Faroe cod!' (As a child, I assumed this to have come from Egypt, caught not in the grey North Atlantic but in the Nile.)

Hoyland also had a number of fish-and-chip shops, at which 'wet' as well as fried fish could be bought. In West Street, facing the top of Valley Way, there was Sanderson's, built fairly recently and run by Mrs Alice Sanderson, one of the daughters of Councillor Crabb. In High Street there was Chambers' (now owned by Higgs). In King Street, between the Co-op grocery store and Hall's, in a shop forming part of Hall's property, was Chappell's. (Before her marriage Mrs Chappell was Miss Minnie Hall.) Green's (later Doyle's) was at the top of Sebastopol, now renamed Millmount Road. Mr and Mrs Fred Sabin's (now the King Fish Bar) was near the top of Gill Street. In addition to these there was a fish-and-chip shop run by a family called Hodgson in Milton Road, facing the end of Millhouses Street.

The standard pre-war price for 'one of each' (a piece of battered fish and a portion of chips) was three old pence (slightly more than a decimal penny). They were wrapped in newspaper and, if to be eaten out of doors, could be sprinkled with the salt and weak vinegar placed to hand on the counter. For an extra penny a slightly larger portion of fish would be cooked at the customer's request. Bottles of Tizer and other soft drinks were usually set out on a shelf. Sausages, pies and other meat products were not, however, on sale at this kind of shop.

The term 'take-away food' had not yet been coined, nor had the take-away habit yet spread to all levels of society and become part of the British way of life. There were still plenty of housewives in those days who thought serving a chip-shop meal a lazy act, excusable only when spring cleaning or during some kind of domestic crisis. Also, before cholesterol hit the headlines, most women liked to do their frying in lard, to which the word 'pure' was usually applied. Hence the fact that some chip-shop proprietors used cotton-seed oil was apt to prove off-putting.

Bakers' Shops

During the 'twenties and 'thirties, Hoyland had several small private bakers. On the corner of West Street and Naylor's Yard, Mr and Mrs Albert Woolley ran a small café and confectioner's shop and also specialized in catering for wedding receptions, funeral teas and social functions.

A plump blonde widow, Mrs Elsie Slowen, had a bakery at No. 40 King Street, between the Co-op boot store and Sayer's frozen meat shop. When she moved elsewhere about 1937, Mr and Mrs Edward Parratt took over the business. Mrs Winifred Parratt, who ran the shop, stressed the fact in her advertisements that she catered for any size of party.

At the start of this period there were two other bakers in King Street. One of my very earliest memories is of going with my mother to buy teacakes from Mr Harold Humphrey, whose premises at the top of Sebastopol later in the 'twenties became Green's fish-and-chip shop.

Lower down, adjoining the playground of King Street School, a confectioner named Willie Storrs had his bake-house and shop (the latter now Harvey and Richardson's). His son Colin was a fellow-pupil of mine at King Street, where the Storrs supplied mid-day meals for those teachers who lived too far off to be able to go home at lunch time. When the Storrs retired during the late 'thirties, the shop was bought by Mrs Margaret Jones, who subsequently moved to St Helen's Street.

In those years of stable prices, a two-pound white loaf wrapped in tissue paper, and sometimes still hot from the oven, cost threepence—halfpenny. Boiled ham, which all bakers sold, cost sixpence a quarter. It was sliced from a juicy ham boiled in the bakehouse and temptingly displayed on a paper doily laid on a white porcelain cake stand. (Though the dangers of eating fat were not yet realized, most customers liked their ham to be lean. My father was an exception. At Slowen's, clutching my sixpence in my hand, I asked for 'A quarter of boiled ham with some fat, please,' and was given the creamy-white disk put on one side when the first slice was cut.)

However, in those days when few married women went out to work, a lot of housewives still baked their own bread, and would not have dreamt of doing otherwise.

Dough was kneaded in a large earthenware 'pancheon', smooth-glazed and cream-coloured on the inside, rough reddish-brown on the exterior, and was then covered with a cloth and left on the kitchen hearth to rise. Some time later, when it had risen, suitably-sized pieces were cut from it, kneaded again and dropped into the waiting loaf tins. (During this second kneading my mother used to recite, 'Two sticks across and a little bit of moss, it'll do, it'll do, it'll do.') A loaf was judged properly baked if, when rapped with the knuckles, it gave a hollow sound.

Yeast (always referred to in Hoyland as 'barm') was sold by most grocers in pennyworths, tucked into little cone-shaped paper bags like those boiled sweets were weighed in. (In my father's youth one private grocer at Hoyland Common, asked by a Co-op customer for 'a pennorth o' barm', is said to have retorted acidly, 'My barm won't raise Co-op flour.')

Besides being available from grocers, yeast was hawked by a

SHOPPING AND SHOPKEEPERS 51

stout man nicknamed 'Fat Jackson' from Longfields Crescent, who used to tour the streets with a rolling gait, a cloth-covered basket on his left arm, shouting loudly and stridently 'Ba-a-a-a-a-a-arm!' Mr Jackson also came round on Sunday evenings, this time in uniform, as a member of the Salvation Army band.

Sweet and Tobacco Shops

Next to their High Street fish-and-chip shop Chambers, like their successors Higgs, had a sweet shop combined with an off-licence.
Another High Street sweet shop was Wilkinson's (now Walker's greeting card and garden shop). At Wilkinson's, besides sweets and tobacco, one could buy cool, bright yellow home-made ice-cream, in twopenny sandwiches or penny and halfpenny cornets. It was usually served from the red cylindrical freezer by one of Mr George Wilkinson's two daughters, pale, fair-haired Betty and her sister Florence (the latter always known by her pet name 'Flossie').

Between the Wars the small building on the corner of Duke Street now known as 'Cottage Flowers' (which had a 'twin' further on Market Street used as a Salvation Army citadel) was a sweet and tobacco shop owned initially by Mr Norman Fisher (a brother of Mr Edwin Fisher of Manor Farm) and for a time during the 'thirties by Mr and Mrs Reginald Hirst Allen (a son and daughter-in-law of George Hirst Allen, the grocer).
At that time it consisted of two separate rooms, divided by a narrow passageway. Tobacco was sold in the room to the left of the door, where a fire was burning in a little grate round which regular customers used to gather. Sweets were sold separately in the room on the right, to which the person serving had to cross when a customer for chocolate or sweets came in.

The sweet shop and off-licence across the street, next to the Infants' School, was run at the beginning of this period by an elderly man named Robinson, whose grey cardigans matched his grey moustache. He was followed by Mr and Mrs Joseph Smith (a brother and sister-in-law of Charles Smith the pork butcher and Mrs Parratt the confectioner). It was from Smith's that my mother and I used to fetch my father an occasional bottle of 'Forest Brown', the only alcoholic beverage he indulged in, with which he liked to refresh himself after a particularly hard, harassing day.

Later the Smiths too started baking, adopting the name 'Field Top Bakery' (the Manor Farm cart track which ran close by was known by everybody as the 'Field Top') and including in their advertisement the words 'Cleanliness is our motto'.

There was another off-licence on Market Street, run by a Mr Dyson, on the corner of that street and Royston Hill, towards each of which it had a window facing. The property formed part of a terrace solidly built of stone, with large sash windows and small vestibules opening on to the street, beyond which stood the little wooden shop occupied by Mr Leonard Whorton, the butcher.

Until wartime Chancellors repeatedly increased the tax on them, cigarettes remained unchanged in price for years. Better brands such as Players and Capstan cost sixpence for ten and a shilling for twenty; when their price rose to a penny each, early in the 'forties, this was regarded as exorbitant. Cheaper brands like Woodbines and Park Drive were ten for fourpence. Those unable to afford even this could buy their Woodbines in green-and-orange paper packs of five.

In each packet there was a picture card, one of a set of fifty. Their themes were mostly mildly instructional: British wild flowers, British fresh-water fish, famous locomotives or, if a Royal occasion such as a Jubilee was imminent, English kings and queens or events in the lives of modern Royalty. Film stars, radio personalities, footballers and cricketers appeared on them, too. Free albums were supplied to keep them in and children collected them avidly, swapping spares. Those whose fathers did not smoke or were pipe smokers begged them from friends and relatives who did. Usually, however, each set contained at least one that nobody seemed able to obtain, a situation leading to accusations of manufacturers' chicanery.

SHOPPING AND SHOPKEEPERS 53

A favourite pipe tobacco in those days, especially with elderly working men, was Thick Twist, which was cheap and burned very pungently. It lay on the shop counter in a rope-like coil, from which lengths were sliced on a hard wooden block over which a small brass cutting knife was hinged, before being weighed on a shining brass beam-scale. The customer then shredded disks into his palm with a clasp knife before filling his pipe.

There were still some old men who smoked white clay pipes. My mother bought me one from Fisher's (where a bunch of them always hung on the wall) to blow soap bubbles with.

Ice-cream Vendors

Although, by the late 'thirties, there were a few Walls' ice-cream vendors riding around on their blue-and-white 'Stop-Me-and-Buy-One' tricycles, whose boxes held both traditional ice-cream and cardboard-wrapped fruit ices (which in those days were still a novelty), most of the ice-cream sold in Hoyland was, like Wilkinson's, made locally.

Tingles, the largest local manufacturers, came from the West Melton area and always attended Elsecar 'Feast', where several of their vans were to be seen parked just inside the main gates of the fairground.

The ice-cream van of those days had a festive air, and also looked distinctly patriotic. It was brightly painted in red, white and blue, its sides were open and its canopy rested upon brass 'barley-sugar' poles. There were no chimes (an innovation pioneered by Walls in the late 'forties), but one enterprising salesman blew a whistle to announce his arrival in the street, following this with a cry which sounded like 'Oosame!' – a name which my amused parents and I were quick to adopt for this commodity.

Vans used during the 'thirties were motorized, though I remember from my early childhood seeing a tall, well-built young woman called Miss Drury sell ice-cream in Booth Street from a pony cart.

54 WHILE MARTHA TOLD THE HOURS

Clothing Shops

Between the Wars both men and women who lived in Hoyland were able to dress smartly from top to toe, without needing either to leave the town or to open a mail-order catalogue.

At No. 38 King Street, almost opposite its grocery branch and next door to Mrs Slowen the baker, the Co-op had a small boot and shoe shop managed by Mr Isaac Liversedge, a short man with glasses and a dark moustache, who was a Methodist lay preacher and, during the First World War, had incurred a measure of opprobrium through registering as a conscientious objector. Before she married Eric Bedford, Mr Liversedge was assisted by blonde, Nordic-looking Miss Muriel Green, who lived further down the hill at High Cottages.

The footwear sold in this dark, narrow shop, with its varnished counter and strong smell of leather, ranged from workmen's heavy, durable boots to the 'Kiltie' arch-heel and 'Startrite' shoes (made in black patent leather or glacé kid) that my mother bought me, afraid that cheaper brands might somehow harm my feet.

For adults, besides a small number of well-known makes, the Co-op sold its own brand of shoes, 'Wheatsheaf', stamped inside with a stylized gold wheatsheaf and tending to be plain and 'sensible' rather than smart.

Except for white sports and gold or silver party shoes, women's footwear, whatever its brand, was for most of this period obtainable in two shades, brown and black. When dark green and navy walking shoes came on the market in the late 'thirties they were regarded as a startling innovation.

Further up King Street, on the corner of Green Street, in premises now occupied by a furniture dealer, was the Co-op drapery store. It was an unusual-looking shop, with two entrances and with part of its ground floor slightly lower than the rest, the two levels being linked by a gentle ramp up and down which, as a toddler, I loved to race while my mother was busy making her purchases.

The shop was two-storey. Downstairs male assistants, including a tall young man whose Christian name was Stanley, measured curtain materials and sold buttons, tape, sewing cotton and other items of haberdashery. Upstairs women assistants, including for a time Miss Edna Shaw of Gill Street, who left near the end of the 'thirties to be married, sold stockings, corsetry, hats and other items of feminine attire.

The manager until 1933 was Mr Christopher King, a short, stocky man who wore glasses. He was the father of Miss Ivy M. King (whose married name was Williamson), a talented musician who played the organ at the Market Street Wesleyan Chapel, was for many years the official accompanist at the Elsecar Midland Musical Festival, made history by playing the piano to accompany a choir broadcasting from the bottom of a mine shaft and, after the Second World War, became the conductor of the Thorncliffe Operatic Society. Mr King's younger daughter, Dorothy (Mrs Gale), who before her marriage worked in the Town Hall, was a gifted soprano and died tragically at the age of forty-two through being struck by an open-cast coal lorry in Cortworth Lane, between Nether Haugh and Wentworth.

When Mr King died unexpectedly in 1933, his successor was Mr William Riley, a tall, good-looking bachelor whose father kept a small private draper's shop in Barnsley. Mr Riley, who lived to a great age, surviving well into the nineteen-eighties, stayed in Hoyland for only a few years. He then moved to the Co-op's main New Street branch, to take charge of the 'Manchester' department selling sheets, pillow cases and other cotton goods.

It was after the death of Mr King that No. 190 King Street, the house in which he and his family had lived, was made into the Hoyland grocery branch manager's official residence, to which Mr and Mrs Harold Copley moved with Brian, their young son.

The double-fronted shop at the top side of Green Street that is now Thawley's newspaper and toy shop was throughout the inter-war period a draper's owned by Mrs Florence Cocker Ottley, a small, elderly woman with a 'light-coloured' voice, who lived in neighbouring Greenfield Cottage with her daughter and son-in-law, Mrs Mabel and Mr George Henry Ernest Hoyland. She was a native of Sheffield and the widow of my Great-Uncle William, who at one time ran the Princess Theatre in West Street, was a former Urban District Councillor and died on Good Friday in 1914.

The shop, the oldest drapery store in Hoyland, had been opened across the road at No. 3 King Street by Great-Uncle William Ottley's first wife, Annie, a tall woman with dark ringlets, who died young and lies buried in St Peters Churchyard. At one time it had specialized in hats trimmed and decorated on the premises. (John Albert Ottley, William and Annie's son, is said as a boy to have excelled at this.) In the 'thirties it still sold dresses and hats, besides haberdashery, stockings and underwear. The second Mrs Ottley's two specialities, however, were knitting wool (the brand she stocked was Copley's, kept in a glass-fronted case near the door) and exceptionally attractive baby clothes (bonnets, matinée jackets, frocks and bootees, all sold at most reasonable prices).

Hoyland's newest ladies' and children's outfitter's, Ford and Marsland's, founded between the Wars, was at No. 2 West Street, one of the two larger of the four shops in the Old Post Office Buildings. Its proprietors were Mrs Eliza Ford (the wife of a newsagent and tobacconist, Mr Fred Ford, who had been in business at the same address) and her auburn-haired daughter, Mrs Doris Marsland, whose good taste was evinced not only by the ladies' and children's clothing on sale there but also by the chapel flower arrangements for which she became noted.

Ford and Marsland were succeeded by May Taylor, whose name became a household word in the town, where she remained in business for many years. When the Buildings were demolished in 1981 her successor, Jessie Ainsworth, transferred the business to No. 46 King Street where it is now run by Mrs Doreen Law.

Another draper's with a 'double-barrelled' name, and by far the best-known in the Hoyland area, was Storey and Cooper's in High Street. Mr and Mrs Harry Cooper had come to Hoyland

SHOPPING AND SHOPKEEPERS

after the First World War, Mrs Cooper and her sister, Mrs Storey, renting a small shop in King Street, near the Maypole, where they sold drapery. In 1927 the Coopers purchased Holly House, a stone residence standing back from the road between the John Knowles Church and Chambers' sweet shop. On to it they built two double-fronted shops, covering the front garden where the holly bush grew from which the property had taken its name. They moved into the one next to the church and let the other to Melias, a firm of grocers. (At Hemsworth, relatives of Mrs Cooper's built two shops almost identical to these in the main shopping centre.)

Run by Mrs Jessie Cooper, a slim, bustling woman with glasses, who usually dressed in dark skirts and twin sets with scissors on a tape round her neck for cutting material, Storey and Cooper's was, as my mother once put it, 'a village shop supplying town quality.' The assistants in their smart matching overalls included three of the Fozzard sisters from Elsecar. Downstairs were haberdashery and curtain fabrics. Upstairs were skirts and blouses, twin sets, dresses, coats and a wide selection of attractive hats. Here, thanks to Mrs Cooper's dependable taste, one could acquire an outfit as smart as any from a Sheffield or Leeds department store, at a considerably lower cost.

The Market Street building that is now a café originally consisted of two shops, each with living accommodation attached to it. No. 12 on the left, nearest to the Town Hall, was a draper's run by Mr and Mrs Norman Fisher, who also owned the sweet and tobacco shop on the corner of Duke Street. It closed during the 'thirties, after Mrs Fisher died following a gall-bladder operation (a procedure which in those days often proved fatal). Some time later her widower married Miss Daisy Lodge (a daughter of Mr William Henry Lodge, who farmed at Upper Hoyland Hall) and moved to Retford. The shop was taken over by the Co-op as a hardware (always called locally a 'tinning') department.

There were also shops in Hoyland supplying clothes for men, and catering for most normal sartorial requirements. Between

Fisher's and the old Wesleyan Chapel, in what is now Clayton's sports and footwear shop, was the Co-op tailoring department, where a man not only could buy shirts and socks but also could be measured for a bespoke suit made at Barnsley by the Co-op's tailoring staff, among whom was Miss Ivy Brooke of West Street. (Until the early 'twenties this shop had been George A. Wellock and Sons' gentlemen's outfitter's. The Wellocks had moved from Hoyland to Hull because of the Depression.)

The first Co-op manager I remember seeing there was Mr Harry Thornley, a stocky man in a blue chalk-striped suit, who wore a measuring tape draped round his neck and walked about the shop with a jaunty air. His wife, a tall, elegant-looking woman with light brown hair drawn back into a bun, presided at the ties and socks counter. They lived over the shop and had an only daughter, Eileen Mary, who closely resembled her mother in looks. Like many northerners in those days, the Thornleys used to spend their summer holidays at Blackpool, Mrs Thornley expressing surprise when my mother told her of our own preference for the Yorkshire coast.

A later manager, Mr Walter Grimes, was a pleasant-faced, obliging young man, whose father had been the Co-op pharmacist in Hoyland until his death when I was very young and whose mother, Edith, still lived at the Co-op house in Booth Street. His assistant, equally helpful and polite, was Mr George Fawcett, whose father was for many years the landlord of the Turf Tavern in King Street. Mr Grimes' wife and Mr Fawcett's wife both taught at Market Street 'Board' School.

Without doubt the best-known of all Hoyland clothiers, however, was Mr Douglas Porteous Beattie, a Scotsman who first came to Hoyland as the manager of John Guest and Sons' pawn shop and outfitter's, between the Queen's Head and Hague's butcher's shop in King Street. Later he had branched out into business on his own, buying No. 13 High Street, a detached, four-square, stone-built property on the corner of Dick Croft (now re-named High Croft) which had housed Moses Fletcher's Old

SHOPPING AND SHOPKEEPERS

Eccles Cake Shop (another speciality of which was its excellent parkin).

Here Mr Beattie and his wife Elizabeth (formerly Miss Elizabeth Askham of Dewsbury), a tall, dignified woman who when I was a child always used to remind me of Queen Mary, resided with their elder daughter Audrey (a school-teacher who married a Sheffield man and settled at High Greave), their sons Donald and Derek (the former of whom was known by his school friends as 'Donkey') and their tall, fair-haired younger daughter Margaret Janet, who attended Ecclesfield Grammar School (where, like me, she was a member of Priestley House, in whose hockey team she played as goalkeeper), worked for a time in Key's Estate Office and, in the Second World War, served as a Wren.

In the shop to the right of the front vestibule, entered through a glass-panelled inner door, Mr Beattie sold shirts, socks and other items of menswear. The iron railings flanking the stone steps leading up to the outer door were hung with caps and workmen's navy-blue overalls. He was also the Hoyland agent for the Yorkshire Traction Company, in whose offices one of his sons worked for a time, and ran a railway booking agency in a most helpful and efficient manner.

It was not, however, as an outfitter that Mr Beattie made his mark on Hoyland. A stocky man with a bald head surrounded by a neat circle of greying hair, who spoke with a lisp and usually dressed in a grey alpaca jacket on working days, he was a born organizer, getting the town a better postal service, helping to make its celebrations of Royal occasions memorably successful, and organizing an annual outing which was the highlight of some working people's year.

Mr Beattie always spoke of his premises as 'Beattie's Busy Corner'. Though still in middle life, he was always referred to with affection as 'Old Beattie'. Hence local children sang a nonsense rhyme, known by boys as far away as Hemingfield, which ran:

WHILE MARTHA TOLD THE HOURS

> Good King Wensless knocked a bobby senseless
> Rahnd Old Beattie's corner.
> Beattie came aht 'n' gave him a claht,
> 'n' knocked him back rahnd t' corner.

In the late 'thirties Beatties retired from business, first spending a holiday in South Africa, where their son Donald had gone to work, and then settling in Mrs Beattie's native Dewsbury. Never a man to be inactive Mr Beattie, when the Second World War broke out, took a temporary post in the Civil Service. When his wife died suddenly a few years later, he took a flat in London near his daughter Margaret, who had married a member of the staff of *Hansard* and lived at Barnes in Surrey. In the early 'fifties, having in the meantime made several welcome calls on Hoyland friends, he too died suddenly, as he would no doubt have wished, collapsing in church during the course of a united Anglican-Methodist service.

When Beatties retired, the 'Busy Corner' premises were let to the Ministry of Labour, from which time they served as Hoyland's Labour Exchange until they were demolished, together with the old Town Hall next door, during the early 'seventies. Mr Beattie's bus and railway agencies were taken over by Walkers, the newsagents across the road from him at No. 22 High Street.

Newsagents and Stationers

Walker's newsagency is a business run by the same family now as fifty years ago. Its founders were Isaac Lichmere Walker, a cheerful, bustling robin of a man whose name was invariably shortened to 'Lichie' and his tall, quiet-spoken wife Annette, whose name was shortened by her friends to 'Netta'. They were the parents of Mr Geoffrey Walker and his sister Mrs Joan Clark, and the grandparents of Mr David Walker, by whom the business is now being run with the help of his team of women assistants. (Mr and Mrs 'Lichie' Walker both came from Barnsley, where Mrs Walker's parents kept the Corner Pin.)

Walker's first shop, where as a little girl I called to buy my comic paper, *The Rainbow*, was a tiny one in King Street, on the end of the row where Maltbys the greengrocers traded. Between it and Mrs Ottley's drapery store were Cross's yard and stable. Upstairs, like the other shops in the terrace, it had small, square-paned, sideways-sliding windows. On the end wall was a large blue-and-white enamelled sign advertising the *News of the World*, one of the Sunday papers whose sale Walkers promoted in the Hoyland area. The previous proprietor of the shop was an aunt of Mr Walker's, Mrs Rothwell.

In 1932 the Walkers moved to their present, much larger premises in High Street, which had previously been run as an ironmonger's by Mr Herbert Garner, who died suddenly on 17th May that year. There they expanded their business by acquiring the travel agencies that Mr Beattie had run, branched out into the sale of chocolates and sweets and later that of gardening requisites, and have now given the shop a smart new look by incorporating into it the areas which were Garner's living kitchen and workroom.

Until the late 'thirties No. 1 Milton Road, which formed part of the Old Post Office Buildings, was run as a newspaper and toy shop by tall, thin Mr John Willie Pickering, whose advertisements referred to it as 'Hoyland's Toyland' and invited prospective customers to walk round, promising that 'We shall not ask you to buy. We shall smile even if you don't.'

Mr Pickering had previously been in business at No. 2 West Street, next door, as the successor to Mr Fred Ford (the husband of Mrs Ford of Ford and Marsland), and had moved into the larger neighbouring shop when this was vacated by Mr Edwin James, a draper and outfitter.

When the Pickerings moved the business was purchased by Mr Ben Smithies, an earnest, cheerful, kind-faced little man who was a Methodist lay preacher and whose daughter Margaret, like Margaret Beattie and me, was in Priestley House at Ecclesfield Grammar School. (Some years later, when the flying bombs or 'doodle-bugs' were falling on south-eastern England, Mr Smithies was among those provincial air-raid wardens who volunteered to spend some time down there helping their hard-pressed London counterparts.)

Besides selling newspapers and toys the Smithies, who retained the Pickerings' advertising slogan, ran a small lending library of popular fiction. When they left Hoyland the business was purchased by Mr Alfred Ellaway, who in turn was succeeded by Mr Brian Dixon. Before the Old Post Office Buildings were pulled down, Mr Dixon moved into the King Street shop where Mrs Ottley had sold drapery. Since his retirement it is being run by Adrian and Wendy Thawley, the elder son and daughter-in-law of Mr Geoffrey Thawley, who farms at Blacker Grange.

Opposite Walker's original King Street shop and next door to David Clayton's furniture store, with which it formed the ground floor of what had once been a Primitive Methodist chapel, was a dark, narrow newspaper and tobacco shop. Its proprietor around 1911 was Mr Arthur Thompson, who advertised a diversity of goods ranging from walking sticks to violin strings. In the early 'twenties it was being run by Mr and Mrs Leonard Scarr of No. 14 Booth Street (a nephew and niece of Edgar Hirst, the proprietor of the Booth Street printing business that my father later took over).

When the Scarrs moved to Mexborough, where Mr Scarr, a short man with a breathless voice, was an agent for the Royal Insurance Company, the business was purchased by a firm called Cotton and was managed by an auburn-haired young woman, Miss Winifred Pye, who lived 'down Milton'. Another assistant at Cotton's was Miss Marion Thickett, whose parents kept the Market Hotel at Elsecar. The shop was also a laundry agency, to which my father's stiff white collars were taken each week in a small leather box shaped like a drum.

About the early 'thirties Cottons were succeeded by Mr and Mrs Harry Dunstone who, however, stayed only a few years. (Besides being a newsagent, Mr Dunstone was a skilled violinist whose services were frequently in demand.)

The Dunstones' successor was Mr Maurice Layte, who brought the wheel almost full circle by marrying Cotton's manageress, cheerful, friendly Miss Pye. He served in the RAF during the War, and stayed in business at the King Street shop until its demolition in 1972.

Besides those newsagents whose rounds were based on these town-centre shops there was, during the years between the Wars, a tall, stooping man with a white moustache, Mr Ted White, who conducted his newspaper trade from a small terrace house part way along the east side of Bethel Street, delivering papers in a box-on-wheels or, in Hoyland terminology, a 'drug'.

Many of today's newspapers already existed before the Second World War. On Sundays one could choose between *The People*, the *News of the World*, *The Observer* and *The Sunday Times*. On weekdays the 'up-market' papers were *The Times*, *The Daily Telegraph* and the *Yorkshire Post*. At a more popular level, and representing all shades of political opinion, right, centre and left, were the *Daily Mail*, the *Daily Express* and the *Daily Mirror*. Morning papers which have since become defunct or have been amalgamated with others included the *Daily Herald*, the *News Chronicle*, the *Daily Sketch* and the more local *Sheffield Telegraph*.

Just as today, there was a circulation 'war', but instead of offering large bingo prizes rival papers used cheap culture as a bait. In return for a shilling postal order and a number of coupons cut from consecutive issues, they would supply one or more books, a process which, when repeated, enabled the reader to build a complete set. The *Daily Herald* was the most prolific source, its publications, printed by the Odhams Press and bound in imitation leather lettered in gold, including the complete works of Charles Dickens, a set of four dozen books by other authors ranging from *Wuthering Heights* and *Ivanhoe* to *Don Quixote* and *The Three Musketeers*, children's encyclopaedias and colourful books containing reproductions of world-famous paintings.

To tempt the young to influence their parents' choice, most papers had a children's page and club, sporting some mascot such as Teddy Tail (a smartly dressed mouse) of the *Daily Mail*, the

Herald's Bobby Bear and Jane Sprogg (a neat, pig-tailed Dutch doll) of the monthly periodical *Modern Woman*. The *Yorkshire Weekly Post*, published each Friday, had its 'Sunshine Circle' (whose friendly motto was 'Spread a Little Happiness'), run by a journalist called 'Auntie Betty' and a newspaper cartoonist, 'Uncle Oswald'. For a small enrolment fee, a child could join one of these and be issued with an enamelled membership badge to wear on its jacket or blazer.

There were fewer 'glossies' than there are today and colour was still in its infancy, tending to be confined to cover pictures. Women's periodicals catered mainly for the cosy-minded housewife, the word 'home' featuring in most of their titles. Popular monthlies included *Woman and Home* and *My Home*. Among the weeklies were *Woman's Pictorial*, *Woman's Weekly* and two smaller publications with the Dum-and-Dee names *Home Notes* and *Home Chat*.

Children's comics, less sophisticated in subject matter and more artistically produced than today's, included *The Rainbow* (which I bought each week from Walker's), *Tiger Tim's* and *Chicks' Own*. The latter had large-print words split up with hyphens into short syllables, to help those tinies just beginning to read.

Hotspur and *Wizard* were favourites with older boys, and the still-popular *Dandy* and *Beano* were launched in 1937 and 1938.

Milk Vendors

Though the Co-op was already marketing bottled milk, the normal way of delivering milk in inter-war Hoyland was still direct from the farm and from the can. It was brought round daily in a pony trap, sometimes by an employee but usually by the farmer or some member of his family.

Farmers selling milk in those days included Horace Thawley of Blacker Grange, Blacker Hill, whose roundsman was Harold, his second son; Wilson Helliwell of Fearnley Farm, West Bank; Edwin Fisher of Manor Farm, Market Street; and, after Mr Fisher moved to Aston, Thomas Lodge, whose youngest daughter

SHOPPING AND SHOPKEEPERS

Beatrice was his roundswoman for a number of years. Another vendor was Harold Dobson of Blacker Hill, whose milk came from the Glebe Farm, Tankersley. A small-scale milk-producer in the 'twenties was William Ottley Parratt, a colliery winder, who lived at a small-holding opposite the junction of Mount Crescent and Hawshaw Lane. His round was done by his daughters, Beatrice (usually shortened to Betty) and Nora.

During the months from April to October, when cows were turned into the fields to graze, milk cost threepence a pint — just over a decimal penny. For the rest of the year, when they were kept indoors and fed on cattle cake, it cost threepence-halfpenny.

The large grey can (resembling those one now sees on wooden stands at the side of country roads, awaiting collection by the dairy lorry) had two metal dippers hooked on to its rim, holding a pint and half-pint respectively. (In Hoyland the latter measure was called a 'gill', a fact which made it most confusing when in cookery lessons at the grammar school our teacher, dictating some recipe, used the word with its correct quarter-pint meaning.)

In those more honest days, when no-one thought of locking their back door except at night (the one Hoyland burglar active in the 'thirties confined his activities to the dark hours, and was deemed a 'one-off' phenomenon), the roundsman or woman walked into each customer's kitchen and poured a measured quantity of milk into a basin or jug left on the table. (This cannot, in today's terminology, have been a 'cost-effective' way to market it, time often being wasted, can in hand, swapping items of gossip with the housewife.)

By the evening a thick, almost solid layer of cream had risen to the top of the jug or basin. (During the Second World War, this could be placed in a screw-topped jar and shaken vigorously to supplement the meagre butter ration.) In thundery or sultry weather, however, at a time when few householders owned a fridge, milk needed boiling at bedtime; otherwise it 'turned' before the morning.

In the late 'thirties, for reasons of hygiene, the Council's Sanitary Inspector attempted to compel farmers to bottle and pasteurize all the milk that they sold in Hoyland. The plan proved most unpopular with both suppliers and their customers who, however, received a 'stay of execution' when the outbreak of war in 1939 caused its implementation to be postponed. Farmers also resented the growing number of regulations concerning dairy hygiene, seeing them as interference and harassment and the Inspector as a meddling busybody. What small milk-producers hated even more was the formation of the Milk Marketing Board, with its red tape and the unwelcome burden of paperwork its forms imposed on them — as unfailing a source of conversation between my mother and the various people who brought our milk as the weather and its effect on the harvest.

Hoyland Market

Opened by a group of local businessmen, the Hoyland Market Company, in 1867, the original Hoyland Market occupied roughly the same site as the present one, between the Strafford Arms (The Beggar and the Gentleman) and the Infants' School (St Andrew's Parish Hall). From about 1920, though, part of the site was occupied by the Cinema, built next door to the 'Strafford'. (A previous market elsewhere in the town had not been a success.)

    The market was held weekly, on Saturdays, staying open until what seems today to be the exceptionally late hour of 9.00 p.m. On winter evenings all the stalls were lit with hissing, bright blue, 'fish-tail' gas-burners. Between the façade of the Cinema House and the street were stalls selling greengroceries, fish, haberdashery, pots and pans, and other household items. The part down the side of the Cinema, however, consisted entirely of meat stalls — permanent wooden structures, built back-to-back, like open-fronted sheds with iron--snecked doors by which the salesmen could gain access to them.

    Besides having shops in the town, some Hoyland butchers used to rent market stalls. Others were let to farmer-butchers, most of whom came from the Hemsworth area. The tale is told of how, one Saturday evening, a country butcher was driving home over dark, deserted Brierley Common in his cart, in the back of which there lay a canvas bag containing his day's takings. Hearing a scrabbling as of somebody struggling to climb aboard, he turned, picked up his cleaver and brought it down where he judged the sound to have come from. Then, without further investigation, he drove on. It was not until he reached home that he found three severed fingers lying near the tailboard.

At the time when refrigeration usually depended on getting a fresh supply of ice each day, it was seldom practicable for a butcher to keep meat over the weekend. Therefore, when the market was about to close, what remained unsold had to be disposed of cheaply. Knowing this, some prominent Hoyland citizens, not poor but clearly living by the adage 'Take care of the pence and the pounds will take care of themselves,' would hang about until 8.55 before stepping up to buy their joints for Sunday.

Built along the boundary wall of the market place which ran at right-angles to the Infants' School there were a few dim, open-fronted shops. In one of these Mrs Scarrott of Hoyland Common, who in my mind's eye is always dressed in black, sold clothes pegs, bars of red and yellow soap, moth-balls, fire-lighters, candles and similar merchandise. She was assisted by one of her daughters, a thin, pale girl with glasses.

End-on to the pavement, next to the school gate, there was a tiny open-fronted shop where, for part of the 'twenties, a Mrs Powell, her son Vincent and his wife Mary sold home-made sweets. They lived in an odd little house on the corner of Green Street, which consisted of a downstairs kitchen and a few rooms over the Co-op drapery store. (It had been the home of the Co-op manager and, after the Powells left, was occupied by other Co-op employees including Tom Meynell or Mennell, who worked in the grocery shop, his wife and their little son, Jacky.)

When I was very young my father used to take me round the market after we finished tea each Saturday, a ritual which always ended with buying a quarter of Powell's bright yellow and pink, acetone-smelling pear drops. I hated them, but did not like to say so. When we got home my mother used to put them on the top shelf of the cupboard, in a tin shaped like a thatched cottage. I never ate any but, as there was always room for more the following week, somebody else appears to have enjoyed them.

At some point after the Powells' time, the sweet shop was converted into a café.

About the start of the Second World War the old market closed. There were probably two reasons for this. An open-air market, with its naked lights, could not be held during the wartime blackout. Moreover, though its opening hours could have been curtailed, after food rationing was introduced there was no meat to spare for casual sale on the butchers' stalls forming a large part of it.

During the War, a roundabout had its winter quarters at the end of the market farthest from the street, giving rides in the evenings suitably blacked out, with its sound clearly audible outside our house. Also, for a number of years, a man called Smithson lived permanently in a maroon-painted caravan behind the Parish Hall.

It was not until the early 'seventies that, despite opposition from Barnsley (which claimed that a medieval charter gave it the sole right to hold markets in the area), the present Hoyland Market slowly evolved, held first on a site behind the old Town Hall, then on a demolition site in King Street between Hall Street and where Barclay's Bank now stands and finally, after the Cinema was pulled down, on permanent stalls at the original Market Street venue.

CHAPTER THREE

Pubs and Clubs

ACCORDING to my parents, the late Victorian Hoyland of their childhood was particularly well endowed with pubs, which early medical officer's reports referred to as 'soul destroyers'. They pointed out to me several old houses in Dick Croft and George Street that had once been licensed. The name of one, I remember, was the Puddlers' Arms, which was obviously derived from iron making.

In Hoyland's heyday as a growing centre of heavy industry, roughly between 1840 and 1880, with employees at the Milton Iron Works needing to drink heavily to slake their thirst and miners at Hoyland Silkstone Colliery seeking relief for their dry, dusty throats, this proliferation of inns and beerhouses was hardly surprising.

During my own childhood, there were still two pubs in Milton Road itself whose names recalled the by then long-since closed Milton Iron Works. Facing towards one of the deep Milton Ponds was the Furnace Inn, which survives to this day, transformed with window-boxes and hanging baskets. Its landlord was Mr Fred Searson, after whose death in 1933 the licence passed to Mabel Searson, his widow. She was a trim, ladylike person who maintained a firm though not unkindly discipline, refusing to allow her 'regulars' to play dominoes on Sundays or Good Fridays. This restriction the old men who seem to have formed a large proportion of her customers, including my mother's father from Armroyd Lane, who went there for his Sunday lunch-time pint, appear to have accepted without resentment.

The shop next door to the 'Furnace', a distinguishing feature of which is its large, square bays, had also at one time been a public house, an erstwhile landlord being Manasseh Cutts, the father of my Uncle Fred Ottley's wife Emily and the coal leader Thomas Cutts, and grandfather of Arthur Cutts who until recently owned the butcher's shop below the Futurist. (He was also the brother of Ephraim Cutts, who kept the little grocery shop on the corner of Elsecar Market Place, and the uncle of Miss Lilian Cutts who, until her untimely death during the 'thirties, taught at Hoyland Common Girls' School.)

The detached, double-fronted house with its front door opening on to the pavement, facing the Milton end of Millhouses Street, was still licensed during the time between the Wars and, like the 'Furnace', had iron-making connotations, being known as the Forge Inn. Its landlord was Mr John Siddall.

At the same side of Milton but higher up, just above the steepest section of the hill, was the original stone-built Gate Inn, which must have been a hundred years old or more, since during the eighteen-thirties a postal service was run from there between Hoyland and Barnsley. The licensee was another widow, Mrs Swift, an elderly woman who walked with a limp. (She was not the first landlady of the 'Gate' — a century earlier it had been run by a Mrs Elizabeth Allott.)

Both Mrs Swift and Mrs Searson took St Andrew's Parish Magazine, which as a teenager I sometimes undertook to deliver for my mother, who at that time was the magazine secretary. Having grown up in a near-teetotal home, I wondered why people engaged in their kind of trade should wish to read religious literature, and always felt slightly wicked when I called at the 'Gate' and the 'Furnace' making my deliveries.

A few yards above the 'Gate' was the Ball Inn, which has recently reverted to its old name after being known for a time as 'Oliver's Ale House'. Its landlord was Mr Walter Sylvester. Appropriately, in view of its name, it was the headquarters of Hoyland Town Football Club, which used to play on the Town Field off West Street in distinctive chequered jerseys and, back in 1901, achieved the double honour of winning the Beckett and Challenge Cups. One of the players in those earlier years in this or some neighbouring team is said to have been 'Chubby' Allott, whose mother patrolled the touch-line and rushed in to belabour with her brolly any opponent daring to tackle him.

(Football 'incidents' are certainly not a phenomenon confined to the second half of the twentieth century. My father remembered printing posters for Jump Red Lion, a club based on a now demolished pub at the junction of Greenside Lane and Church Street, Jump, warning that 'Anyone caught throwing stones, glass jars or other missiles at the referee will be prosecuted.')

Another woman licensee in Hoyland in the inter-war years was Mrs Charlotte Titcombe of the Queen's Head, on the corner of Victoria Street and King Street. A stately-looking woman with bright golden hair, she was the widow of a former landlord, John J. Dewhirst, and some time between his death in 1905 and 1911 had married a comedian, Fred Titcombe, who took part in variety shows at the Princess in West Street. An advertisement dated 1911 describes the 'Queen's' as 'central, cosy and comfortable' and calls attention to its excellent cigars, finest ales and stouts, and choicest wines and spirits.

Mrs Titcombe, who kept the 'Queen's' licence on until 1933, had two sons by her first marriage. The elder of them, Mark Dewhirst, a thoughtful-looking young man with a facial resemblance to the Prince of Wales (later the Duke of Windsor), at one time ran a small grocery and general store on the other corner of Victoria Street, though he later worked at the Hoyland Cinema. The shop, which had a window facing each street and double doors up two steps across the corner, had once been run by Edwin Thompson, the father of Mr Robert Humphreys Thompson, an organist, and Miss Florence Thompson, his violinist sister. (My father recalled how, in the Thompsons' time, the place had been so full of merchandise, boxes and barrels stacked up on the floor and brooms and brushes hanging from the ceiling, that it was difficult on entering to chart a course towards the counter.)

Mrs Titcombe's younger son, Reginald Dewhirst, fair-haired and more closely resembling his mother in looks, was a colliery electrician who gave up his job for reasons of health and in later years kept a small grocery shop at the far side of King Street. It formed part of a group of buildings owned by the Firths, facing the Bethel or 'New Connexion' Chapel, and is said in earlier days to have been run by a Mrs Smith as a confectionery and toy shop.

Mrs Titcombe's sister, Mrs Elizabeth Ann Solomon, was the wife of Mr William Solomon, who was for many years the organist at Hill Street Congregational Chapel.

During the 'thirties the old Queen's Head was pulled down, as were the Gate Inn at the top of Milton and the Gardeners' Arms in High Street. The latter, on the opposite corner of Dick Croft to Beattie's outfitter's, was a double-fronted beerhouse, built of stone, with a two-up-and-two-down house attached to it. Among its earlier landlords had been a Mr William Goldsborough.

Between the Wars its licence was taken over by Thomas Doyle, who had formerly been a travelling greengrocer.

Each was rebuilt in brick, the 'Queen's' in a pleasantly unremarkable style, the other two in the streamlined, flat-roofed idiom of the day.

A pub threatened with closure since my parents' childhood (so long, in fact, that the subject had become something of a joke in the community) was the Turf Tavern in King Street, across the road from Mrs Florence Ottley's shop, the blind corner it caused, with no pavement at that side, being said to constitute a traffic hazard.

Formed from two cottage houses knocked into one, the 'Turf' had four rooms up and four rooms down. Its tap room and saloon each had its own street door. Licensed under the Beer House Act of 1830, which enabled any householder to become licensed to sell beer on his premises by applying direct to His Majesty's Customs and Excise, without needing the Licensing Justices' approval (a concession later rescinded), it sold beer, ale and porter but not spirits and wines. The landlord from 1910 till the late 'forties, Mr George Fawcett, took over the licence from an aunt of his.

Another joke was that the 'Turf' sold 'singing beer', the cheerfully raised voices of the old men who formed the nucleus of its customers often being audible in the evenings to passers-by. Its original supplier is said to have been the Cubley Brook Brewery at Penistone, which later changed to the manufacture of vinegar. By my childhood, however, the Turf Tavern was owned by Samuel Smith's Brewery at Tadcaster, whose red, round-fronted steam delivery lorry with its glowing fire and rattling driving chain, its paintwork matching that of the 'Turf' itself, was a familiar sight unloading barrels and forming an additional hazard to passing cars.

Despite the pessimists' prognostications, no fatal collision ever occurred outside the 'Turf', the reason perhaps being that Mrs Ottley's plate-glass windows proved excellent albeit unofficial driving mirrors. Nevertheless it was vacated in 1960, and replaced by a fully-licensed house built in Green Street on part of the gardens of Rowland Cross's former residence, Greenfield House. The new 'Turf' was subsequently re-named 'The Kestrel' in honour of Hoyland's novelist Barry Hines, whose best-known work, *A Kestrel for a Knave*, was made into the widely-acclaimed film *Kes*. The break with the old 'Turf' became complete when, in October 1986, the ownership of The Kestrel was transferred from Samuel Smith's Brewery to Samuel Webster's.

A similar-sized beerhouse to the 'Turf', like it possessing two front doors, stood on the corner of Bethel Street and King Street opposite to that then occupied by Clarkson's fruit shop. Its name was 'The Five Alls', and the right-hand ground-floor window as seen from King Street consisted of a single pane of glass which was engraved with five symbolic heads: that of bearded King Edward VII (its caption 'I rule all'); that of a bishop in his robes ('I pray for all'); that of a wigged barrister ('I plead for all'); that of a uniformed soldier ('I fight for all'); and (a cynical touch lacking at those pubs which are known as 'The Four Alls') John Citizen with the words 'I pay for all'. (One wonders how long the ornamental pane would have lasted in the glass-breaking-happy Hoyland of today.)

The licensee was Mr Frank Robinson, the son of Edward Robinson, a previous landlord. His wife was a sister of Mrs Winifred Parratt the confectioner, Charles Smith the pork butcher and Joseph Smith, the off–licence proprietor and baker. One year in the early 'thirties Miss Teresa Robinson, his petite, dark-haired daughter, wearing an ice blue dress, head-dress and train, was the May Queen who walked in the Roman Catholic procession round Longfields Crescent from St Helen's Church.

The Five Alls ceased to be occupied as a pub about 1939, but continued to be lived in as a house until, along with neighbouring properties, it was demolished during the early 'seventies.

Further down, between the 'Queen's' and Barber Street, a few yards below William Hague's butcher's shop, there was a former pub called the 'Rock Inn', which at some time prior to the Second World War had been made into a private residence. (I remember that, when I was a pupil at King Street School, a younger girl called Betty Brown lived there.)

Basically a small, double-fronted, stone-built house, with a stable joined on to its lower end, it gave the appearance of having once, like many pubs in country areas, had a small-holding attached to it. Records show that it was there as long ago as 1858. It was pulled down about the same time as The Five Alls, when the Victoria Street area was being cleared.

Two pubs structurally much the same now as they were then, though one has had its stonework smartened with paint and the other has been given new windows and smart louvred shutters, are the Prospect Tavern on the corner of Brooke Street, a few yards from the former Kino and, where Hoyland joins Elsecar, the Clothier's Arms, on the corner of St Helen's Street and King Street. When buses first started to run through Hoyland the latter, said to have acquired its name because its first landlord was also a clothier, soon became a well-known fare stage on the Rotherham, Circular and other bus routes passing it.

This led to some confusion on one occasion when my parents were coming home from Barnsley by bus. A passenger who was a stranger to them asked for a ticket to 'the clothier's' and then complained that he had been over-charged. The conductress was adamant that he had not. The reason for his indignation was revealed when the stop where he alighted proved to be Booth's clothing factory at Hoyland Common.

Hoyland's largest, most prestigious pub, however, was the Strafford Arms between Rowland Cross's shop and the Cinema, its long, low, elegantly-proportioned frontage giving it the appearance of having strayed from some English country town.

It was in the concert room there on Friday evenings that the Hoyland Town Silver Prize Band (which some unkindly alleged to have won this title by taking the third prize in a competition where there were only three competitors) held its weekly practices. A name closely associated with the Band was Hickman. Hence a sound often heard in the Booth Street of my childhood was that of one of Matthias Hickman's younger sons practising scales on the cornet in the attic of No. 17, their three-storey home.

It was at the 'Strafford' too that, in the days before it was usual for pubs to advertise 'inn food', bank clerks and similar white-collar workers, including visiting commercial travellers, could obtain what would now be known as a business lunch.

Originally called 'The Beggar and Gentleman' (a picturesque name it has now reverted to, with the addition of an extra 'the'), either in late Victorian times or during the early years of the present century it had acquired the more august name 'Strafford Arms', apparently in memory of Thomas Wentworth, Earl of Strafford, the ill-fated adviser of King Charles I, who lived two miles away at Wentworth Woodhouse and was executed in London for abetting his sovereign's plan to implement despotic rule. Owing to the proximity of the Market Place, however, from which the ground between it and the street was separated by fluted iron posts, most people simply called it the 'Market House'.

The landlord of the Strafford Arms between the Wars was Mr Reginald Hinton, a member of the Hinton family which pioneered bus services in Hoyland. His wife, formerly Miss Amanda Evans, who is said to have looked rather like the then Duchess of York (the present Queen Mother), was the thirteenth and youngest member of a family brought up in Fitzwilliam Street at Elsecar. They had three children, two golden-haired daughters, Barbara and Joan (the first of whom was a fellow-pupil of mine at Miss Caws' little school in the Wesleyan Manse, from which the Hintons' maid collected her each lunch time) and a son Percy who was his sisters' junior by several years, and as a child is reputed to have been a skilled billiards and snooker player.

In those days most pubs in and around Hoyland were owned by local breweries, some in Sheffield and Barnsley. Tennants owned the 'Strafford', Wards the 'Furnace' and Clarksons, with their elephant trademark, the 'Gate'. The majority, however, including the 'Queen's', belonged to Whitworth, Son and Nephew Ltd. of Wath-upon-Dearne (later absorbed by John Smiths of Tadcaster).

A cousin of my father's told the story of how a layabout named Tommy Ashton (who even when inebriated seldom lost his flair for smooth, nonchalant repartee) was once found lying drunk in a Hoyland gutter. The police ordered him brusquely to get up. 'I can't,' replied Tommy, 'I've got three men holding me down.' 'Nonsense,' snapped the sergeant, 'Who are they?' 'Whitworth, Son and Nephew,' Tommy answered blandly.

For those preferring to drink and socialize in a club there were in the 'twenties and 'thirties, as there are now, two working men's clubs in Hoyland itself, besides those in Hoyland Common and Elsecar. The Belmont, a large, gaunt-looking stone house down Belmont Yard, with its front windows looking across towards Wentworth and Scholes, was the predecessor of the purpose-built club which now stands back from West Street. Its steward was Harry Birkinshaw, whose second wife was the widow of Fred Miles, the fruiterer on the corner of Belmont Yard. When he came to order printing for the Club, sometimes accompanied by his small son Carl, he caused my father much amusement by his down-to-earth, racy comments on people and events.

The Hoyland Nether Working Men's Club in Broad Street (usually known simply as the 'Prospect Club' through being in the part of Hoyland called Prospect) occupied the same premises then that it does now.

There was also a small Roman Catholic Club, not so well-appointed as the present one, behind St Helen's Church.

During the grim Depression of the 'thirties, the former Conservative Club off Hoyland Road (named colloquially the 'Blue Club' or 'Blue Pig') was made into a club for the unemployed which, through being unlicensed and selling only gassy soft drinks, soon came to be known as the 'Belchers' Club'.

One memorable day it received a visit from Prince George, the Duke of Kent (husband of the elegant Princess Marina), who took a keen interest in social welfare and under whose aegis clubs of this kind were being set up. To add some local colour to the occasion, His Royal Highness was regaled with a rendering of 'On

Ilkla Moor Baht 'at', which a local councillor promptly stepped forward and offered to translate. The Duke declined his services with thanks, explaining that he did not need an interpreter.

On another occasion the Club was visited by the Rev. Ian Moffat, carrying a zip-topped bag full of bottled beer bought at Hutson's Stead Lane grocery shop and off-licence. While the Vicar was engaged in conversation, some club members removed the bottles and replaced them with 'woods' from the bowling green — a substitution the reverend gentleman did not discover till he had toiled with his load up the 'Law Hill' to St Peter's Vicarage.

The club building was bought in 1945 by H. Booth & Son Ltd. of Huddersfield and was subsequently extended as a factory for the manufacture of their 'Talamade' range of suits and overcoats. As Booth's 'Hector James Menswear' factory, it is still one of the main employers of labour in Hoyland township.

CHAPTER FOUR

Trade and Industry

The Iron Industry

IN SOME PARTS of South Yorkshire iron ore, smelted in the early days with charcoal, has been mined even longer than coal. (In medieval times Monk Bretton Priory owned forges, which used local iron, in the part of Barnsley that is still known as Smithies.) The earliest way of mining iron was by digging bell-pits. It is the overgrown remains of some of these which have given its unusual name to the Bell Ground, the wooded area between Tankersley Hall and the old turnpike north of Wentworth Station. There were also numerous bell-pits at Thorpe Hesley.

Within the memory of older people living during the 'twenties, there had been an iron ore or 'iron-stone' mine situated near Wentworth Station. It was known as the Skiers Spring Iron-stone Pit and was owned by Earl Fitzwilliam. (My mother's father, who often spoke of it, always pronounced it 'inest'n'.) Its workings, like the old bell-pits, must in places have been very near the surface, since the story goes that, hidden behind a bush, the men had made a hole they could slip out through to go for a quick drink in the pub at Harley.

Some of this locally-mined ore had once supplied the hand nail-making industry flourishing in the yards (alleys flanked by low-roomed, stone-built cottages) in the neighbourhood of Market Street and High Street. (Other villages engaged in this rural craft included Ecclesfield, Darton, Hoylandswaine and Oxspring.)

Predictably, this cottage industry had died out about 1880 following the invention of factory-based nail-making machinery. Another blow to Hoyland's prosperity was the final closure in 1884 of the Milton Iron Works, which earlier in the century had been a mainstay of the town's economy and also a cause of its rapid expansion. The elderly ironmaster, it appears, could find nobody to take over his lease.

By the 'twenties, like the forge at Elsecar, the works was a fast-receding memory, though some traces of it could still be seen. The ponds which were dug to supply it with water remained, as two of them do to the present day. There was then a total of four at different levels, two to the west of Milton Road, one to the east and, a hundred yards or so along Millhouses Street, what was called macabrely the 'Cat and Dog Pond'. (Presumably in times past it had proved useful for the disposal of unwanted pets.)

The blast furnaces had been dismantled and of the iron works buildings two parts only remained, a high retaining wall of dark red brick where, before being levelled to make playing fields, the ground rose vertically some forty feet part-way between Millhouses Street and the LMS railway, and a long, low building, facing towards the Cat and Dog Pond, that between the Wars the Urban District Council used for storage purposes.

The works, opened by Walkers of Masborough at the beginning of the nineteenth century, had been owned by several firms and had known lean times. At the start of the 'fifties it was taken over by two Midlanders, George and William Henry Dawes, the former a more-than-life-sized character of whom tales were still in circulation during my childhood. Mr Dawes who lived, I am told, at Milton House, the large property with its outbuildings and trees on the ridge between the railway line and Armroyd, built equally handy though more modest dwellings to house his workforce on the steep hillside overlooking the works. Dating from the time of the Crimean War, the development was named Sebastopol after a siege which took place on the Black Sea coast from 1854 to 1855.

He also built workmen's terraces at Jump which were given such aristocratic-sounding names as Milton Square and Fitzwilliam Road, but acquired nicknames like 'Inkerman' and 'Turkey', likewise dating from the Crimean War. At Jump he also gave the site for the village church, consecrated in 1881 and, in his honour, dedicated to St George, and gave generously towards the building of the original village school (later the church hall), which the grandfather of a friend of mine used to pay ninepence a week to attend, at the other side of Church Street.

To judge from the stories which survive about him, Mr Dawes seems to have been highly irascible. One day a woman called at his office to ask for the tenancy of one of his new houses. 'You can have a house in Hell!' the ironmaster thundered. The applicant was walking dejectedly away when another woman came running after her. 'Missus,' she asked breathlessly, 'where's the house he's let you?' 'Why?' came the startled query. 'Because,' replied the other excitedly, 'he says I can have the one next door to it.'

Sometimes, however, his mood could change dramatically. On one occasion, a foreman went to ask him to treat the workforce to a seaside trip. 'You can have a trip to Hell and back!' Dawes exploded. 'Well, Mr Dawes,' the foreman answered mildly, 'I'm glad to hear you're going to bring us back.' His employer so appreciated this repartee that he relented and the men were given their outing.

Though the Milton and Elsecar forges had long since closed, between the Wars a number of men were still employed by two iron-working businesses in Elsecar, Davy's and Lax's foundry in Foundry Street.

Both were family concerns. J. Davy & Co. Ltd. had been founded in 1869 by Jonathan Davy, a former moulder at the Thorncliffe Iron Works, who lies buried under an obelisk appropriately surrounded by iron railings in Elsecar Churchyard. The business was run by four generations of his family, trading as general ironfounders and making castings in a variety of patterns and sizes, some weighing ounces, others hundredweights. The foundry closed early in the nineteen-eighties on the retirement of Mr Ryan Davy, the sole surviving partner, but the lozenge-shaped Davy logo can still be seen, especially on manhole covers, in places throughout the Hoyland area.

Lax's foundry, which closed some years earlier, had been opened in 1876 by William Lax, a former partner of Jonathan Davy, and likewise produced such useful articles as cellar grates and 'Yorkshire' kitchen ranges. After it closed, its building was acquired by Baxter and Weekley (structural, agricultural and vehicle welding engineers specializing in the manufacture of fencing and gates) and was given the name Cardigan Works.

Mines and Mineworkers

Throughout the 'twenties and 'thirties, Hoyland was still essentially a place dependent on coal for its livelihood. Its transformation from being an area of scattered farms and cottages had started rather more than a century earlier, first with the opening of the Milton Iron Works, then with the sinking prior to 1840 of the Hoyland and Elsecar Colliery.

Re-named Hoyland Silkstone after a new shaft was sunk to the Silkstone seam 508 yards below the ground, but often referred to as 'Platts Common Pit', this colliery loomed darkly to the left of the road going towards Platts Common from Market Street. Sometimes, too, it was known as 'Vizard's', since its first owner had been a Mr William Vizard. (When dark clouds piled up behind the colliery tip, my father would say, 'It looks black over Vizard's.')

The new shaft was opened in 1876. The following year coal began to be despatched via a mineral line constructed to link the pit to the Manchester, Sheffield and Lincolnshire Railway (later re-named Great Central and later still London and North Eastern) near High Royd. There was already a rope-operated incline which passed beneath Jump (now known as Greenside) Lane and down the valley between Jump and Hoyland to the Dearne and Dove Canal at Cobcar Ings. (When the Midland Railway line from Barnsley to Sheffield was opened in July 1897, a spur was constructed to link up with this, the momentum the waggons had acquired on their way down the valley raising them to the height of the viaduct crossing it.)

During the colliery's later years, the engine working the steel cable was operated by a local 'character' known as 'Old Gedney', an eccentric who towards the end of his life dressed in tatters with a sack clutched round his shoulders. After the pit closed in the 'twenties, he became a threshing machine contractor. He also made a hobby of restoring roundabouts and old threshing machines to working order. Two of the latter he kept in Jump Valley for many years, until the Government commandeered them as scrap iron during the Second World War.

The village of Platts Common with its three pubs, the Royal Oak, the Pheasant Inn and the Star (once known as 'Dinah's' since its landlady was a Mrs Dinah Roodhouse), its tiny chapel across the road from the pit and its mission church near the working men's club, had grown up in late Victorian times to house the Hoyland Silkstone miners and their families. Beyond the pit a long, gaunt-looking row of dark brick houses, some of which were standing until recently, stretched up the right-hand side of Hawshaw Lane. Hawshaw Terrace was its official name but, as it was first occupied mainly by families which had come over from Lancashire seeking work, it was disparagingly known as 'Lanky Row'.

At a time when it was still regarded as the managerial class's prerogative to take a leading part in local affairs, Hoyland Silkstone's top officials were prominent in the town's civic and religious life. The Hoyland Silkstone Coal and Coke Co. Ltd.'s General Manager and Agent, Mr Christopher W. Fincken, brought in as liquidator in 1883 when the colliery was being threatened with closure, was Chairman of the Local Board which was formed (a precursor of the Urban District Council) in 1891. For a time he lived near the town centre at Netherfield House, which was formerly the home of Dr Booth. Then he moved to the more prestigious Hoyland Hall, which became the managerial residence. (Perhaps he had reason to welcome the move, since his wife is alleged to have become over-friendly with Captain Bartlett, the sea-faring husband of Mrs Elizabeth Bartlett, founder of the John Knowles Memorial Church, who lived conveniently near at Greenfield Cottage.)

A later manager and occupant of the Hall was Mr Lazenby, who was a warden at St Andrew's Church where he crossed swords with Mr Edgar Hirst, the printer my father was apprenticed to, who at that time was the church's choirmaster.

Among the Hoyland Silkstone miners themselves, a man who achieved distinction was Mr Francis Frank Chandler, awarded an Edward Medal in 1908 for his heroism in a rescue operation after an underground boiler exploded. The occasion was celebrated in Hoyland by the printing of a commemorative postcard depicting Mr Chandler and his medal with the caption 'Hoyland's Hero'. (His son, Francis George Chandler, showed courage too when, in his late forties during the First World War, he volunteered for army service, falsifying his age.)

During its roughly ninety years of life, Hoyland Silkstone experienced a succession of owners. The last of these, Newton Chambers & Co. Ltd., found it no longer profitable to work and in 1928 without ceremony closed it. Perhaps because of the demoralizing failure of the national coal strike two years previously, this action seems to have met not with militant opposition but merely with resignation and apathy.

The blow shook Hoyland's entire economy, the smoke cloud from the pit's cluster of chimneys giving place to a pall of gloom and despondency. There were middle-aged and elderly miners who after the closure never worked again, with no redundancy payment and also no offer of redeployment. The resulting shortage of money in the town also affected its small businesses. Indeed, so widely was the trauma felt that people of my parents' generation in later years tended to date events from 'after Platts Common closed.'

Two of the pit's three shafts were later sealed, but a third was kept open as an additional entrance to the adjacent workings of Rockingham (Rockingham Colliery, likewise owned by Newton Chambers, being barely one mile distant at Birdwell), and Hoyland Hall became the official home of a succession of Rockingham managers. The winders retained included my uncle Edwin Ardron, who worked on at Platts Common until he retired after the Second World War.

Misfortune was piled on misfortune when, while a shaft was being sealed in 1936, a gas explosion took place which killed three men, one of them a Mr James Dunning of Hoyland Common, a fellow-pupil of my father's at the old St Peter's School. Dr Joy Allott, at that time a medical student, was driving through Platts Common with her mother just after the explosion occurred. Their car was stopped, and they were the first to arrive to administer first-aid.

Its smooth vermilion chimney contrasting sharply with the rolling green backdrop of Beacon Fields, Elsecar Main, sunk for Earl Fitzwilliam between 1905 and 1908 to a depth of 350 yards and later extended by means of drifts, was newer than Hoyland Silkstone but not so deep. In the inter-war years, to distinguish it from older mine workings at Elsecar, it was still being referred to as the 'New Pit' — a name which stuck to it until its closure in 1983. (A sidelight on aristocratic attitudes at the beginning of the century is provided by the fact that, whilst Elsecar Main, hidden in its valley from Wentworth, was equipped with a tall, conspicuous chimney built of brick, Earl Fitzwilliam's New Stubbin Colliery near Rawmarsh had two short iron ones — the top of a taller chimney sited there would have spoilt the view from the east-facing rooms of the Earl's stately home.)

Among the predecessors of those guests whose sensibilities this eyesore on the sky-line might have offended were several kings and princes. At Wentworth House there was a long tradition of entertaining England's royalty, and offering it conducted tours of the Earls' industrial undertakings. Back in 1828 the Duke of Clarence, afterwards William IV, 'The Sailor King', stayed at Wentworth and visited the Old Milton Pit. In 1891 the Prince of Wales, ten years later to become Edward VII, paid a visit to Elsecar while staying at Wentworth. My parents recalled the excitement when King George V, destined to reign till 1936, kept up the tradition by visiting Elsecar Main with his consort Queen Mary in 1912, the winder who safely lowered them down the shaft and brought them back to the surface being rewarded with an inscribed gold watch.

Just as 'Vizard's' had attracted Lancashire men, Elsecar early this century experienced an influx of miners from Staffordshire. Like 'in-comed-uns' the world over, they appear to have met with suspicion and hostility. According to 'locals' living at the time, the newcomers had three distinguishing features: a liking for giving their children Old Testament names such as Enoch, Ezra and Amos; excessive thrift bordering on parsimony; and an obsessive desire to acquire real estate in the form of cottage property which they could profitably let to other workers. (My mother claimed to have known one Staffordshire family which bought five pikelets for Saturday tea. The parents ate two each, whilst the eight children were each in turn given the remaining one.) An old man with the uncompromisingly English name John Wood displayed no love towards the Irish either, going so far as to say that, if he had his way, every Irishman working at Elsecar would be made to swim home with a Staffordshire man on his back.

Though, unlike Hoyland Silkstone, Elsecar Main was kept open despite the lean years, by the 'thirties the export market for coal had so dwindled that the pit was able to meet its order book in half a working week. Instead of half the workforce being laid off, the whole of it was kept, working part-time, the pit buzzer being sounded in the evening to let men know when they were needed the following day. (Another use to which mine and factory buzzers were traditionally put was to signal the start of the New Year, but this custom was dropped during the Second World War, when they were doing duty as air-raid sirens, and it was never afterwards revived.)

Though, unlike some collieries such as Lundhill in the Barnsley area, Elsecar Main never experienced a major tragedy, an unusual accident happened there one evening during the summer of 1934, when a cage full of workmen being drawn up the shaft overshot the landing stage and ended up among the winding gear. After being given on-the-spot medical treatment by Dr J.H. Fairclough, summoned to the scene, several men were taken to hospital. Among them was Samuel Burdin, a deputy, whose serious back injury prevented him from ever being able to work again, though despite this disability he stayed cheerful and survived to a great age, dying in February 1986 in his mid-nineties.

Though Hoyland did not become heavily industrialized until the nineteenth century, coal is thought to have been mined in the area at least as early as the seventeen-fifties. The original pits were all drift mines, driven into hillsides, and were usually called 'footrills' or 'day holes'. The entrance to one, sealed with an iron grille, can be seen in the grounds of Footrill Cottages, where Broad Carr Road descends steeply towards Skiers Spring. There is a similar opening in the hillside between Wentworth Road and Forge Lane at Elsecar.

In the 'twenties a drift mine was being worked near the edge of Spring Wood, its buildings lying to the left of the path which dips from Kitty Hague Lane, crosses a stream and climbs steeply towards the tree line. From the gaping black entrance, laden corves came clanking out on an endless belt between two low brick walls, giving the colliery one of its nicknames, the 'Nibble and Clink'. Nobody used its official name; I doubt whether there were many who even knew it. This small concern supplying local customers was for some reason usually known as the 'Kipper Pit'. ('Kipper Pit hards' were said to make excellent house coal.) A low, square concrete building sunk among undergrowth in the middle of the wood, looking rather like some garden air-raid shelters erected during the Second World War, was the colliery's powder magazine.

This pit had been opened in 1919, to work the pillars of coal which were left in the old footrill mine off Broad Carr Road, by a Barnsley man, Mr Adamson, and his partner. (Mr Adamson lived at Holly House in High Street, a property made in 1927 into part of Storey and Cooper's drapery shop.) It was afterwards taken over by Earl Fitzwilliam, whose under-manager, responsible to the manager of the larger Elsecar Main, was Mr Reuben Simpson, who lived at an old house on Primrose Hill and whom I remember as a thickset, dark-moustached man in knee-breeches and leggings.

Mr Simpson was killed by a fall of roof at Christmas 1930. The 'Kipper Pit' closed soon after and most signs of its existence were erased. The offices, however, were left intact and converted into Skiers Spring Bungalow, which faces Hoyland with its back towards the wood, its nearest neighbours Footrill Cottages.

Beside the old Barnsley to Sheffield turnpike, just north of Wentworth Station railway bridge, is the site of the former Lidgett Colliery, whose engine house is now the Lidgett Garage. Since its owner was a Dr Clark or Clarke of Bell Ground House, it was nicknamed 'The Pillbox'. The doctor is said to have owned a parrot whose cage hung in his surgery. When a miner reported there with a crushed finger or toe, the bird would eye it judiciously, head on one side, and exclaim, 'Cut it off! Cut it off!'

A rope-operated waggon line used to link Lidgett to the goods station at Elsecar. For some distance its course ran parallel to that later followed by the Midland Railway Company's Sheffield to Barnsley branch line, crossing Stead Lane by a bridge just above the present one, and Broad Carr Road and Armroyd Lane at road level, and then crossing the passenger line, when that came to be built, by sharing with other traffic the final bridge before Elsecar and Hoyland Midland Station. Thence it ran downhill to Fitzwilliam Street, where the crossing keeper was housed in a hut of the same orange-red brick as the engine house, and so between hedges down the 'Ash Gates' to Wath Road. There a man in a second cabin had the job of shunting the waggons on to the branch railway line.

The Fitzwilliam Street keeper in my mother's childhood was an elderly man called George White, who spent a lot of time chasing off boys who put objects to be flattened on the rails. A narrow lineside path along the 'Ash Gates' was used by some children from Fitzwilliam Street as a short cut to school.

In Dr Clark's time it was not unusual for 'contractors' to work sections of a mine, supplying their own men to get the coal. One such contractor was my great-grandfather, dark, curly-haired George Ottley of Stead Lane, about whom a horrendous story has been passed down. For shot-firing purposes he owned a keg of gunpowder which, perhaps for reasons of security, he kept at home under his bed. One evening my Great-Uncle Frank came home late, after going out for a few hours with his friends, to find that the rest of the household had all gone to bed and that washing on a clothes horse round the fire had caught light and was starting to blaze. With great presence of mind (he was in his late teens at the time) he filled the sink with water and tipped the burning laundry into it. Had he not come home until later, there might have been an explosion of the kind Guy Fawkes was vainly endeavouring to achieve, and I might never have been born to chronicle the story.

As a widower in his late sixties, George Ottley did experience a tragedy when in July 1894 his son Walter, a bachelor of thirty-five, was killed at Rockingham. I am told the first news the old man received of this was when his son's body was brought to the door in a coal cart which had been swept out and then lined with clean straw.

Preceding Hoyland Silkstone's closure by two years, the event of the 'twenties in the coal industry not only in Hoyland but throughout the land was the miners' strike of 1926, which lasted an unprecedented six months, twice as long as the strike of 1921, from April till October.

The summer was a hot one during which people were able to

keep warm without lighting fires but, as most Hoyland families still used old-fashioned 'Yorkshire' ranges, they needed coal for cooking purposes. For those whose stocks ran out, a solution was to burn colliery slurry.

To the right of the road at the foot of Greenside Lane, as one faced towards Jump, in those days there was a pond where as a child I sometimes searched for tadpoles. It was fed by a stream into which water ran from the Hoyland Silkstone washer. Hence, over the years, a thick deposit of coal dust had settled under and round the fringe of its shallow water.

Each morning before my father started his work he and my Grandfather Ottley, who lived with us, armed with a shovel and zinc bucket each, trudged down the steep hillside known as Jump Fields, where cows from Manor Farm grazed placidly, and dug squares of the oozing black substance as crofters dig peat, to provide my mother and grandmother with a day's burning. Anxious to do my bit, I walked behind carrying a small 'pot-hole' shovel.

Dubbed inelegantly by most people 'bull muck', this make-shift fuel burned without a flame but with a fierce red heat which ruined grates and shortened fire pokers. However, as a neighbour in Green Street, John Kennerley, remarked, burning evenly and without flame it 'made grand toist'. (No doubt what also endeared it to him was the fact that it was free. Nicknamed 'Saddler Jack' because his father had been a saddler, though not poor he stingily mended his own boots with such odds and ends as bits of motor tyre, his approach in consequence being signalled by the plopping sound they made. Also it was rumoured that, in his bachelor days, his mother had grown so weary of his meanness that one day while he was away at work she 'flitted', leaving nothing in the house but a poker-work text, 'What is Home without a Mother?')

Though, with no Welfare State to ease the load, conditions then were grimmer in many ways, the 1926 strike did not produce the violence seen in 1984. Sometimes groups of miners took to the road, not to picket in less militant areas, but playing and singing to earn a little to support their families. The name given to this activity was 'busking'.

Free teas were served to Hoyland strikers' children in the playground of St Helen's Catholic School, where a huge black boiler, like those used for tar, had been placed in a corner to supply hot water. Tickets were issued to those children eligible, one of them being surrendered for each meal. Fascinated by seeing the preparations for tea when I passed with my mother on our way to an uncle's at West Bank and frustrated by being unable to join in, I was appeased by being given a string of cloakroom tickets, and solemnly handed one over to my mother when we sat down each tea time.

It was not only miners and their families who suffered deprivation during the strike. Hardship was felt by some small shopkeepers whose customers needed extended credit. Similarly affected were those buying small properties, on which mortgage repayments still fell due though tenants could no longer pay their rents. (A friend of my mother's, whose parents-in-law at that time were buying a few cottages, commented on how the standard of the meals they served on her visits at weekends had fallen.)

Until well into the present century, the Hoyland area still lacked pit-top baths. Groups of men coming home at the end of a shift in their 'pit muck' remained a common sight. Through no fault of their own, if they got on a bus, they tended to leave gritty smears of coal dust on the Traction Company's blue-and-fawn moquette and on the clothes of fellow-passengers, who would consequently try to avoid travelling on any bus passing a pit between two and two-thirty in the afternoon, when the day shift was 'lawsing'.

When Earl Fitzwilliam, always an enlightened employer, had pit-top baths installed at Elsecar during the early 'thirties, they were hailed as a splendid innovation and opened with fitting ceremony. The showers had three temperatures, hot, cold and tepid. One speaker, unused to the latter word and swept away by his own eloquence, made a point of mentioning those ingenious taps which ran 'hot, cold and putrid'.

Pit canteens, where a hot, filling meal could be obtained for a reasonable price, were introduced during the Second World War, when the sparseness of the basic civilian rations, especially that of the meat ration, made it essential for miners and others doing heavy work to have an additional source of nourishment.

Brick Making and Pottery

By the end of Hoyland's first century of expansion, a period when brick started to oust local stone as a material for building homes, ample supplies of bricks could be obtained within the township's boundaries. At Shortwood, between the hamlet of Upper Hoyland and the old Barnsley to Sheffield railway line, were the kilns of the Hoyland Brick Company whose ochre-coloured clay pit, like the Law Stand on the sky-line above, was a landmark discernible from Ward Green and Worsbrough.

The works, founded over a hundred years ago by two partners named Chambers and Dawson, was in my youth operated by the Thompson family, which had managed it ever since its opening, and in the nineteen-twenties was being run by tall, bearded Mr Ralph Thompson and two of his sons, Augustus (usually abbreviated to Gus) and Herbert (similarly shortened to Bert).

Besides supplying Hoyland with building bricks, 'multi-coloured, red facings and common', this family made its mark on local life. Mr Herbert Thompson, who after his marriage lived in Tankersley Lane, was for a number of years a churchwarden at St Peter's, Tankersley. In the Second World War, Major Augustus Thompson, who lived in Kirk Balk at the house named Kirkwood, played an important rôle on the home front, being in command of the Hoyland Home Guard. Their relatives included that other well-known family, Parkins the pharmacists.

In the early 'thirties, with trade in the doldrums, Ralph Thompson left his sons to run the firm and moved to North Yorkshire, first managing a brick works at Grosmont, seven miles inland from Whitby, and then moving into Whitby itself, where he and his wife ran the Queen's Boarding House on the West Cliff near the Spa.

Change of a different kind came to Shortwood when, in 1957, the works became a subsidiary of Thomas Marshall and Co. Ltd. of Loxley, who re-named it Hoyland Marshall. Today it is owned by GR – STEIN Refractories Ltd., which uses it for the manufacture of foundry products.

In 1877 three partners leased some land on which they opened a brick works near Stead Lane along a track, beside which a few houses were built, branching off above the bridges on the side opposite Spring Wood and nearest to the turnpike.

Though I am told that some of its output was used to build the old part of Strafford Avenue, this Skiers Spring Brick Works tended to produce bricks of a very poor quality, porous and rough and often distinguished by having a dark blue round or oval blemish. (It is thus still possible to detect some buildings which were constructed with bricks from Skiers Spring. One is the kitchen wing of my own house, a later addition contrasting sharply with the original Blacker Hill sandstone.)

The cause of these defects was probably the fact that the bricks were made not from traditionally excavated clay but from black shale and chips of iron-stone which were salvaged from the waste heaps of the Skiers Spring Iron-stone Pit. This may also explain why my father always called the works Goschen, after the place at which the Israelites had to make bricks for Pharaoh without straw.

This works is said to have closed in 1919 (its end was perhaps hastened by these shortcomings), though a retired builder tells me that in fact it stayed in business for a few years more, not making new bricks but re-dressing old ones.

Near the brick works was Earl Fitzwilliam's Milton Pottery, one of many small potteries which once existed in this area of South Yorkshire and which, unlike the Rockingham Pottery at Swinton, specialized not in delicate hand-painted ware but in plain, useful objects such as plant pots, dishes for apple and 'meat-and-tatie' pies and the huge 'pancheons' used when kneading bread dough.

The pottery was run by two Cumbrian brothers named Keir

the elder of whom, Mr David Keir, would arrange for items to be manufactured to customers' requirements. In those days, before battery hens and mass marketing ensured a good supply of eggs at all seasons, my mother pickled some twelve dozen each year, for use in cakes and puddings, while they were cheap and plentiful in spring. (Pickled eggs were unsuitable for boiling, since standing in water-glass made their shells brittle.) I remember, at the age of three or so, being wheeled in my push-chair down the hill and up the lane to the pottery one afternoon. There my mother spoke to a tall, grey-moustached man from whom she ordered a large earthenware bread crock, to stand the eggs in under the stone table that food was stored on in our keeping cellar.

The pottery, like the adjacent brick works, is no more. I am told that it closed in 1938. It is, however, commemorated not only by any of its artefacts which survive but by the name of the Potter's Wheel inn on the Cloughs Estate.

Printing and Publishing

One of Hoyland's most frequented business places during the period between the Wars, and one with a very varied clientèle, was my father's printing office here in Booth Street. The business carried on there had been founded in 1882 at Batley in the heavy woollen district, and later moved to Hoyland, by Mr Edgar Hirst, who in looks closely resembled Sir Adrian Boult, the orchestral conductor. In 1897 he purchased Netherfield House, which at some stage he altered to suit his needs, from Mrs Ann Harrison of Milnthorpe, Westmorland and formerly of Carleton, Pontefract, the daughter to whom its first owner, Dr Booth, bequeathed this real estate. (For some years previously he had rented the house, a receipt from October 1893 showing that he paid £5 a quarter for it.)

Three small bedrooms facing towards the street, used by the Booths' resident maidservants, were made into a long typesetting room. The doctor's consulting room, facing towards Green Street (the plate glass window where his remedies were displayed since replaced by a bay), became a machine shop. The adjacent waiting room with its side door was turned into an office. Also the brick-built kitchen wing was added, incorporating an outside lavatory to replace the earth closet the doctor had made do with.

Mr Hirst had two sons, William and Hubert, one of whom served as a Royal Flying Corps pilot during the First World War. He too changed the appearance of the place when, as a sentimental gesture while home on leave, he planted the sycamore which has now grown tall in the corner at the angle of Booth Street and Green Street.

The method of printing used here differed little from that first introduced by William Caxton at Westminster in 1476. When my father joined Mr Hirst in 1905 as a fourteen-year-old apprentice lad, he had to learn how to set type by hand. Two shallow wooden cases held each type face, at an angle to each other like a partly-opened book, the upper one holding the capitals, the lower the small letters — hence the expressions 'upper case' and 'lower case'. Both cases were divided into sections, some oblong and some square, one for each letter of the alphabet and one for each of the punctuation marks. Like a typist, the compositor worked by touch, picking out the letters and aligning them in a small metal tray called a setting stick. A groove along one side of each piece of type told him whether the letter was the right way round. If by some mischance he upset the case, the resulting jumble of type was called 'printer's pie'.

The completed lines were carefully transferred to an oblong frame or 'chase', in which lines of varying lengths were held in place by small wooden wedges called 'quads'. This form of type was laid face upwards on the press, ready to be printed from.

Though the large 'Wharfedale' press in the bay-windowed room, started by spinning a flywheel, was powered by a panting gas engine, the small press was still operated by hand and looked very like those shown in history books to illustrate the life and work of Caxton. It was used for posters ('crown' or 'double crown' according to their size). First the type (wooden, not metal, for this kind of job, since for larger letters wood gave a better impression) was placed on the bed of the press, and evenly inked with a hard rubber roller rather as pastry is rolled. A sheet of paper was laid over the type. Then the sheepskin lid of the press was lowered on to it and (hence the name of the machine) paper and type slid under a large weight and were pressed together when a lever was pulled forward. A life-sized metal eagle on the frame above exerted pressure to assist the process.

Upstairs was a small, treadle-operated press always known as the 'platen' or 'Heidelberg' (the latter name being given to it since it was made in that German centre of learning). It was used mainly for cards and small handbills. A treadle-operated perforating machine, one of whose jobs was to punch holes along the sides of counterfoils, produced fine 'confetti' like computer 'chads'. What fascinated me most as a child, however, and at the same time horrified me after we learned about the French Revolution at school, was the rumbling guillotine which cut paper to size, its heavy blade gliding diagonally down with an air of quiet menace. It never failed to astonish me to see my father use this murderous-looking piece of equipment to shave a mere fraction of an inch from the edge of a stack of cards or a pile of concert programmes.

Before the Second World War, printing was still a trade requiring a seven-year apprenticeship. As a teen-age apprentice, my father walked from his Hoyland Common home six days a week in time to begin work at 7.00 a.m., and from Monday to Friday he worked until 6.00 in the evening. Three nights a week he then walked to the Midland Station to catch a train to Sheffield, where he studied typography at the School of Art. Other evenings, before being free to go home, he sometimes had to push a heavy barrow loaded with parcels of printing to Birdwell where a newsagent, Samuel Wildsmith, on the corner opposite the Travellers Inn, ran a printing agency. (Another printing agent for many years was Mr Harry Haywood of Hemingfield, a well-known credit draper.)

Later, with my father 'out of his time', Mr Hirst retired first to one of the Chalfonts, then to Hastings (where he was able to pursue two of his interests, playing bowls and listening to orchestras), leaving his now fully-qualified assistant to move into Netherfield House and take charge, and finally selling out to him in

1931. Having taken control, my father proudly displayed on the office wall, for customers to see when they brought their orders, the First Class Certificate awarded to him by the City and Guilds of London Institute at the end of his arduous period of study.

For two years, between 1902 and 1904, Mr Hirst had produced a weekly newspaper named the *Hoyland and Wombwell Advertiser*. The few yellowed copies of this which survive contain a modicum of local news and fascinating advertisements by Hoyland traders, some apparently intent on impressing by their weight of verbiage, for goods ranging from corsets to coffee and potatoes to pills, at prices which astonish when compared with those charged in today's inflated currency.

Also, one year, he published an almanac whose title reads, *E. Hirst's South Yorkshire Almanac for the Year 1897, Price One Penny*. In its hundred or so closely-printed pages are combined calendar and diary, moon guide, year book and magazine. Each page is headed by a proverbial saying or by a joke of the Christmas cracker kind. There are also steel etchings of such varied subjects as battlefields, oriental princes holding court and schooners in full sail, features including 'The History of Wigs' and 'The Origin of Tithes' and (doubtless of more interest to Hoyland people then than now) a discreet six lines on redeeming pawnbrokers' pledges.

The almanac also throws interesting light on local happenings, with references to a Thorncliffe riot in 1870, a sheep-stealing at Darfield, and the last bull-baiting held in Barnsley, surprisingly as recently as 1831. Another entry runs, 'Great Strike of Miners in 1893. Military called in. Great destruction of property in the district'. Moreover, day-to-day life at that time clearly possessed its hazards. In an exemplary copper-plate hand, in the only copy I have ever seen, the original owner records how, in one of three gas explosions all of which took place in Hoyland during the same week, Elijah Fletcher was blown into the roof of his shop and was injured for life. Another local worthy, he records, was 'thrown out of his conveyance and killed,' whilst a macabrely enigmatic entry states simply, 'Jack Rawson dug his own grave and was paid for it.'

By the 'twenties the Booth Street printing business was engaged mostly in general and commercial work. Some jobs were regular and seasonal. Every month church magazines were printed for St Peter's, St Andrew's, Elsecar and John Knowles, the distinctive colours of their covers being sky blue, salmon pink, white and green respectively. Each of these had a view of the church on its cover and contained a letter from the incumbent, a list of officials and activities, details of baptisms, marriages and deaths and an 'inset' (supplied by a London printing firm) with religious articles, questions-and-answers, and homely recipes and remedies. Each church employed a band of volunteers to distribute magazines to householders. The price of each issue was two old pence.

The chapels, too, were valued customers. May and June were their Anniversary months, when posters advertising dates and preachers' names, practice sheets for use at rehearsals, and hymn sheets for use on the day itself were supplied not only to Hoyland, Hoyland Common and Elsecar chapels, but to some in villages further afield including Hemingfield, Blacker Hill, Birdwell and Pilley. The Anniversary season often meant working late to ensure that orders were ready on time.

The most frenziedly busy month of all, however, was March, when the Urban District Council elections were held and my father did not only the official printing (ballot papers and notices of poll) but also posters and election addresses for most of the eight or more candidates optimistically contesting the four wards.

My father held firm political views and never failed to vote in an election, parliamentary or local government. Beyond that he did not take sides. Each candidate, whatever his allegiance, was a customer for whom only the best possible job should be done. A potentially embarrassing situation could therefore arise when, as sometimes occurred, my father was talking to one candidate in the office and my mother to his rival in the living room. (She always made excellent coffee, simply by scalding in a brownware jug freshly ground beans bought from Mr George Hirst Allen or, after he retired, from Mr Wilton Brooke. Some 'regulars' therefore always took care to bring their orders between 10.30 and 11.00 a.m., to make sure of being asked in for 'elevenses'.)

Nor was any job too trivial to do well, or mistake too unimportant to rectify. One evening, to get the ink on them to dry faster, my father put some notices of poll over a clothes horse by the open fire. With childish glee (I was nine at the time) I pointed out that a 'Cherrytreet' Street was listed among those whose polling station was at the Miners' Welfare. Though it was late and he was very tired, father promptly vanished into the machine room and did not emerge until he had run off some new, corrected copies.

My mother and, as I grew older, I myself helped with the business in various small ways. We were frequently called on to read proofs (a job less easy than it may appear, since one tends to see not the printed word itself but what one knows the printed word should be). We also folded programmes and church magazines on the living-room table. My favourite job was silvering wedding invitations and the small cards sent out with wedding cake, conveying the happy couple's compliments and traditionally showing the bride's maiden name boldly crossed out with a thick silver arrow. They were printed in black and then lightly dusted over with silver powder while the ink was still wet − a job needing just the right amount of pressure to ensure that the powder adhered without smudging the words.

Funeral cards, embellished with ornamental crosses, lilies or ivy leaves, stating the name and age of the deceased and place of burial, and conveying pious platitudes enshrined in sentimental verse, were no longer fashionable as they had been a few decades before. Some mourners nevertheless still had funeral ribbons printed to distribute in their loved ones' memory. These were wide satin ribbons, lilac or grey, fringed at the ends like book marks and giving names, ages and dates just as the cards had done.

In my childhood there was another printing works in Hoyland, likewise housed unexpectedly in premises originally built for a different purpose. Run at separate times during that period by two men named Newton and Gelder, it occupied the top floor of No. 9 King Street, the former chapel whose ground floor comprised a newsagent's and Clayton's furniture shop. It was entered via a steep, enclosed flight of outside steps, at the end of the building nearest to the 'Turf', through a door at the outer edge of the pavement.

The second of these two printers was succeeded by his assistant, a young man named Stanley Green, who moved into another former chapel along the lower side of Bethel Street, named his works 'The Caxton Press' and displayed a sign, like those hung outside inns, showing William Caxton operating his press. In the 'thirties, however, Hoyland was unable to provide a living for two full-time printers. The Caxton Press in consequence stayed open for only a few years. My father's business proved more viable. Despite the Depression, followed by paper rationing and other problems in the Second World War, it enjoyed a modest prosperity for another quarter of a century, eventually closing on his retirement in 1958.

Painting, Decorating and Plumbing

Another Hoyland business with a link, albeit indirect, with Netherfield House was that engaged in by C. Firth and Sons, painters, decorators, plumbers, electricians and glaziers, whose founder, Charles Firth, married Mary Booth, a daughter of Dr William Smith Booth, its builder. This couple's first home was at No. 6 Booth Street, whose front room owes the size of its window to the fact that it used to be their wallpaper and paint shop.

By the 'twenties both these elder Firths were dead and the business had moved to No. 46 King Street, where purpose-built, stone-fronted premises had been erected back in 1907 facing the large, ornate Mount Tabor Chapel. The senior partners during the inter-war years were Charles and Mary's sons. The elder, short, grey-bearded William, a bachelor who ran the new shop and was one of the first Hoyland people to venture on a cruising holiday, lived at No. 10 Booth Street with his sisters, Miss Ann or Annie Firth and Mrs Florence Westwood, the second of whom sometimes brought me magazines sent from New Zealand, where she had spent her early married life.

His deferentially polite brother Arthur, a tall, thin man with very bright dark eyes, who was an exceptionally skilled wood grainer, lived with his wife and family over the shop. Their eldest and third sons were plumbers. Charlie, the eldest, was a bachelor and, like his uncle, enjoyed travelling abroad. Harry married Miss Phyllis Dale of Elsecar, and lived in Armroyd Lane. George, a cheerfully garrulous character who served in the Navy in the Second World War was, like his father, a painter and decorator. Arnold, the fourth brother and the only one to marry and have children, managed the shop after his uncle retired. Their elder sister, Florence, stayed at home. Their younger sister Edith, a schoolteacher, married Mr (later the Rev.) John Charles Hardy and moved to Chorley over in Lancashire.

In their heyday during the period when, with labour costs much lower than today's, more people employed professional decorators, Firths had a large workforce based on their yard, with its range of storerooms and offices, in Bethel Square behind the King Street shop. They also owned property in Booth Street and on the far side of King Street. Among their decorators in the 'twenties were the two Coulson brothers, Colin and Tommy, who on completing their apprenticeships built up a successful business of their own. (On the last occasion when I saw Tommy Coulson, which was two years or so before his death in 1987, he said he had vivid memories of how on the first day that he went to work for Firths, early in August 1927, the job that he was given – a daunting one – was to sandpaper our hundred-and-one banisters, before they were stained and re-varnished. I remember with equal clarity how this smiling, teasing, curly-haired apprentice dabbed some red paint on my teddy bear's nose. The paint, which proved impossible to remove, gave it a permanently bibulous look.)

With the exception of William and George, who moved with his sister Florence to Lancashire to be near their married sister and her children, during the 'seventies, none of the second and third generation of men in the Firth family lived to enjoy retirement. Arthur Firth died in 1941. His burial took place at St Peter's Churchyard in the grave of his eldest daughter, Violet Mary, who died in her seventeenth year while still a pupil at Barnsley Girls' High School. His parents, Charles and Mary, lie next to them.

The younger Charles died when about sixty. Harry, an Inspector in the Special Constabulary, collapsed and died at a War Memorial service on an exceptionally frosty Remembrance Day. Arnold, too, died prematurely.

After George Firth's retirement the King Street shop, which had sold paint, wallpaper and hardware and had also provided a useful service by supplying paraffin for oil heaters, was taken over by a Mr Hepworth, who was always quietly helpful and polite. He, however, did not stay long, and the shop is now run by Mrs Doreen Law as a ladies' and children's outfitter's. Some of the property in Bethel Square, including four cottage houses without front doors, was pulled down several years since. The rest is being used as the headquarters of the Hoyland Nether Community Service. The Booth Street yard where Firths kept their plumbing lorry and private cars (and, in the Second World War, fattened a pig) is now owned by Mr Peter W. Shaw, a building contractor.

Higher up King Street on the other side, facing the Barnsley British drapery store, was a soundly-built stone terrace of three houses owned by Hoyland's other old-established firm of decorators and plumbers, the Rawlins, whose business was founded in 1856. Mr Wilfred Rawlin, in charge of the firm, lived in the house on the corner of Hall Street, which had a sloping side wall and was therefore a little smaller than the other two, with his wife Agnes (one of the Whittlestones of Jump Pit) and their small daughter Enid. The front room of the middle house was used as a wallpaper and paint shop. In the 'twenties the top house of the three was occupied by Mr and Mrs William Bowden and their two children. (Mrs Cissie Bowden was one of Mr Rawlin's sisters.) After the Bowdens moved to Hawshaw Lane, the new occupants were Mr Rawlin's mother and his brother Frank, a tall, thin-faced man who after the Second World War was for a time a churchwarden at St Andrew's.

Approached through a pair of large gates to the side of this house, the yard where Rawlins stored ladders and other gear was behind a terrace, joined on to the 'Turf', comprising two houses and the little shop that until the late 'twenties was Charles Smith's pork butcher's.

Down the years, Rawlin's advertisements incorporated the words 'All Work Done by Qualified and Experienced Workmen'. Among these were Mr Edwin Fletcher, now of Platts Common but for a number of years a neighbour of mine in Booth Street, who later worked for the Urban District Council, and Mr Hubert Sands of Cherry Tree Street, who married my father's assistant, Miss Hilda Jones and, after doing wartime work in Scotland, took a job with the Dearne Valley Water Board.

The Rawlins were connected by marriage to other well-known families in the Hoyland area. Old Mrs Rawlin was a sister of William Allen the architect and George Hirst Allen the family grocer. Another of her daughters, Clara, was the wife of Robert Humphreys Thompson of Milton Road, the music teacher and church organist.

Like most large families in years gone by, the Rawlins suffered early bereavement. There is in St Peter's Churchyard a touching memorial, its verse expressing a simple, trusting faith, to two Rawlin children, Henry and Edith, a brother and sister of Wilfred, Clara, Cissie and Frank, who died in early childhood. This family also lost a son, named Walter after his father, during the First World War, killed on the first day of the Battle of the Somme. His name is included in the lower panes of the war memorial window at St Andrew's.

Though painting and plumbing are traditionally linked, during the inter-war years, just as today, there were some firms which did decorating only. One such decorating business was that run by Frank Ashton, brother of Herbert Ashton, a schoolmaster. His double-fronted paint and paper shop, at which he prided himself on keeping the best-quality materials in stock, was in Fitzwilliam Street at Elsecar, between Armroyd and the corner of Wentworth Road.

When Mr Ashton died in middle life, his wife Mary took the then unusual step of deciding to keep on the business and run it herself. One of the more unusual jobs my father did was to print handbills for her to send out advising customers of her intention.

Conversely, not all plumbers were decorators. At No. 47 Milton Road, in a detached pebble-dashed house built about the early 'twenties, lived Mr Thomas Limb, a small, elderly man with a grey moustache, who with his son Jesse traded as T. Limb and Son, advertising 'A plumbing service that satisfies'. He also had a daughter, Edith a schoolteacher, who after marrying a Mr Green moved from the Hoyland district.

Although the Limbs did not do decorating, they had an indirect connection with it, Mr Jesse Limb marrying Miss Phyllis Coulson, a sister of the two Coulsons, Colin and Tommy, the second of whom a few years after the Second World War, during which he had served in the RAF, moved from Elsecar to live at Rock House, built high between No. 47 and the Gate Inn.

CHAPTER FIVE

Road and Rail

Paths, Lanes and Turnpike

EXCEPT for a few tracks and lanes connecting it to neighbouring villages (the path from Upper Hoyland to Worsbrough Village was one of them, and Burying Lane between Wentworth and Alderthwaite another), before the railways came Hoyland's sole link with the outside world was the Wakefield-Barnsley-Sheffield turnpike which passed through Hoyland Common and Chapeltown. Inaugurated by an Act of Parliament in the late seventeen-fifties, 'The Turnpike', as it was still being called during my childhood, had once carried stage coaches plying between London and Leeds. The last long-distance coach to pass through

Barnsley, however, ran in August 1840, three years after Queen Victoria came to the throne and a month after the opening of the railway line which linked Leeds and Rotherham via Cudworth, connecting with the Rotherham to Derby line, though the mail coach service between Barnsley and Sheffield continued until 1854.

People of my parents' generation remembered how 'The Turnpike' also served a less romantic purpose as the route regularly followed by tramps or 'roadsters' on their way between the workhouse at Fir Vale and that at Gawber, on the far side of Barnsley, the institution on whose extensive grounds the Barnsley District General Hospital now stands.

My father told of how two friends from Hoyland Common, the surname of one of whom was Robinson, decided to visit London by train. They spent so much on sightseeing that they found themselves without the means to pay their rail fare home, and had to walk – which took them quite a time. It was as he toiled wearily up the turnpike road, his even more footsore friend not yet in view, that Robinson was spotted by a crony from the flight of steps outside the Prince of Wales.

'Here comes Robinson Crusoe,' the man called to friends drinking inside, 'I wonder what's happened to Man Friday.'

The Railways

There were also people alive during the 'twenties who could just remember the excitement when, in 1854, the South Yorkshire Railway (later absorbed by the Manchester, Sheffield and Lincolnshire, in 1897 re-named Great Central, which became part of the London and North Eastern network in 1923) opened a branch from Aldham Junction near Stairfoot, on its Barnsley to Doncaster line, to Blackburn Junction just north of Sheffield, whence trains could continue to the Wicker Station. (This branch was later linked via Woodburn Junction to Sheffield Victoria.)

Following the easiest contour of the land, to avoid the need for the construction of difficult and costly viaducts and tunnels, the new line did not pass through the villages it served but skirted them, mostly some distance off. The station serving Hoyland was Dovecliffe, halfway between Blacker Hill and Worsbrough Dale, where the line crossed the road linking these two places. The rails then described a long curve via High Royd to Birdwell, where Birdwell and Hoyland Common shared a station as near to Pilley as to either of them, a fact which emerges from some verses written by John Woffenden, Tankersley's sexton-poet, about a Wharncliffe Silkstone Colliery outing to Scarborough. On his way home a workman whose name was Wood somehow boarded the wrong train. Then, the versifier tells us:

> Wood fell asleep and off the train went,
> And when he woke up they cried 'Burton-on-Trent!
> Out with your ticket man, don't be so silly!'
> 'Nonsense,' said Wood, 'I'm for Birdwell, near Pilley.'

(A station opened at High Royd, near Upper Hoyland, was closed for some reason in 1856.)

From Birdwell the line went through Sowell, Westwood and Newbiggin to Chapeltown, crossing the old turnpike there, skirting the western edge of Hesley Woods and coming via Smithy Wood to Ecclesfield and Grange Lane (the station for Scholes and Thorpe Hesley). High Green passengers had a long, lonely walk to Westwood, a station approached along a curving woodland track bordered in spring by golden pussy willows.

Named because of the sandstone bluff rising steeply above it and the River Dove on the valley floor below, Dovecliffe was a Toy Town layout halfway down a steep hill at the edge of Wombwell Wood, with a lattice-work footbridge and a level crossing controlled from a tiny wooden signal box perched high above the end of the station buildings. (One of the signalmen during my childhood was the brother of Annie and Wilfred March, two Hoyland teachers, and the elder son of Mr Edwin March, a signalman at Elsecar and Hoyland.) On the 'down' platform, past the signal box and small, white-painted, swinging entrance gate were a waiting room and railmen's cottages. On the 'up' side, fronting a stone-edged flower-bed, was a small buff-coloured shelter with fretwork eaves, covered in summer with pink rambler roses.

While the M.S.& L. was the sole form of public transport of which they were able to avail themselves, Hoyland people had perforce walked to Dovecliffe, a distance of over two miles from the centre of the town, through Blacker Hill and past the triangular stone edifice known as the 'Smoothing Iron', undeterred by the state of the weather or by perhaps having to walk at least one way through woods and open country in darkness. Or, if bound for Sheffield, they might choose instead to walk to Chapeltown, which was further still but from which the fare was cheaper.

The train service appears to have been quite frequent. My father had a great-uncle, Tommy Carr, who kept a pawn shop in St Philip's Road at Neepsend and was renowned for his tight-fistedness. When he came to Hoyland Common visiting, Great-Uncle Tommy would, as my grandmother put it, 'ride a station and walk a station', seemingly without any lengthy waits, the object of this eccentricity undoubtedly being to 'save his brass'.

Because of its attractive situation, thirty or forty years ago my father and I often walked round Dovecliffe on fine weekends. The only time we tried to ride from there was a May Saturday in 1947, six years before the old line received its 'coup de grâce' at the hands of British Railways. A study of the timetable had shown that, if we booked to Chapeltown, we could get a connecting train back on this scenic and, to us, thoroughly fascinating line. When we tried to book however the station staff, nonplussed perhaps by what had become a rare request, confessed to having lost contact with the train – it had 'got lost' somewhere on the way from Barnsley! Disappointed, we trudged home in the sticky heat. There was nevertheless one positive result. A friend, highly amused by the episode, compiled a book of full-colour cartoons which he entitled 'One Sunny Day in May', illustrating its ludicrous aspects. Today this is one of the possessions I cherish most.

Though it was the proliferation of bus services that took the last passengers from the old line, the first blow to it had already been struck in 1897, when the wealthy and ambitious Midland Railway, partly in response to official representations received from Hoyland, opened a rival Barnsley to Sheffield route. By building an imposing viaduct across the valley of the Dove near Swaithe and a shorter viaduct at Elsecar, and tunnelling almost a mile under the hill between Tankersley Old Hall and Chapeltown (engineering feats that the M.S.& L. was unable or unwilling to attempt), the Midland not only reduced the total journey by a mile and a half but touched the fringe of Wombwell, where it built a station, passed between Hoyland and Elsecar, where Elsecar and Hoyland Station was built, went through the centre of Chapeltown and was able to have a station slightly nearer to Ecclesfield than that of its older rival.

The new line had little of the visual appeal of the old. There was nothing in its whole length to compare with the long, gleaming curve between Dovecliffe and High Royd, or the sensuously sinuous bends between Sowell and Westwood. Moreover, its buildings were starkly utilitarian. Bridges and stations, the latter with their long platforms each the mirror image of that facing it, were built not of local brick or mellow stone but of ugly though durable Staffordshire blue (usually known as 'engineering') brick.

Nevertheless, for Hoyland passengers, it was infinitely more convenient. Predictably they abandoned Dovecliffe. (Hoyland Common people were now offered the choice between Birdwell and Hoyland Common on the old line and Wentworth and Tankersley, later re-named Wentworth and Hoyland Common, on the new, living roughly halfway between the two and not conveniently situated for either.)

My grandmother who lived at Elsecar had a mother and sister at Spitalhouses, a hamlet between Wentworth and Hood Hill. She once told me how, soon after the new line was opened, she rode from Elsecar and Hoyland to Wentworth Station taking with her my mother, then aged fifteen months, and walked from there up the old turnpike road and then along the coach road to Spitalhouses. It would have been little further for her to walk from her home in Fitzwilliam Street via 'Watery Lane' — she just wished to enjoy the novelty of the ride.

In the 'twenties and 'thirties, however, despite being in opposition to each other and the fact that more and more of their passengers were being lost to the buses, which had by then come on the scene, both lines appeared to flourish. Though worse hit than its rival passenger-wise, the LNER, as the Great Central had now become under the amalgamation of 1923, had the advantage of passing several pits: Barrow Colliery and the adjacent chemical works, in the valley between Worsbrough and Blacker Hill; Rockingham Colliery to the left of the line between High Royd and Birdwell; Wharncliffe Silkstone Colliery close to whose yard it ran at Tankersley; and Smithy Wood Colliery and Coke Ovens just north of Ecclesfield. It also, like the Midland (re–named LMS), served the Thorncliffe Iron Works. In addition the LNER had a single-track freight line coming up the valley from Wath to Elsecar, its terminus being a small goods station along Wath Road opposite Station Row. (Similarly, the LMS had a mineral line from Wharncliffe Silkstone joining its Sheffield-Barnsley line just to the south of the Swaithe Viaduct, much of its course running parallel to and in places only a few yards from the Dovecliffe line.)

In those days, before motorways were dreamt of or streets choked with towering container vehicles, the railways were the country's 'common carriers', bound by law to transport anything and everything. The freight they handled ranged in size and weight from cardboard boxes full of day-old chicks to waggon-loads of coal weighing ten tons. The goods train service tended to be slow. It was faster although costlier to send small or perishable items 'passenger'. At Elsecar and Hoyland, there was a parcels office where they could be handed in and weighed adjacent to the booking hall. A service popular during the summer months was 'Luggage in Advance', holiday-makers' trunks and suitcases being conveyed from door to door for two shillings each, and collected and conveyed but not delivered, or not collected but conveyed and delivered, for one. The station also had a sizeable goods yard, on the site that City Steels now occupies, with large white-painted gates opening off Hill Street. The siding leading to it was controlled from a signal box beyond the south end of the 'down' or Barnsley platform.

ROAD AND RAIL

A familiar sight in Hoyland between the Wars was the maroon-painted delivery van, with 'L M S' in white lettering on its cab, in which goods sent by train were delivered round the town, a typical load including perhaps tubs of butter and crates of eggs for a grocery store, and cartons of ladies' clothing for a draper's. Its driver, Mr Reginald W. Hendy (who was universally referred to as 'Reg'), was a chirpy character, who looked slightly bandy-legged (perhaps through carrying such heavy loads), appeared to have some Cockney in his make-up, and partnered his long-sleeved railway waistcoat with a sensible black apron.

Reg frequently called at my father's office, delivering cumbersome bales of printing paper whose wrappings often exuded an odour of fish, through being stowed near fish boxes in transit. Using the concessionary tickets the Company gave them, he and his wife were pioneers of holidaying in such distant and, to most Hoyland people in those days, still unknown resorts as Brighton and Penzance, from which each year they sent my parents a postcard initialled 'L.M.S.'

The LNER made its Hoyland deliveries not from Dovecliffe but from Birdwell and Hoyland Common, a station approached up a steep track from the minor road which, before the M1 Motorway was built, led from Birdwell Police Station to Pilley Green, skirting the base of Wharncliffe Silkstone spoil heap.

The driver of Birdwell's round-fronted, royal blue van was Mr 'Jimmy' Johnson, a tall, broad-shouldered giant of a man with a round rosy face and grey moustache who would have made an ideal Santa Claus, and who could hoist a full cabin trunk on to his shoulder using only one hand. Like many LNER men in South Yorkshire, he came from Lincolnshire and had joined the railway down in his native county in his youth. A champion skater, he took winter holidays in order to be able to take part in skating contests on the frozen fens.

Horse-drawn Transport

On Hoyland's roads, in the two decades leading up to the Second World War, the era of the horse had not quite passed. Not only did the travelling greengrocers Thomas Doyle, Herbert Ibbotson and Albert Miles hawk their wares from door to door by horse-drawn dray. There were coal leaders, including an elderly man named John Senior and Tom Cutts, my Uncle Fred Ottley's brother-in-law, who used horses and carts for making their deliveries. Each load was restricted to a single ton, since it would have placed too great a strain on the horse to haul a heavier load from Elsecar Main up the steep slope of either Cobcar or Hill Street. (It was John Senior's proud boast that no horse in Hoyland could beat his at pulling a load up what he pronounced 'Copter'.)

Another coal leader was Brightmoor Moody, a member of a staunch Congregationalist family. He always worked wearing a trilby-style hat and, I am told, lived in a large old house, along the path leading from the bottom of George Street to Dick Croft, some of whose windows had been blocked up in the days of the much-resented Window Tax.

When I was very young there was also an old woman called Mrs Dunn who drove a flat cart round the town selling firewood, going at a smacking pace.

Moreover, horses were still used on local farms, some to pull the traps the milk was brought round in, others to do the work now done by tractors. Most days a pair of them from Manor Farm was led along the field track past our house, in autumn to plough, the following summer to pull the swaying hay cart or the clacking, flailing reaper-and-binder, which seemed to break down at each circuit of the field. (My father took advantage of their passing to keep our 'Excelsior' rambler rose well fed. In those days it was so laden with crimson flowers that the trellis it grew on was invisible.)

To shoe all these hard-working animals, there was a blacksmith at the top of Milton Road. He was named George Fleetwood and his smithy was near what is now the junction of Milton Road and Southgate.

My mother, born in 1896, recalled a time when the family doctor made his rounds, as if in a novel by Jane Austen or Trollope, on horseback.

Both my parents often spoke of waggonettes which, from their description, appear to have been large carts or drays with benches round and across them, each drawn by a team of horses. A family called Marsh at Pilley used to own a number of waggonettes, which were available for private hire. Also, each Friday evening, they ran a service from Pilley to Hoyland Common Market, smaller than that at Hoyland and situated on the site between Hunt Street and Central Street now shared by a baker's and a supermarket. (The habit of shortening its name by omitting the 'Hoyland' led to confusion when, years later, some elderly people in the area were asked their opinion of the Common Market.) Other waggonette-owning families were the Smiths of the Crown Inn at Elsecar, and George Dallison and Sons of Linthwaite Lane.

Before the coming of the char-a-banc and its ubiquitous successor, the motor coach, waggonettes were often hired for Sunday school outings, favourite destinations for which, being picturesque but not far enough off to tire the horses, were Conisbrough Castle and Wharncliffe Craggs. Dallisons also used to advertise that they supplied carriages for picnics, birthday parties, balls and evening parties at the shortest notice.

Even after the 'horseless carriage' made its début, the use of horses on special occasions was kept up by ordinary people for some years, as it is to this day by Royalty. When an older sister of my mother's, Aunt Edith, was married at Elsecar in 1914, she rode to church in a wedding carriage with white ribbons plaited in the horses' manes. Also I remember how impressed I was, as a child during the 'twenties, by once seeing a line of black, horse-drawn cabs setting mourners down outside the station in Hill Street, to catch their trains home after attending a funeral. (I am told that the hearse which was used with these cabs probably had engraved, frosted-glass sides and a flat roof surmounted with black, nodding plumes to enhance the solemnity of the occasion.)

The Coming of the Buses

By the 'twenties, the waggonette had been superseded by its motorized counterpart, the char-a-banc (always pronounced in

Hoyland 'sharrer-bang'). A Spartan precursor of the motor coach, this had a row of doors along each side, bench-type seats and, to protect passengers from the rain, a canvas hood, folded down at the back, which could be pulled over them on wet days.

Pioneers in this field in the Hoyland area included the Bedford Brothers, one of whose char-a-bancs enjoyed the name 'Whippet' with its implication of stream-lined, graceful and seemingly effortless speed.

Buses, too, had made their appearance. They were the small, 'long-nosed' variety, with dusty window curtains looped inside, which still ran in Swaledale until recent years and were seen in the television version of *All Creatures Great and Small*. A service was started by the Hinton family to which Reginald Hinton of the Strafford Arms belonged. For people forced to rely on public transport, the sole way to reach Rotherham from Hoyland till that time was to take a train to Brightside and change there to a main-line train for Masborough. The Hintons abolished the need for this by running buses to Rotherham via Wentworth. (In those days an arm of Elsecar Reservoir extended on the Wentworth side of 'Watery Lane'. Since the single-arched bridge carrying the road over it had been weakened by mining subsidence, passengers when buses became bigger and heavier had to alight, to lighten the load, and walk across.)

Hintons had two buses, each painted yellow, which allowed them to run an hourly service. One was driven by Mr Percy Hinton, the other by an employee, Thomas Hodgson, whose father, George Hodgson of Barber Street, worked in the Urban District Council's highways department. When, after a few years, the expanding Yorkshire Traction Company took over Hinton's route, which it extended from Hoyland to Barnsley, it took 'Tommy' Hodgson into its employ. One of its longest-serving, best-trusted drivers, he eventually came to work full-time on the express route from Newcastle-upon-Tyne to London. (When I was working in the London area, during the nineteen-fifties, and was going back by train after spending a few days at home, his mother if she saw me always asked, 'Why don't you go by bus?', adding meaningly, 'You'd be safe behind our Thomas.' I had to explain that, since time was of the essence and the train much faster, one could only hope that the British Railways driver on duty that day proved as expert and reliable as Tommy.)

The Yorkshire Traction Company

Gradually and inexorably, during the inter-war years, the Barnsley-based Yorkshire Traction Company took over scheduled bus routes in the Hoyland area, and most small operators went out of business — the kind of process that de-regulation is seeking to reverse. A notable exception was Burrows of Wombwell, who stayed independent, running a service from Rawmarsh to Leeds via Cortworth and Coaley Lanes, with a detour into Wentworth.

Some routes were shared by other major operators. Sheffield Corporation's cream-and-navy double-deckers ran one hour in four on the No. 70 route from Sheffield via Hoyland to Upton. Both these and the bright green West Riding buses based on Wakefield, besides the Traction Company's scarlet ones, ran through Hoyland Common on the old turnpike route between Sheffield and Barnsley. Also the service between Rotherham and Barnsley that had been taken over from Hintons was run on alternate hours by Rotherham Corporation Transport.

A typical Traction Company bus in the early years was a single-decker and had a folding central door. In front of this was a no-smoking area; it had six double seats, which were upholstered in blue-and-fawn moquette. The sideways seat facing the door, and all those to the rear, were covered in easier-to-clean brown leather. When double-deckers were first introduced, they had an open platform at the rear whence the steep, narrow, twisting stairs ascended. The upstairs seats held four passengers each and had a narrow aisle to the right of them, which made collecting fares at busy times a difficult procedure. As the aisle was recessed into the roof of the lower saloon, it was also a hazard to passengers on the off-side when they rose to alight.

To collect its fares, the Yorkshire Traction Company employed both conductors and conductresses. In winter the women wore thick, dark brown uniform coats piped with scarlet upon their collars and cuffs, and dark brown 'pork pie' hats likewise trimmed with scarlet. In summer they wore light brown dresses of a strong cotton-like material. Perhaps because blue is cooler-looking than red, these and the matching summer hats had saxe-blue piping.

Throughout those two decades when prices were stable fares remained static, as did the cost of staple foods. Some short journeys, including that from the Milton Hall at Elsecar to the Town Hall at Hoyland, cost only a penny (less than the short-lived decimal halfpenny of recent years). Single tickets were white. For double journeys one could buy a pink return, which cost appreciably less than two singles. The return fare from Hoyland Town Hall to Wombwell was fivepence, that to Barnsley tenpence and that to Sheffield one shilling and threepence. On the way back the pink return ticket was surrendered and a green 'exchange' one was given in its place. The fare paid was shown by the length of the strip clipped from the edge of the ticket.

By 1930 the Traction Company had launched out into running a daily service in the summer to the more popular north-country coastal resorts — a move which was to knock a further nail into the coffin of South Yorkshire's railway network. This new mode of travelling proved popular because it was cheaper than going by rail, it cut out irritating changes and waits and, both journeys having to be booked in advance, seats were assured and overcrowding was avoided. ('It's Quicker by Rail' was the slogan adopted by the railway companies in retaliation, and illustrated on their posters by children sliding down a stair rail.)

When my parents and I went to Scarborough each July for our customary two weeks' holiday, we went by rail, leaving Barnsley Exchange in a sulphur-smelling non-corridor train and changing at Wakefield and Normanton. In 1930, when the Depression was at its worst and the self-employed were hit like everyone else, we booked rooms at nearer Cleethorpes for a week and went by bus, almost from door to door, picked up with other people outside the John Knowles Church. (There was a slight 'hiccup' on this occasion. A passenger too many had been booked, so a man waiting further along the route had to sit in the aisle on a kitchen chair, which gave rise to a number of 'corney' jokes about his being the 'chairman'.) When business improved slightly the following year we spent a fortnight at Scarborough again but still chose to travel by road, instead of availing ourselves of the LMS and LNER's joint services.

The 'Tracky' Company also ran a parcels service with an agent (often a small shopkeeper) in each of the villages its routes passed through. This was particularly useful for items whose shape or size prevented their being sent by post. A family friend living at Elsecar, for whom I acted as a child bridesmaid, had her bouquet of pink carnations sent from Horsfield's in Barnsley, on the morning of her wedding day, by bus; it arrived on time despite last-minute fears of a breakdown or some other delay. Once a friend of my mother's living in the country sent a pair of rabbits for our Sunday lunch. This time the outcome was less fortunate. They arrived on Saturday evening and the agent (at that time a Hoyland boot and shoe repairer), seeing no light from our shuttered living room, assumed that we were out and kept them till Monday – which did nothing to enhance their freshness or to endear him to my mother when she at last received them.

Mr Ernest W. Tipler

No account of Hoyland transport between the Wars would be complete without mentioning Mr Ernest W. Tipler, a self-employed motor coach proprietor who lived in Longfields Crescent with his wife and schoolboy son Bernard. Mr Tipler's mother, left a widow when he and his sister (whose married name was Thickett) were young, lived in Cherry Tree Street with her second husband, Police Constable Woodall.

A quiet, thin-faced man of medium build who always dressed in sober brown or grey, Mr Tipler was a consistently smooth and steady driver, rarely exceeding thirty miles an hour. Mrs Tipler, who frequently rode with him, bore a marked facial resemblance to the Labour politician Miss Ellen Wilkinson, who was the Minister of Education in Mr Clement Attlee's post-war government.

She was a close friend of Mrs Walker, the wife of Mr 'Lichie' Walker, the newsagent.

Mr Tipler's cream-coloured luxury coach, which he garaged in Hall Street, could be hired for such private outings as Sunday school and choir excursions. It was always immaculately maintained. (The cleaner for some years was a widow named Methley who lived in the house, now a dental surgery, on the corner of Spring Gardens.) To keep the atmosphere inside it fresh, passengers were forbidden to bring fish-and-chips on board. If there were too many intending passengers to fill the coach for a particular trip, Mr Tipler hired a second one for the day, complete with driver, from some other private firm.

Two Tipler outings I remember clearly from the 'thirties were organized by the Hoyland and District Chamber of Trade. The first was to the Lincolnshire tulip fields and the Royal family's home at Sandringham, where we admired the gardens and greenhouses and went into the little village church, but could not see inside the house itself, where all the blinds were drawn. The second, not long before the War broke out, was to Llandudno and other places in North Wales, where we admired the famous Swallow Falls and at Llangollen had an excellent tea, including fresh Dee salmon. Descending a hillside in Wales that morning, we passed a column of 'militiamen', the twenty-year-olds belatedly called up for military training after the Munich 'Peace in our time' debacle.

During the War, Mr Tipler and his coach were commandeered for 'work of national importance'. When peace came he was soon on the road again, working a seven-day week in the holiday season, on some days being hired for private trips, for others advertising trips of his own which might be to the Peak District, to either coast or to one of Yorkshire's inland beauty spots such as Harrogate and Knaresborough. On summer and autumn Saturdays he also ran a holiday service between Hoyland and Blackpool.

Cars, Bicycles and Motor Cycles

Comparatively few people, either in Hoyland or in the rest of the country, owned motor-cars during the period between the Wars – even the Leeds-based commercial travellers who visited my father seeking orders for ink and paper used to come via Barnsley on the service bus. Most car owners in the area were either professional or business people who needed this convenient form of transport for their work, and to be able to run a car purely for pleasure was considered a sign of affluence.

Until the 'thirties most cars had 'artillery' wheels, which were fitted with thick iron spokes and many, like that of the Rev. Ian Moffat, the Vicar of St Peter's, had canvas tops and mica windows, which tended to crack and turn a brownish yellow. During the 'thirties iron spokes were replaced by intricate wire ones. Popular models during that decade were the little Austin Seven or 'Baby' Austin (known as a 'hatbox' in my family), the blunt-nosed Morris Cowley whose rear passengers sat in the open on a pull-out dicky seat, and the larger Morris Oxford. I have vivid memories of visiting an aunt and uncle at Oxspring, when I was eight, and being taken for a drive across the moors, where the ventilation shafts of the old Woodhead Tunnel smoked like sleeping volcanoes, on the dicky of their dark blue Morris Cowley. Fords were regarded ambivalently. Their engines were acknowledged to be good; however, their bodywork in those days was rather too showy for some people's liking. At least in Hoyland, no-one ever saw a Swedish, Japanese or Italian car.

There was no driving test to be taken until, with more and more vehicles appearing on the roads, the Road Traffic Act of 1934 was passed introducing one. Few learners had previously taken professional tuition. Most of them either had lessons from their friends or were self-taught, like the Hoyland Common farmer who drove his new car round and round a field until he had 'got the hang of the thing.'

By the same Act, a thirty-mile-an-hour speed limit was introduced in built-up areas, the approach to a restricted stretch of road being shown by a scarlet-and-white lollipop-shaped sign.

Another safety measure was the introduction of pedestrian crossings, striped in black and white, their presence indicated by amber globes known as Belisha beacons. (The Minister of Transport who devised them was Mr Leslie Hore-Belisha.) For some years there were two of these in the centre of Hoyland, one crossing High Street from Beattie's to Walker's shop, the other crossing the lower end of West Street from the Gas Office (now Taylor's Electrical) to the Old Post Office Buildings.

Petrol cost about a shilling a gallon, including tax. In Hoyland it could be obtained either from George Neil and Son's Aero Garage on Market Street (now the headquarters of D. Pearson [Electrical] Ltd.) or from Frank Marsh's garage at West Bank. (Like his successor, Mr W.C.W. Wordsworth, Mr Marsh was also a coal leader.)

Next door to their garage, Neils had a shop (now a video centre) where they sold bicycles, radio components, flash-lamps and batteries of various kinds. Part of it was partitioned off into an office. This was the domain of Alfred Williamson, who was Mr Neil's book-keeper and the husband of the well-known musician Miss Ivy M. King.

The founder of the firm, the elder Mr George Neil, was a chain-smoker with a rapid, staccato way of speaking. Before acquiring the garage he had run a cycle shop in lower Hill Street at Elsecar, at the bottom end of the tall row of houses between Church Street and the cottages known as 'The Barracks'. At his Hoyland shop, at a time between the Wars when inflation in Germany was soaring madly, he kept a bucket of Deutschmark notes on the counter and, as a sales gimmick, gave customers handfuls of them in their change.

At one time Mr Neil also employed an assistant named Joe Beeston, who lived with his plump, auburn-haired, stagey-looking wife in a flat over the shop. It fascinated me as a child to see Mr Beeston measuring a yard of wire. He would simply hold one end against his nose, stretch out the wire as far as he could reach, and snip it at that point.

There was another cycle and wireless shop in Hoyland at

No. 48 King Street, opposite the Mount Tabor Chapel and next door to C. Firth and Sons' paint and wallpaper shop. It was run by Mr and Mrs Arthur Bircher, who came there during the 'twenties, following a jeweller and watch repairer named Taylor who was also an optician and whose granddaughter, Margaret Woodcock, sometimes came to play with me. The cost of a cycle was about £3, payable in small weekly instalments.

The Birchers, who retired to Chesterfield after the Second World War, had fair-haired, blue-eyed twin daughters, Beryl and Cora, who were my contemporaries at King Street School and were scarcely distinguishable from each other except by people who knew them very well. 'The Twins', as everyone at King Street called them, both trained as teachers of domestic subjects. One of them taught for a time at Kirk Balk School and the other at the Technical College in Barnsley.

In retrospect there appear to have been fewer motor-cycles on the roads then than there are now. Perhaps this is an illusion caused by the fact that those which were around were far less noisy. The *Barnsley Chronicle* and the *Hoyland Express*, as the *South Yorkshire Times* was known in Hoyland in those days, often had short news items about young men summonsed and fined for riding motor-bikes 'not fitted with effective silencers'.

The motor-cycle with a side-car attached was still a fairly common form of transport. In the 'twenties, my Aunt Doris and her husband (who later owned the Morris Cowley) sometimes came to visit us from Barnsley, where they lived before moving to Dundee and then to Oxspring, rattling and jolting down the street on a machine like that owned in *Last of the Summer Wine* by Walter Batty. To shield their eyes from the draught they wore goggles rather like those that skin-divers now wear. As a toddler I ran and hid when they arrived, scared by these monstrous-looking apparitions.

The Dearne and Dove Canal

By the 'thirties, the time at which I first recall it, the short Elsecar branch of the Dearne and Dove Canal, which was cut in the late eighteenth century as a link with the South Yorkshire Navigation, was already disused, neglected and weedgrown, though the dripping, worn lock gates were still in place near the road bridge at Royds Lane.

At one time the picture had been a very different one, the canal carrying coal not only from Elsecar but from Hoyland Silkstone, from which it was brought down for loading in rope-operated waggons. It also transported the products of the Elsecar Iron Works. It had faced competition since the eighteen-fifties, when the South Yorkshire Railway built its branch line up the valley and creamed off much of this lucrative mineral traffic. Nevertheless, as recently as my mother's Edwardian childhood, barges had still come up to Elsecar.

The children of one barge owner named Hood, who travelled on the water with their parents, attended Elsecar Church of England School on those days when the barge was moored nearby. One of the girls was in my mother's class, and is said to have looked neat and spotlessly clean, wearing a starched white apron over her frock. Canal folk, however, seem to have been regarded mainly as a disreputable lot, the name 'bargee' that was applied to them carrying derogatory overtones.

It was to keep the Elsecar branch topped up by replacing the water lost through its locks that Elsecar Reservoir (locally known as the 'Reservoy' or 'Big Pond') had been made, damming the waters of the Harley Dyke. In its heyday it stretched well to the Wentworth side of 'Watery Lane', which crossed it on a single-arched stone bridge, and also past the stone bridge on Burying Lane. In the period between the Wars, however, when it no longer served a commercial use, its level was allowed to fall drastically to avoid the risk of a disastrous flood, since the dam head, which had assumed a switch-back shape, had been seriously damaged by subsidence.

The name 'Elsecar Lido' had not yet been coined, but the reservoir already attracted anglers. In hard winters like that of 1938 it was also a popular venue for skaters, the more skilled of whom liked to show off their prowess. Its presence and that of the adjacent park, complete with café, bandstand and landscaped stream, helped to establish the sobriquet 'Elsecar-by-the-Sea'. (Not only local people knew of these charms. Coming home by train from Sheffield once during the 'fifties, having seen me off on a London express, my father was surprised when his compartment was invaded by 'inner city' children asking: 'Mester, does this train go to Elsecar-by-the-Sea?' and then speculating nervously as to whether it would pass through a tunnel on the way.)

Aeroplanes and Air Travel

To most people living in Hoyland as elsewhere, during the 'twenties and 'thirties, aeroplanes were inventions to read about and marvel at, but not to think of travelling in oneself or in one's wildest dreams to associate with cut-price holidays. Most models seen over the town were biplanes. When one of these droned slowly overhead (incredibly so when compared with the speeds of today) it was an occasion for rushing out and staring. One Sunday, after it was rumoured that a plane had made a forced landing in Jump Fields, people came hoping to view this phenomenon.

I also dimly remember, from the 'thirties, seeing the German airship 'Hindenberg' pass over early one evening on its scheduled crossing to the United States, weeks before its career was tragically cut short by catching fire on landing. To adults, it brought memories of the Zeppelin raids during the First World War. To all who followed the international news, it brought chill forebodings of less peaceable flights over Britain if ever war broke out again.

All Hoyland took a proprietary interest in the daring exploits of Miss Amy Johnson, the pioneer woman aviator, of whom we felt particularly proud since she was a Yorkshirewoman (though, coming from Hull, she would nowadays be called a Humbersider).

This adulation was not confined to Yorkshire. A popular song declared, 'Amy, wonderful Amy, I'm proud of the way you flew,' adding 'Believe me Amy, you cannot blame me, Amy, for falling in love with you.' Children at King Street School sang a less complimentary jingle to the tune of 'Daisy Belle'. It ran as follows:

> Amy Johnson flew in an aeroplane,
> Flew to China and couldn't get back again.
> She flew in an old tin Lizzie,
> Enough to make you dizzy,
> But she'd look sweet, sat on a seat
> In the Manchester Ship Canal.

(I got scolded for singing this at home, my mother asseverating that it was vulgar.)

Amy Johnson's most spectacular achievement was her solo flight to Australia. After she had blazed the trail, an England to Australia Air Race was organized in 1935. People followed its progress keenly both in the papers, where each day it constituted front-page news, and on the 'wireless', which most homes possessed by then. Among names filling the news bulletins were those of Kingsford Smith, after whom Sydney airport was subsequently named, Cathcart Jones and Waller, flying as a team, and a solo competitor called Wiley Post. (My parents, who had a flair for finding nicknames, promptly bestowed that of 'little Wiley Post' on a small black 'hearthrug' dog which used to strut, self-assurance making up for its lack of size, on the track going past our house from Manor Farm. It may have borne no resemblance to the airman, towards whom no disparagement was meant — the unusual-sounding name just happened to fit this most unusual-looking animal.)

CHAPTER SIX

Education

King Street School

THE HOYLAND SCHOOL I knew from the inside was King Street, to which I was taken at the age of six and where I stayed until ten-and-a-half, when I moved on to Ecclesfield Grammar School.

Standing at the junction of King Street and Millhouses Street on a large site sloping down towards the LMS railway, and flanked on one side by the council tennis court and bowling green and on the other by the premises of the baker and confectioner Willie Storrs, King Street was a 'mixed' school which originally catered for all ages from five to the school-leaving age of fourteen. Though its official name, as pupils were always reminded, was the

Hoyland — Elsecar King Street Council School, from its being built in 1909 till its demolition in 1985 it was generally known as 'The New School' (just as Elsecar Main was always 'The New Pit').

Approached by two steep flights of steps down from the street, it was a large, many-gabled, slate-roofed building of smooth red brick, with seven classrooms grouped round a high central hall. There were two entrance doors, one with 'Boys' and the other with 'Girls' inscribed on a semi-circular stone over it. The cloakrooms, one for boys and one for girls, had rows of iron pegs for hanging coats and a few wash–basins whose taps always ran cold. The asphalt-surfaced playgrounds, used both for 'drill' during lesson time and for playtime games such as hide-and-seek, skipping, 'tig' and 'What time is it, Mr Wolf?' were likewise one for each sex, and were separated by a high brick wall. The only sanitary facilities were a short row of lavatories in each. At playtime the queue at the girls' side was always so long that it was not always possible to go before a teacher's whistle signalled the fact that lessons were due to begin again.

The headmaster, Mr Hugh Buxton, was a short, middle-aged man with spectacles and a bristly moustache, who wore brown tweedy suits, sat at a large desk on a platform near the back of the hall with a brass handbell in front of him, and irritated his fellow headteachers, most or all of whom were training-college taught, by signing the notes that he sent them, 'Hugh Buxton, B.A.' His wife, a thin, dark-haired, bespectacled woman who wore a somewhat disapproving look, sometimes did supply teaching, for which she dressed in a green overall.

The Buxtons lived at the large house called South Grove, between the end of Broad Street and the Cloughs. They had two daughters, Dorothy and Winifred, and also a son named Sidney. Mrs Buxton died while they were still at Hoyland, and was buried in the Kirk Balk Cemetery. (I was saddened, on a visit to the cemetery a few years ago, to see that the inscribed kerb had been taken from her grave as part of a tidying–up exercise and was lying discarded by the gravediggers' hut.) Mr Buxton, who lived to a great age, moved from the district after his retirement (I believe that it was either to North Wales or to some place in the north-west of England) to join one of his daughters, and wrote frequently to the *Hoyland Express* giving his latest news.

The rest of the teachers were mainly local. Mrs Braham, who taught the five-year-olds (known as the 'baby class') was brought up at Hoyland Common. Formerly Miss Effie Murfitt, the daughter of Russell Murfitt, a butcher, she was a large woman with a florid face suggestive of high blood-pressure and legs permanently encased in bandages. Her husband, who had lost a leg in the First World War, drove her to school in an old Jowitt car. It was said that he kept a furniture shop. The Brahams had twin sons and a daughter, herself a school-teacher, who married Mr Douglas Davy, a member of the Elsecar ironfounding family of that name.

Mrs Braham's room, the middle one of the three at the Millhouses end, had a coal fire in one corner with a tall guard, and little chairs for the tinies to sit on. It also boasted a rocking-horse and other toys, while the blackboards along two of the walls were covered with friezes depicting scenes from nursery rhymes, skilfully executed in coloured chalks, presumably by Mrs Braham herself.

I was not however, on joining the school, allowed to savour these delights for long. When Mr Buxton found that I could read, I was sent to join the other six-year-olds (whose class was not distinguished by a name or number). Our teacher, Miss Baker, soon afterwards left to be married. After an interval during which Mrs Buxton taught us she was followed by Miss Saunders, a strong-featured woman with horn-rimmed spectacles who usually dressed rather 'tweedily'.

The six-year-olds sat primly, two at a desk. In the mornings we did simple sums and learned to print. The afternoons, I recall, were devoted to such lighter activities as hearing the teacher read from *The Water Babies*, *Gulliver's Travels* and *The Song of Hiawatha*, or folding squares of brightly-coloured gummed paper and cutting bits from them with blunt tipped scissors. If this was done carefully, the paper when unfolded formed a pretty, symmetrical pattern. At the end of the autumn term, we also cut out plum puddings and Christmas trees. The best specimens were stuck on the classroom windows, from which no doubt the caretaker eventually had trouble removing them. A useful teacher's stand-by towards 'home time' was 'the clay'. Kept in a dustbin this grey, putty-smelling substance could in theory be used to model anything from a cow to a cottage loaf. In practice it was invariably either so dry that it crumbled into hard, currant-sized lumps or so slimy that one's fingers got coated with it.

Standard 1, which comprised the seven-year-olds, was taught in the room across the hall from Mrs Braham's by Mrs Brown, a stout woman who lived in a council house in the part of West Street running parallel to Fearnley Road and who, like Mrs Braham, was driven to school by her husband. In Standard 1 pupils began to learn the elements of human geography, bossy-voiced Mrs Brown broadening our horizons by teaching us about American Indians, Eskimos and the nomadic herdsmen of the Steppes, and handicraft time being devoted to making cardboard igloos and cotton wigwams. She also taught us such little ditties as 'A carrion crow sat on an oak' and 'There was a tailor had a mouse', and became explosively angry when some of us sang 'I-diddle-um-tum-feegle' instead of 'feedle'.

Standard 2's teacher was Miss Norah Utley from Church Street, Elsecar, a short, plump, round-faced woman with dark brown hair. Confusingly, Standard 3 was taught by Miss Bessie Eileen Uttley of Hoyland Common, a tall young woman with fair, wavy hair whose parents, staunch Methodists, kept a wallpaper and paint shop on the corner of Hunt Street and Hoyland Road. The confusion was resolved when Miss Bessie Uttley left to be married and her place was taken by Miss Edith Brooke, who had formerly taught in Sheffield and whose parents, Mr and Mrs Wilton Brooke, kept the grocery store in West Street. (The 'supply' teacher who filled the gap before Miss Brooke came was Mrs Annie White, a sister of the local historian, Mr Arthur Clayton.)

Standard 4 was in the care of Miss Marion Hough, who wore spectacles, had neatly trimmed brown hair and was a sharp-voiced disciplinarian, rapping one's palm with a ruler for the slightest misdemeanour or carelessness. In 1935 Miss Hough married Mr

Arthur Parkin, the eldest son of Mr Ernest Parkin, Sr., a King Street pharmacist, and went to live at Ipswich.

Standard 5 was taught by Miss Annie March, who lived in Barber Street, the only daughter of a signalman at Elsecar and Hoyland LMS Station. Miss March had a heavy responsibility, since hers was the 'scholarship' class, whose members took the examination which decided whether they would go away to grammar school or finish their education at King Street itself. Also she and Mrs Braham took turns at the hall piano to 'play in' the pupils lined up in the yard at the start of each school session and after each playtime.

Those who stayed at King Street after the age of eleven were instructed by the school's two male assistants, Mr Fred (always referred to as 'Ferdie') Wrightson, who wore horn-rimmed glasses and ill-fitting tweeds and Mr Herbert (nicknamed 'Cobby') Ashton, tall, stooping and professorial-looking and, standing before the class in his grey suits, bearing a marked resemblance to a heron. Mr Wrightson was an Elsecar man whose father managed the Electra Palace (which was later re-named the Futurist), halfway between the school and the railway station. Mr Ashton, who lived with his wife and small daughter Sybil at 'Culham', a detached house at the junction of Kirk Balk and Royston Hill, was a local man too, being the brother of Frank Ashton, the Elsecar painter and decorator.

Lessons in all Standards followed a set pattern: scripture followed by the 'three r's' (including reciting multiplication tables) at the start of the day, then lighter subjects such as geography and history and, in the afternoon, painting, crayoning and handicrafts. The girls did some elementary needlework, a typical exercise being to make either a pincushion or a kettleholder of dark green or rusty brown calico, embroidering the edges with simple stitches in contrasting (often clashing) shades of silk. The older girls also learned country dancing to such lively tunes as 'Sir Roger de Coverley', 'Sellinger's Round' and 'Gathering Peascods'.

Classes were large, with about fifty pupils in each. Holidays, compared with those of today, were short, comprising four weeks in the summer, two at Christmas and one only at Easter.

Because there were nine classes to seven rooms the hall, divided by mobile wooden screens, served as two extra classrooms, Standards 6 and 7 occupying the Elsecar end in turn, Standards 3 and 4 the Hoyland. Lessons in the hall were subject to many distractions, including those from pupils passing through to 'leave the room' through not having time (or being too lazy) to go at playtime.

The hall was also used for morning assembly, at which we sang 'Stand up, stand up for Jesus' or some other rousing hymn and then stood, hands together and eyes closed, reciting the Lord's Prayer. Sometimes there was evening assembly too, at which 'Hushed was the evening hymn' was sung frequently. (The six-year-olds had their own home-time prayers, singing something more suited to their age, 'Gentle Jesus, meek and mild', 'Jesus, tender shepherd, hear me', 'There's a friend for little children', 'We are but little children weak' or 'When mothers of Salem'.)

Most of the songs learnt higher up the school had a moralizing, didactic tone. I still clearly remember two of them:

> We'll go to our places with bright smiling faces
> And pay great attention to what we are told,
> Or else we shall never be happy and clever,
> For learning is better than silver or gold.

and

> He who would thrive must rise at five.
> He who has thriven may stay till seven.
> He's a thriftless loon who lies till eleven.

The entire school also gathered in the hall each Armistice Day, which was 11th November, wearing the tiny penny poppies sold to children, to keep the Two Minutes' Silence with bowed heads and a puzzled, uncomprehending feeling of guilt.

Owing to the sloping nature of the site, there were two basement rooms which were entered from the playground. One was used for cookery, the other for woodwork, the senior pupils from both King Street itself and other schools attending one day a week for instruction in these subjects. There was also, beneath Mrs Braham's room, a dark boiler house, containing the iron boiler which supplied water for the school's huge black radiators. The caretaker, Mr Walter Shepherd, stoked it. He was a small, mouse-coloured man who lived in Booth Street, in one of two cottages facing towards Jump. His hobby was woodwork, so my parents got him to make an ornate dolls' house for my sixth birthday and a desk with a sliding blackboard for my seventh.

Until the Second World War, when some children's 'mums' started going out to work, there were no meals provided at the school. There was, however, mid-morning milk. Until about 1930, this took the form of greasy, lumpy, cardboard-tasting Glaxo dried, served in an enamelled mug with a Marie biscuit (presumably supplied to remove the taste). Then a farmer, Mr Horace Thawley of Blacker Grange, was given a contract to deliver fresh milk in bottles, each holding the statutory third of a pint. There was also pungent-smelling cod-liver oil (which when very young I called 'oliver fish') for children judged to be in need of it. This was served at playtime in pitted grey teaspoons, which were afterwards taken by one of the more backward older girls and rinsed in cold water in the girls' cloakroom — a procedure which even as a child I thought most unhygienic.

The school's official visitors included the occasional councillor or Education Committee member, whose presence in a room was greeted with embarrassed awe, although even on normal occasions discipline seems in retrospect never to have been a problem. It was only rarely that some older boy was beaten with a wooden blackboard duster. A punishment used lower down the school was to be hauled out in front of the class and made to stand in disgrace behind the blackboard.

A more regular visitor was the school nurse, stern-looking in her navy uniform. We had to sit with heads resting on desks while she ruffled our hair looking for 'livestock' — something that could easily be passed on since the desks, with their iron supports lettered 'WRCC', each had a bench-like seat holding two pupils. Less often the school doctor (stout, grandmotherly, dressed in ankle-length black and looking as if she ought to have retired long since) came to examine us, commandeering the women's staffroom for this purpose.

Truants were chased up by Mr William Coggan, who was called the School Attendance Officer but was universally known as the 'school bobby' and lived in a semi-detached house between the terrace called 'Church View' and Skiers View Road. Looked on as something of a bogy–man, he trudged round the area knocking on doors and asking the whereabouts of absentees, which he duly recorded in his notebook. His daughter had a baby-linen shop on Hoyland Road at Hoyland Common.

During my years as a pupil there the school experienced two tragedies. Jolly, round-faced, sandy-haired Betty Burdin failed to return after a school holiday when she was seven and we were both in Mrs Brown's class. The rest of us were never officially told in school but got to know from our parents that she had died. The cause was said to have been meningitis – something still fairly common in those days. Some time later five-year-old Betty Brack of Elsecar died of Bright's disease in term time, and pupils were asked to take pennies to buy a wreath. (Memories of this occasion were brought back when recently, walking along Wath Road, I glanced over the churchyard extension wall and saw her grave, marked with a little stone and a bunch of fresh flowers.)

Our main source of contact with other schools was the annual School Sports which were held on Elsecar Cricket Field. A King Street girl from Jump Pit named Bessie Worthy always distinguished herself on these occasions. Each school was allocated a colour for those taking part to wear. Because there were not sufficient traditionally used colours (red, blue, yellow and green) to go round, King Street competitors wore green and white.

Market Street School

The pupils at King Street came mainly from the King Street – Cherry Tree Street area. There were also some who came from Milton Road, and some from Elsecar. Most of those from Platts Common and the rest of Hoyland went to the original Market

Street, part-way between Royston Hill and Hawshaw Lane and opposite the grounds of Hoyland Hall. Having been founded under the provisions of the Education Act of 1870 and, unlike the church schools in the area, been administered by a local School Board, it was generally referred to as 'The Board School' – a title which seemed more appropriate still when the inscribed stone bearing its name and the date 1874 was boarded over during the Second World War so that German paratroopers could not read it and find which part of England they were in.

Built of stone in a style reminiscent of Victorian church Gothic, Market Street too was an all-ages school. It was not, however, 'mixed'. On the contrary, segregation was complete, boys and girls each occupying a series of classrooms in one of two symmetrically balanced wings. There was also a neat stone-built residence to house the caretaker, who at one time was Mr Andrew Taylor and, at the top side of the playground away from the street, a shed to shelter under during rainy playtimes – an amenity that King Street did not boast. (Another way in which Market Street once scored was by the adoption of certain items of uniform – how I envied its girls in their 'pork pie' hats of navy blue with yellow monograms and piping!)

The boys' headmaster was a tall, thin, scholarly-looking man, Mr Joseph E. (usually known as 'Joe') Watkinson. His wife Elsie, whom he married late in life, having met her while on holiday at Whitby, was a Sheffield school-teacher who, when she moved to Hoyland, became a well-known Methodist church worker and also a J.P. After Mr Watkinson's death his wife remarried, her second husband being a Mr Wood, a most polite and gentlemanly person, and became known as Mrs Watkinson-Wood.

One of the assistants in the boys' department was Mr Wilfred March, a brother of Miss Annie March of King Street and, like her, tall and dark with a thin, good-looking face. Because in his first, inexperienced teaching days the pupils had found Mr March a source of amusement, they had given him the nickname 'The Penny Gem', the title of a children's comic then being published. It stuck to him throughout his teaching life.

Another assistant was Mr Charles Stuart ('Charlie') Guest, a small man with a dark moustache and a fussy manner.

The headmistress of the girls' section was Miss Jessie Guest, Charles Stuart Guest's sister, an upright, grey-haired, capable-looking woman who, I am told, had been an army nurse in the First World War. The Guests came of a local family. One of their brothers had a butcher's shop a short distance from the school. Another had a pharmacy in High Street, Wombwell. The two teaching Guests retired to Worthing on the south coast, where Charles died in March 1964 and Jessie in October 1969. Neither of them ever married. Memorial tablets to them can be seen in the Guest family plot near the main gates of Kirk Balk Cemetery.

One of the girls' assistant teachers was Mrs Beatrice May Lax of Elsecar, a tall woman who wore dark-tinted glasses and plain, rather masculine-looking clothes. She was the wife of Mr Arthur Lax of Strafford Avenue, and was for many years the Secretary of the Elsecar Midland Musical Festival.

Among Market Street's pupils during the 'twenties was Miss Mary Nightingale who, after studying at Barnsley Girls' High School and Lincoln Training College, taught at her old school for many years as Mrs Fawcett and became its deputy headteacher.

A teacher whose career was contemporary with that of Mrs Fawcett was Miss Margaret Mary McPartlain, a small woman who wore 'tea cosy' hats. She was the second of the six daughters of Mr Paul McPartlain, a highly-skilled plasterer whose services were much in demand when Hoyland was expanding during the period between the Wars.

The Infants' School attached to Market Street was a separate building at the Hawshaw Lane end of the girls' playground. Its headmistress in the 'thirties was a Miss Walker whose sister, small, grey-haired and bespectacled, kept a wool shop for a time across the road from Hoyland Post Office. The two of them lived in the little school house between the infants' building and the street. They were pacifists and in 1939, after the outbreak of the Second World War, incurred a great deal of opprobrium by displaying Peace Pledge Union posters in their sitting-room window.

'The Little Infants' School'

There was also another school on Market Street. Throughout most of the years between the Wars the mullion-windowed building with fish-scale slates adjacent to the Hoyland Market Place and now used as St Andrew's Parish Hall was a school for children aged from five to seven. No-one seemed to know its official name. It was always called 'The Little Infants' School', leaving one in some doubt as to whether the 'little' described the infants or the school.

It had been built in 1853 by Earl Fitzwilliam as a church infants' school. During the nineteen-forties an old woman proudly showed me a photograph of herself taken there with other pupils in starched white pinafores. Their headmistress, pleasant-faced Miss Oscar, who seems to have been very popular, sat wearing long skirts in the middle of the front row.

A typical school building of its time, the Infants' School comprised a small cloakroom, a medium-sized classroom and a larger room, one end of which could be screened off by closing a folding varnished-wood-and-glass partition. (Originally there was the long room only, the one nearer the street being a later addition.) The two classrooms were heated by open fires. The only lavatory was in the yard at the back of the building.

The headmistress during the school's later years was Miss Gwen Parkin, who lived with her widowed mother at Elsecar in a semi-detached house in Armroyd Lane, where her next-door neighbour was appropriately Mrs Doris Hague, who was the headmistress of Elsecar Infants' School. Miss Parkin's two assistants were Miss Eddy and Miss Irene Hague, who married a Barnsley accountant, Mr Maurice Howard, in 1938 and was a keen worker at St Andrew's Church, where she and her husband ran the Sunday School. Maurice Howard, who bore a marked facial resemblance to the television personality Cliff Michelmore, was also a lay reader.

In 1934 the little school was closed when, to take its place, the West Riding County Council built West Street Infants' School, to which the staff and pupils were transferred. Before St Andrew's

Church was opened in 1890, services for people in what became its parish had been held in the school, conducted by a curate. The owner of the school building, Earl Fitzwilliam, now gave it to St Andrew's to be used as a parish hall where meetings, sales of work and other parochial activities could take place.

The new West Street school with its assembly hall, airy rooms opening off a glass corridor and spacious grounds was hailed as a model of its kind. (Because so much wood was used in its construction, my father always disrespectfully called it 'Uncle Tom's Cabin'.) Under Miss Parkin's successor, Mrs Magson, it built up a reputation for giving its pupils an excellent basic grounding in the 'three r's'. Ironically, it was destined to enjoy a far shorter life than its cramped predecessor, being pulled down as a redundant school in 1985, at the same time as King Street.

St Peter's Church of England School

Situated slightly lower than the Law Stand, St Peter's Church of England School stood near the highest point in Hoyland. A bungalow now occupies its site, next to the Water Authority's property. The stone–built house between the bungalow and the corner of Upper Hoyland Road used to be the headmaster's residence.

Once the sole school in the area except for the infants' school on Market Street and Elsecar Church School, towards the end of its time St Peter's catered mainly for those pupils from Hoyland Common, Platts Common and the top end of Hoyland itself whose parents preferred a church school education to that provided by Market Street and the (then separate) boys' and girls' schools situated near Allott's Corner at Hoyland Common. It was commonly referred to as 'The Law School', just as St Peter's was called 'The Law Church', and is thought to have been built about 1835, though some authorities would place it even earlier. A document I have seen dated 1903 calls it 'Hoyland National School', 'National' being a name church schools were generally known by.

A smallish, mullion-windowed stone building with double doors at the top of a flight of steps parallel to the road, St Peter's was 'mixed' and, like Market Street and King Street, taught pupils up to the school-leaving age. Its children were reputed to excel at singing, one writer fancifully comparing them to skylarks hovering above the town. Perhaps an example was set by those of the boys who were also members of St Peter's choir.

The headmaster during the 'twenties was Mr Thomas Rawling Fletcher. He was a son of Mr Moses Fletcher, who kept The Old Eccles Cake Shop (later Mr D.P. Beattie's outfitter's) at No. 13 High Street. (Moses Fletcher was also a former churchwarden at St Peter's.) Those people of my father's generation who were pupils at the turn of the century spoke reverently of a former headmaster, Mr Holdsworth, who appears to have been a stickler for tidiness, inspecting his charges' boots and shoes each day to see whether they had been cleaned both front and back.

Mr father also remembered how, in icy weather, his mother pulled old socks over his boots to enable him to walk safely up and down the snow-covered Law Hill and how, after singing 'Now the day is over' with its words 'Shadows of the evening steal across the sky', he came out of school glancing apprehensively up, expecting to see a steel shutter slide overhead.

One of the assistant teachers at St Peter's was tall, dignified-looking Mrs Florence Westwood, a member of the Firth family which ran the plumbing and decorating business in King Street. After her marriage to Harry Westwood she had spent a number of years in New Zealand (which seemed much further away in those pre-airline days), later returning to live with her bachelor brother William and her unmarried sister in Booth Street.

Possessing limited amenities and with its catchment area overlapping those of other, more modern schools, St Peter's was closed about 1934, at a time when Hoyland's educational system was undergoing various important changes, and was pulled down in 1939.

St Helen's Roman Catholic School

The first children to receive a Roman Catholic education in Hoyland were taught in the original St Helen's Church, which was constructed in 1866 between the top of St Helen's Street and Cobcar. Among them was Mr Frederick Kelly, whose younger daughter, Mrs Winifride Hawksworth, taught at King Street for some years after the Second World War.

By the 'twenties, however, the purpose-built St Helen's School erected in 1897, with its playground adjacent to the Town Field in West Street, was already a familiar part of the Hoyland scene, the crosses crowning its vermilion gables serving to emphasize its identity.

Like King Street and St Peter's, St Helen's was 'mixed', and like them and Market Street it taught all ages. The headmaster, whose features I remember as having a distinctly Churchillian cast, was Mr Vincent James Houlton, who lived in a nearby council house in West Street and was for many years a Labour member of the Urban District Council. Some of his assistants, not surprisingly, had Irish-sounding names. Two whom I particularly remember were a vivacious dark-haired girl called Miss Costello (who lodged with an uncle and aunt of mine, and tried to persuade my staunchly Church of England mother to allow me to join her infants' class) and Miss O'Sullivan. There was also a Miss Hickey.

In those non-ecumenical, intolerant days, the instruction given at St Helen's School was as much a dark mystery to the Protestant majority of the community as the worship in St Helen's Church itself. There were rumours that children educated there were taught 'nothing but religion'. This separateness was perpetuated at the grammar school stage, the brighter Roman Catholic boys going to the De La Salle College in Sheffield, the brighter girls to the Notre Dame High School (always pronounced in Hoyland 'Noatrer Darm'). Some non-Catholic families too chose to send their daughters to this Sheffield convent school, which not only had a good academic record but seems at that period to have enjoyed a certain social cachet.

'Passing the Scholarship'

To be eligible to enter a grammar or high school in those days, one had either to pay (the fees were £3 a term — an average weekly wage) or to win a County Minor Scholarship. Standard 5 pupils automatically took the County Minor Examination, regardless of their chances of success. (Those who did not fancy going to a school where they were given homework to do each evening sometimes played truant or pretended to be ill on examination day.) The time at which the examination was held was a Saturday morning in February. There were papers in English and arithmetic, and also a written intelligence test. The results did not come out till May or June. Each child was entitled to make two attempts, taking the Junior Examination at ten and, if unsuccessful or for some reason unable to sit, the Senior Examination at eleven.

It was considered a distinction to have 'passed the Scholarship'. On the back wall of the central hall at King Street was a black-painted honours board on which Scholarship winners' names were painted in gold, the older ones already dull and tarnished. I assume that there were similar boards at other local schools.

Until 1931, Scholarship boys went to Barnsley Holgate Grammar School and girls to Barnsley Girls' High School, commuting from Elsecar and Hoyland LMS Station by train, the boys in green and royal blue blazers and caps, the girls in navy coats and matching 'pudding basins'. (Some years later these colours were changed, Holgate pupils wearing black and High School girls grey.)

Then, in September 1931, largely through the efforts of Lady Mabel Smith (who, though a sister of the Seventh Earl Fitzwilliam, served as a Labour County Councillor), a new grammar school was opened at Ecclesfield (or, more precisely, halfway between Ecclesfield and Chapeltown). Its catchment area included Hoyland, Hoyland Common, Elsecar, Wentworth, High Green, Grenoside, Chapeltown, Thorpe Hesley and Ecclesfield itself. Hoyland children already studying at Barnsley stayed there. Subsequent Scholarship winners went to Ecclesfield, conveyed from the Town Hall and back again in Traction Company buses.

The new system split some families in two. Among them were the children of Mr and Mrs George Chambers, who kept the fried fish and off-licence shops in High Street that are now owned by Higgs, two daughters and a son (Ida, Irene and Horace) going to Barnsley, a daughter and two sons (Joyce, Eric and Harold) to Ecclesfield. Two sons of Mr and Mrs George Wilkinson, who kept a sweet and tobacco shop in High Street, were similarly separated.

Nor was the change universally popular, some parents including my own maintaining (quite without justification, in the event) that 'this new place of the West Riding's' would never attain the high standard of academic excellence for which the two Barnsley schools had become noted.

Kirk Balk School

Of the changes and innovations which took place in Hoyland's educational system between the Wars, the most momentous was undoubtedly the building of Kirk Balk. Initially known as a 'middle' school and then, after the Education Act of 1944, referred to as a 'secondary modern', Kirk Balk was opened in 1933 to provide a secondary education and improved surroundings and amenities for those pupils in the Hoyland area who, in a phrase which was in those days in common use, had 'failed the Scholarship.'

A handsome pale brick building with stone detailing, it was like Market Street two schools in one, a boys' school and a girls'. The boys' headmaster, a bachelor named William Roby, stayed there for the remainder of his teaching life, retiring some years after the Second World War. He lodged in West Street with Mr and Mrs Samuel Burdin (the parents of Betty Burdin, who died while a seven-year-old at King Street). The first headmistress of the girls' school was Miss May, a martinet who was not very popular and stayed only a short time. (A favourite punishment of hers is said to have been to make offenders stand on bitterly cold days in the freezing vestibule between the school's inner and outer entrance doors.)

Kirk Balk's first uniform was navy blue, with Hoyland's neighbouring landmark, the Law Stand, embroidered in turquoise blue on the blazer and cap.

When the new school was opened, King Street and Market Street changed their status to that of primary schools, taking pupils up to the age of eleven, and Market Street in addition became 'mixed', with Mr Watkinson as its headteacher. Some teachers moved to Kirk Balk from other schools. They included Mr Ashton, Mr Wrightson, Miss March and Miss Norah Utley (who became the girls' physical training mistress) from King Street, and Mr Raymond Belk from Elsecar.

Miss Alice Emily Caws

No mention of Hoyland education between the Wars would be complete without a reference to Miss Alice Emily Caws.

Educated at Cambridge University (a rare distinction for a woman in those days), Miss Caws came to Hoyland during the late 'twenties. She supplemented the annual allowance that her family gave her by opening a small school, sometimes jestingly called 'Miss Caws' Academy'. The first place where this was held was the Wesleyan Manse (the detached stone house in King Street just above the Miners' Welfare Hall). Later the school was moved across the road to the front room of No. 192, a semi-detached house at that time occupied by Mr George Young and his family. (Mr Young was a pharmacist whose shop was further down the street.) Later still, it moved to a council house across the road from the Princess Theatre in West Street.

The pupils, numbering about ten in all, were for the most part five- and six-year-olds, and came mainly from business and professional families. They included tall, dark-haired, intense-looking Monica Roome whose father, the Rev. James Vesey Roome, was at that time the Vicar of Elsecar; tall, dignified-looking, brown-haired Margaret Young, the chemist's daughter; pale Georgie Parkinson, one of the Wesleyan Minister's twin sons (who once terrified me by telling me that a piece of toffee paper I had swallowed would wrap itself round my heart and make it stop and − no doubt having heard this from his elders − that there would be another war when I grew up), whose rosy-cheeked, more robust-looking brother Billy was banished to King Street School because Miss Caws found him too rough to handle; golden-haired Barbara Hinton, whose parents kept the Strafford Arms — now The Beggar and the Gentleman; Denise Utley, a fair-haired, frail-looking child who lived near Milton Ponds; blonde Madge Chadwick, a Roman Catholic child, whose brother Dennis became the Council's Estates Surveyor; and a boy from Harley whose Christian name was Gilbert but whose surname I seem never to have known.

Some pupils attended because they were not well enough to stand the rigours of full-time State education. One of them, older than the rest of us, was Beatrice Ibbotson, a daughter of the Elsecar LNER station-master. She was always said to be 'delicate'. My parents chose to send me there because, having had severe whooping cough at the age of three, followed by broncho-pneumonia at four, at five I was not considered well enough to receive full-time schooling.

Miss Caws' pupils attended in the mornings only, writing with scratchy slate pencils on little slates and learning to read from books with pictures under which were short cat-on-the-mat type sentences. She also taught us how to tell the time, using a cardboard clock-face, told us comforting stories about Jesus and God and frightening ones of how ill we would feel if ever we tried to smoke cigarettes, and played the piano with ring-encrusted hands while we sang traditional songs such as 'John Peel'. We even learned a smattering of French.

Taking her duties as instructress seriously, Miss Caws issued a lengthy, detailed report on each of her small charges every term-end. A few years ago I discovered two of these, carefully kept by my mother over the years, in an old tea caddy. In her bold, squarish handwriting Miss Caws waxed lyrical on my scholastic achievements, and made predictions which have since come true regarding the course of my future career. With my conduct, however, she was less pleased, pronouncing me 'too restless and erratic to be exemplary.'

One of the world's eccentrics, Miss Caws attracted a certain amount of ridicule. Crudely made up, with her dark hair in heavy braids, she wore flowing black draperies, jangling beads and a quantity of bejewelled rings — indeed her appearance was considerably more like that of a fairground fortune-teller than like that of a schoolmistress. She always spoke in a deep 'plummy' voice and walked with an incredibly slow, swan-like glide.

Some children who did not attend her day school were sent to Miss Caws in the evenings to learn elocution. They displayed their newly-acquired expertise by taking part in sketches at the concerts Miss Caws laid on in church and chapel halls. (I remember how, one foggy November evening, I acted the part of the farmer's wife, brandishing a silvered-cardboard carving knife, in a sad little play based on a poem called 'The Goslings' at the Hill Street Congregational Chapel schoolroom. This is a poem I never heard again till it was sung recently on television in the 'Choir of the Year' competition.)

Though she became such a well-known figure in Hoyland, Miss Caws did not in fact remain there long. Her career as teacher and impresario ended sadly, cut short when she died during the late 'thirties at St Helen's Hospital, Barnsley, to which she was admitted suffering from gangrene.

CHAPTER SEVEN

Church and Chapel

DURING the 'twenties and 'thirties, before the Second World War further undermined the faith shaken by the First which it so closely followed, and at a time when there were no television programmes peddling evolutionary materialism, and few cars and coaches to take people from home on Sundays, nearly everyone in Hoyland took part in some form of public worship and was known to be 'Church', 'Chapel' or 'Catholic'. A resident who openly confessed to atheism, or merely to being an agnostic, would have been regarded at best as a crank and at worst as a lost soul heading for perdition.

My family was Church of England on both sides, my father having been a chorister, Sunday school teacher and sidesman at St Peter's, my mother a Sunday school teacher at Elsecar.

St Peter's Parish Church

Despite its venerable looks, St Peter's Church was barely a hundred years old in those days. It was constructed in 1830 at a cost of about £2,000 in a plain, pseudo-Perpendicular style to replace the 'Hoyland Chapel' built by the Townends, a family various of whose members lived at Upper Hoyland, Blacker and Stead Farm. Begun about 1720 and consecrated in November 1740 by the Bishop of Gloucester in a service lasting some three-and-a-half hours, and endowed by the Townends with the income from various fields and farms, including a farm at Worsbrough Dale and one at Ben Bank in the Parish of Silkstone, this original church had been built as a chapel-of-ease in the Parish of All Saints, Wath-upon-Dearne. By the present century, however, St Peter's had acquired its own parish with the then lordly stipend of £500 a year — twice that of St Andrew's or Elsecar.

People of my parents' generation still talked about the Victorian clergy who had held office there. One was Mr Cordeaux (pronounced by his flock 'Caddoo'), whose family was so large that the Vicarage (which has now been converted into Woodlands Lodge) had to be enlarged to make more room for it, who refused to christen babies with such names as Sam, Tom, Joe and similar abbreviations, and who lies under a roof-shaped memorial, with the inscription 'In Hope of Eternal Life', between the east window and the churchyard wall.

Another incumbent was Mr Sale, after whom a Hoyland Common street is named, a henpecked bachelor whose sister kept house for him, rationed him at tea time to half a mince-pie, and when she was going to make broth asked the butcher for bones from which every scrap of meat had been pared, saying that the Vicar's stomach was delicate.

There was also Mr Steele, who spent his Monday mornings chasing up those who had failed to attend church the previous day, who forbade his choirboys to sing 'Good King Wenceslas', saying it was not a carol and who, too, gave his name to a Hoyland Common street.

From 1915 until 1927 the Vicar was the Rev. Thomas Godfrey

Rogers, the son of a Cambridgeshire incumbent and himself a graduate of Queens' College, Cambridge, a tall, dark, heavily-built man who wore spectacles and married Miss Doris Cleaver Steele, Mr Steele's elder daughter. When he was serving as an army chaplain during the First World War his father, who is said to have looked rather like the German Admiral Alfred von Tirpitz, had come to St Peter's to take services.

It was during Mr Rogers' incumbency that, at the age of three, I first went to church, accompanying my father to Morning Service. We arrived slightly late and, since the nave was full, had to find places in the gallery. Most of the service passed over my head, but I was fascinated by the repetition of a phrase which to me sounded like 'letter spray'. Another time, at Harvest Festival, we found the gallery as packed as the nave – there was literally standing room only.

In 1927 Mr Rogers moved to St Margaret's at Swinton, a living which, like that of St Peter's, was in the gift of Earl Fitzwilliam. In 1942, with his family of six sons, he moved back to the Hoyland area as the Rector of Tankersley, a parish where he stayed till his retirement in 1958. He was also appointed a Canon of Sheffield Cathedral.

Mr Rogers' successor at St Peter's was the Rev. William Ian Grant Moffat, a tall, thin-faced, bespectacled Scotsman who usually dressed in dark suits and overcoats. He had trained at the College of the Resurrection, Mirfield, had spent four years as Vicar of Elsecar and, like Mr Rogers, was an Honorary Chaplain to the Forces.

Mrs Moffat, a dark-haired, round-faced, vivacious woman, had before her marriage been on the stage and was younger than her husband by some years. Her name was Margaret Mary, but he always spoke of her and addressed her as Pearl. They had three children, Margaret Bailey (always called Peggy), Bernard and Catherine Mary Rose (whom at first I always confused with Princess Margaret Rose, since they were both born in the same year, 1930).

A tragedy struck this little family when, while a pupil at Ecclesfield Grammar School, fourteen-year-old, sandy-haired, freckled Peggy died of diphtheria. She was buried outside the east wall of the church. Her fellow Girl Guides were among the mourners.

Another member of the Vicarage household was Mr Moffat's aunt, Miss Catherine Moffat, who had been governess to Lady Elfrida, Lady Joan, Lady Donatia and Lady Helena, the daughters of the Seventh Earl Fitzwilliam. Consequently, boxes of discarded clothing were sent from Wentworth Woodhouse to the Vicarage, for distribution to the poor of the parish.

The Moffats ran an ancient Austin Seven with discoloured mica windows, and shocked their more strait-laced parishioners by smoking, drinking and frequenting public houses, one of their favourite calling places being the Cock Inn at Birdwell.

Towards the end of 1937, Mr Moffat exchanged his living for one at Mirfield, being succeeded at St Peter's by the Rev. Algernon Bertie Pratt, an Oxford graduate. Mr Pratt, tall, aquiline-nosed and scholarly and, like his two predecessors, wearing glasses, was in his early years at Hoyland always accompanied on his outings by a black Labrador called Jimmy. He stayed at St Peter's till the mid-fifties and took a keen interest in local history, about which he wrote in his Parish Magazine, dealing with such topics as the origin of 'Hoyland Chapel' and the exact location of the Battle of Tankersley Moor. During the Second World War, he carried on an argument in letters to a local newspaper with a Hoyland Common physician, Dr Philip Lewis, about Britain's alliance with the Soviet Union, the doctor heaping praises on that country, the Vicar predicting that, once the War was over, she might turn upon her allies.

Mr Pratt and his quiet, pretty, ladylike wife had two daughters and a son. Catherine, the elder daughter, was a nurse at St Thomas's Hospital, London, which suffered damage in the London 'blitz'. Joan was a schoolteacher. Richard, several years younger than his sisters, worked as a 'Bevin boy' during the War, being one of the young men chosen by lot to work as miners instead of being drafted into the Forces.

Mr Pratt retired to Edale in Derbyshire and died soon afterwards. Mrs Pratt returned to Hoyland as companion to Dr Joy

Allott, a staunch member of St Peter's congregation, with whom she eventually moved to Sidmouth.

The incumbencies of Mr Moffat and Mr Pratt brought some significant liturgical changes. During the 'twenties, High Church practices were still uncommon in the Hoyland area. It was customary to have Holy Communion at 8.00 a.m., Mattins at 11.00 and Evensong at 6.30. There was therefore some murmuring at St Peter's when Mr Moffat introduced Sung Eucharist (in those days styled 'Choral Communion') on alternate Sunday mornings. Though by no means a High Churchman, Mr Pratt went still further, having Mattins only on the third Sunday in the month. This upward trend is one which has continued.

For those too old, young or infirm to climb the hill from Hoyland Common, there was in those days a small Mission Church (always referred to as the 'Mission Room') at the junction of Hoyland Road and Tinker Lane. Holy Communion was celebrated there on certain days and, during the 'thirties, other services were taken by a young lay reader, tall, studious-looking Mr Norman Chappell, who worked in the Town Hall accounts department. There was also, at one time, a Church Army Captain resident at Hoyland Common. Early in Mr Pratt's incumbency the Mission Church was closed, and the building was made into a Parish Hall. (The idea behind the closure seems to have been that its congregation would then be compelled to start attending the Parish Church itself. In the event many of them stopped going anywhere.)

For two hundred years after the first 'chapel' was built, St Peter's was not only a place where the living worshipped but also a place of burial for the dead. The earliest burials, including those of some members of the Townend family, took place around the church. Until most of them were removed about 1960 as part of a 'landscaping' exercise, the ground on each side of the building was filled with austere ranks of headstones, many of black, durable Greenmoor stone. It also contained venerable trees, felled at the same time that the stones were moved.

With Hoyland's population fast expanding in the nineteenth century, this original burial ground soon filled, and across the

CHURCH AND CHAPEL

road from it an extension was opened. Comprising approximately five acres, with a stone wall and two pairs of iron gates, a gridiron of paths and, in the top corner nearest to the road, an iron tank supplying water for flower vases, this remained in use until 1924, by which time the shortage of space was so acute that new graves had to be dug along a path. To provide land for future burials, the Hoyland Nether Urban District Council laid out the neighbouring Kirk Balk Cemetery, which was duly consecrated that year by the first Bishop of Sheffield, the Right Reverend Leonard Hedley Burrows, D.D.

Churchyard burials continued in existing graves till the 'sixties, when the churchyard was officially declared closed and handed to Hoyland Council for maintenance. A quick, inexpensive tidying job was done in which some stones were buried beneath earth and grass. The graves they marked cannot therefore now be traced. Fortunately others remain standing and provide an invaluable record of the names, and tastes in sculpture and memorial verse, of the people of Victorian and Edwardian Hoyland.

Few people were cremated who died in Hoyland in the years before the end of the Second World War. The practice was commonly regarded until then as new-fangled, repugnant and even sinful. Also, however their bodies were disposed of, a greater reverence was shown towards the dead. It was customary for people to stand still when a funeral cortège passed them, and for men to remove their hats and caps as a mark of respect for the deceased.

The hill on which St Peter's stands is named Hoyland Law (from the Anglo-Saxon 'hlaew', meaning a hill), just as Stainborough Law is the name correctly given to the boldly-rising wooded hill at Stainborough. It is still customary for older people to refer to St Peter's as 'The Law Church' (a name which in my childhood made me think it must have some connection with the legal profession) and the end of Hawshaw Lane descending sharply towards Hoyland Common as 'The Law Hill' – an example of tautology comparable to that in the famous Wensleydale name Penhill (both of them literally meaning 'Hill-hill'). The area at the base of the Law Hill is known as 'The Law Foot'.

It was in one of the Law Foot cottages that there once lived Rupert Burtoft whose memorial, excellently preserved, is to be seen in the churchyard extension. He was the verger at St Peter's, and an irascible character who hated having to clean and sweep the gallery. If there were empty seats down in the nave at the start of a service, he would stand in the middle of the aisle and shout to anyone sitting up there, commanding them to 'Coom dahn inter t' body.'

The story is told that, one New Year's Eve, he was in the church tower ringing the New Year in, on the three bells transferred from the original 'chapel', when a young man staying at the Vicarage thought to play a practical joke on him. Suddenly Rupert heard a moaning sound, and a white-sheeted figure appeared on the belfry staircase. He stood up, flung his three-legged stool at it and went on with his peal. Caught off-balance, and crashing down the stone steps to the floor below, the joker was lucky to escape with his life. As things were, he spent several weeks in bed. No action, however, appears to have been taken against the agent of his downfall.

A later verger, Mr Albert Garnett, whose young son Harry was a chorister, lived at Hoyland Law Stand, which had been made into a dwelling-house, from 1911 until he moved to Thorne in 1926.

St Andrew's Parish Church

Hoyland's population continued to increase and, towards the end of the nineteenth century, it was obvious that another church was needed, preferably nearer the centre of the town. At first Sunday services, taken by a curate, were held in the Infants' School on Market Street. Then Earl Fitzwilliam gave a piece of land, further along that street, on which a church was constructed at a cost of approximately £1,400. Some money was given by the Earl himself. (Hence, like Elsecar, St Peter's and other churches towards which the Fitzwilliams have been generous, this one now receives a Christmas tree each year from the Wentworth estate.) The rest was provided by public subscription, a donor giving the then generous sum of £100 being Mrs Martha Knowles, who also built

CHURCH AND CHAPEL

the Town Hall clock tower and gave the tower clock to St Peter's.

The new church, whose foundation stone was laid by Lady Fitzwilliam in April 1889, was for obvious reasons dedicated to St Andrew, the fisherman brother of Simon Peter. Designed by the Hoyland architect Walter John Sykes, it was built of dressed stone in the Gothic style and comprised a chancel, a vestry and a nave, with double lancet windows in the nave and a handsome five-light east window with flowing tracery. The consecration service took place in September 1890.

Until it was removed during the 'thirties, rendered unsafe by mining subsidence, there was a bellcote situated on the roof at the junction of the chancel and the nave, the single bell being tolled by a ringer standing near to the chancel steps. It was also owing to subsidence during this period that the three massive stone buttresses were built at the east end of the church.

Until 1916, St Andrew's had no parish but was a chapel-of-ease to St Peter's, just as St Peter's itself had once been a chapel-of-ease to Wath, and couples from the whole of Hoyland still had to go to be married at 'The Law'. It was run by a curate-in-charge, a small man surnamed Wilson, whose appetite for cakes and pastries when invited out to tea, or attending a wedding reception or funeral feast, is said to have been prodigious.

When St Andrew's Parish was eventually formed, its Vicar's stipend, £250 a year, was taken from that of the Rector of Tankersley (once one of the richest livings in the North). To compensate the Rector for his financial loss, he was made the patron of St Andrew's living.

The name of the first Vicar was Charles Tremayne. He did not stay for long and very little, either good or bad, seems to have been remembered of him. He was followed in 1920 by the Rev. Harold Augustus Crowther-Alwyn, whose father was reputed to have been a Professor of Music at Oxford who was killed, crossing the famous High Street there, by a motor-cyclist. Mr Alwyn, a mathematics graduate of St John's College, Oxford, had once been a schoolmaster. He had also been the curate at Tankersley for most of 1919, to which fact he seemingly owed his preferment.

A stocky man with steel-rimmed spectacles and a head of

untidily-cut greying hair, he had a booming voice and sarcastic tongue, and used to advertise in the local paper the startling titles of forthcoming sermons. (One, comprising a line from a comic song, was 'The parson in a long white shirt turned up.') His comments in the Parish Magazine on local affairs and the activities of certain Urban District Councillors bordered on the libellous.

Mr Alwyn and his wife, Mrs Ruth Alwyn (a small, mousy-looking woman who always sat in the back pew wearing a grey fur coat, was said to have been a West Yorkshire mill-hand and seemed in awe of her more intellectual husband), were vegetarians, something widely regarded in those days as the hallmark of a crank. The choirboys used to complain bitterly that, at choir suppers held in the Vicarage, they were fed oatcakes and Marmite sandwiches.

The Alwyns' only son Vivian, small like his mother, studied at Wath Grammar School, Durham University and the Theological College at Ely and was subsequently ordained, serving in the West Indies for a time and then becoming Vicar of Leighton Buzzard. He was made much of by his parents, perhaps partly because their other child, Lettice, had died when very young. In 1939 he married a nurse, Miss Jessie Hough, a sister of Miss Marion Hough who taught at King Street.

It was largely owing to his son's influence that during the early 'thirties Mr Alwyn, previously a Low Churchman, started introducing High Church practices and pronouncing himself to be a Catholic. He substituted Sung Eucharist ('Sung Mass', he called it) for Mattins, acquired a set of vestments, started reserving the Sacrament, taught the congregation to cross themselves and genuflect, placed a statue of the Virgin and Child on a window sill, and preached the doctrine of the Real Presence. These changes were not universally liked (the introduction of the statue gave rise to accusations of breaking the Second Commandment), but such was the power of his personality and the hypnotic effect of his 'hell-fire' preaching that on Sundays the church continued to be packed.

The Alwyns owned a small holiday cottage at Mumby, near Alford in Lincolnshire, to which they drove in an old motor-car, crudely painted in a bright turquoise green and the subject of some merriment in Hoyland and also of a humorous feature in the Wath Grammar School magazine. It was there that Mr Alwyn, still in his fifties, was taken ill and died after a short illness in the late summer of 1939, within days of the outbreak of the Second World War. Mrs Alwyn, already seriously ill with anaemia, did not survive him long, and never returned to the Vicarage.

The next Vicar, inducted that same autumn, was the Rev. Geoffrey Surtees, who came from Newcastle-upon-Tyne and was a Durham University graduate. A slender, good-looking bachelor aged thirty-three, he bore a noticeable facial resemblance to a film star of the 'thirties, Leslie Howard, and his appointment caused a fluttering in the hearts of certain single ladies in the parish. He introduced further High Church practices, to which his successor, the Rev. Alan Greaves Hurst, in turn subscribed, with the result that St Andrew's is among those of South Yorkshire's churches in which High Church ritual is today most firmly established.

Unlike Mr Alwyn, who had never troubled about the appearance of either his church or his home, Mr Surtees proved to be intensely house-proud, and liked pale colours and plain surfaces. Soon after he came he took the controversial step of having the interior of the church painted cream, thus obliterating an interesting mural decorating the walls of the sanctuary. Painted by Harry Uttley, a Hoyland Common man who had won a scholarship to study fresco painting in Italy, it depicted angels in pink, mauve and blue, carrying palm fronds and with golden haloes, against a stylized background of Italian arches. Likewise following an Italian tradition, the church ceiling had been painted dark blue, spangled with silver stars.

The organ in the chancel at St Andrew's was built by Albert Keates of Sheffield. The organist until 1936 was Robert Humphreys Thompson of Milton Road, who also gave private piano and organ lessons. He was the son of Mr Edwin Thompson, who kept a small grocery and general shop in King Street, and the brother of Miss Florence Thompson, a violinist. After Mr Thompson's untimely death in 1936, the organ was played for a short time by John Parkin, one of the twin sons of Mr Ernest Parkin, Sr., the King

Street pharmacist. When Mr Parkin's work took him elsewhere he was succeeded by Miss Irene Seymour (after her marriage Mrs Harry Mills), who when she first came to Hoyland taught music at the Raley School (since re-named Honeywell) in Barnsley. Later she was appointed Lecturer in Music at the Teachers' Training College which, after the War, Barnsley Education Committee opened at Wentworth Castle.

St Andrew's had a Mission Church at Platts Common which was closed in the late 'thirties, about the same time as St Peter's Mission Church. Its site is occupied by the small public garden at the side of Platts Common Working Men's Club.

The John Knowles Memorial Church

About 1910 a new Vicar, the Rev. Charles William Bennett, was appointed to St Peter's. He had been the curate at a church in Barnsley, where the parishioners when he left presented him with a brass cross and two brass candlesticks. Mr Bennett put these in the most fitting place for them, on St Peter's altar, which had previously been devoid of all ornaments except an alms dish.

Nobody in the congregation at St Peter's seems to have objected strongly to this action, but at St Andrew's (which at that time was still in St Peter's parish) the effect was cataclysmic. Led by Mrs Elizabeth Bartlett, the only daughter of Mrs Martha Knowles and one of the wealthiest people in the town, most of the congregation there exclaimed in horror that this constituted an initial step on the road back to Rome. Mrs Bartlett, a benefactor of St Andrew's, who had given the stained glass in the east window in memory of her mother and that in the two west windows as a memorial to her brother John, who died in 1899 at the age of fifty-two, did more than merely object. On a plot of land in High Street, in between Holly House and Garner's ironmongery shop, she caused to be erected at her own expense a place of worship for the Free Church of England, a small church, with a strong following in Lancashire, whose doctrines and practices approximate those of Low Church Anglicanism.

The two foundation stones of 'The New Church', as it was

widely known for many years, were laid one by Mrs Bartlett herself and the other by the Right Reverend William Troughton, Bishop Primus of the Free Church of England, on 20th September, 1911. A neat stone building with double lancets, a small porch and a louvred, lead-covered bell turret, the church was designed by Mr William Allen and was constructed by John Parr and Sons, a Hoyland firm of builders. Mrs Bartlett named it after her brother John, in whose memory she had given St Andrew's Church its west windows.

She also bought a house for the minister, a detached stone residence, which she named Church House, standing at the lower end of Vernon Street. In addition she made provision for his stipend, largely by making over to the church various cottage properties in her possession, including a number at Blacker Hill and two in Booth Street, one occupied during my childhood by her former companion, Miss Lydia Ramsey, the other by Mr and Mrs Walter Shepherd, who were the caretakers at King Street School. The income from these various sources came to £250 a year – an affluent sum in those days. What Mrs Bartlett could not have foreseen was how its value would be eroded by rising inflation after the Second World War, until it dwindled into a mere pittance.

The first Rector, a small man named Hermon, stayed only a few years, leaving to join the Church of England and becoming the vicar of a parish in the Wirral. His successor, a heavily-built man named Turner, wore glasses and usually dressed in a light-coloured trenchcoat. Mr Turner's most lasting claim to fame in Hoyland came from owning a sulphur-crested cockatoo, which sat on his shoulder as he walked down West Street, occasionally flying off to perch on a chimney but never failing to find its master again, however crowded the pavement. It was a performer, not a talking bird. Sometimes it would pretend to smoke a pipe, the stem gripped firmly in a grey, scaly claw. Asked, 'What does this little boy do when his mother wants to wash him?' it would promptly imitate a crying child, turning away from the speaker and wiping its eyes with a wing.

Mr Turner left Hoyland and went 'down south' about the late

'twenties. He was succeeded by the Rev. William Whitehead, a small, gentle, silver-haired, bespectacled Scotsman who spoke with great precision, always referring to himself as 'one', and who stayed at John Knowles until his retirement during the early 'forties.

Not only did the John Knowles Church, in its first years, provide a haven for the disaffected from St Andrew's. It became a fashionable church to attend, its congregation boasting a fair number of business and professional people including members of the family of Mr and Mrs George Hall, the greengrocers, and Mr Edgar Hirst, the printer to whom my father was apprenticed. Until his death in 1932 the treasurer, Sunday school superintendent and one of the wardens was Mr Herbert Garner, whose ironmongery shop was next to the church. Later wardens included Mr Ernest Parr, a member of the firm which built the church, and Mr Frank Haywood, a checkweighman at Elsecar Main Colliery. Mr Haywood's brother, Mr Ernal Haywood, was for some years the organist at John Knowles, as later was Mr Ernest Thomas Ferris, who worked at the Hoyland Labour Exchange in High Street.

It was also a church with a warm, friendly and welcoming atmosphere. During the 'thirties one of its fringe attractions was a small concert party, 'The J.K.s', drawn from young members of the congregation and including Miss Annie Hall, Mr Frank Haywood's daughter Connie, Mr Ernal Haywood's daughter Phyllis and her husband, Mr Herbert Dickinson, Mr Ernest Parr's elder daughter Eva and her fiancé, Mr Clifford Penn, and the lay reader, Mr Joseph Hinks, the comedian of the group. Performances were given in the schoolroom. Mrs Dickinson had a rich contralto voice. I can still hear her, dressed in the concert party's colours of brown and gold, singing the ballad 'There's an old-fashioned house in an old-fashioned street', one of my childhood favourites.

It was always a pleasure on Christmas Eve to receive a visit from the John Knowles choirboys, who came carol singing at selected homes, never failing first to knock and ask permission. The choir's boy soloist during the 'thirties was Victor Maltby, the son of Mr and Mrs Weadon Maltby, the King Street greengrocers. It was also customary in the small hours of New Year's Day, after the Watchnight Service, for young people from the congregation to come round singing 'Sweet is the work my God, my King' to the tune 'Deep Harmony'. One of their stopping places was the home of Mr and Mrs Owen Hazell, faithful members of the John Knowles congregation, whose house was in the old part of Green Street near my home.

St Helen's Roman Catholic Church

The number of Roman Catholics in the Hoyland area grew rapidly during Victorian times owing to an influx of Irish labourers, who came to work in its heavy industries or on building South Yorkshire's intricate railway network, some settling there and marrying local girls. Consequently, by the 'twenties Hoyland had acquired a sizeable Catholic minority, further increased by the arrival of Polish servicemen in 1939.

The first Roman Catholic church to serve the township was built at Elsecar in 1866, the austere-looking building, with its high-pitched roof, between the top of St Helen's Street and the railway. Like several medieval churches in South Yorkshire, it was dedicated to St Helen, the mother of the Emperor Constantine. Among the first worshippers were some who came, walking each way, from as far off as Wath-upon-Dearne. To fortify them for their journey home, a Catholic shopkeeper in St Helen's Street, Mrs Kelly, supplied them with cups of tea. The church also served on weekdays as a school for Roman Catholic children. The original presbytery was Prospect House, next to the Clothier's Arms. To replace this the wooden-framed bungalow was built which stands between the church and the top of Hill Street.

By the 'twenties, however, church, house and bungalow had all been sold to the Midland Railway Company, which in the eighteen-nineties drove a line through the land lying between them and Cobcar Street. The church building has since played several rôles. For a time it was used as the Midland Club. For a few years after the Second World War it was the DHSS's Hoyland office.

In their place the Church had bought a site in West Street, where it had built a presbytery and school and consecrated a small cemetery. Just as lessons had been held in the old church, now Mass was celebrated in the new school in a room set aside for this purpose, until in 1929 the present church, built in the Italian Tuscan style of rustic brick with a tall campanile, was consecrated. The new church's opening was delayed for a time because the pews which were going to be installed were destroyed in a fire.

The priest in whose time these changes were put in hand, Father Smith, who was Rector of St Helen's from 1880 until 1918, became something of a legend during his lifetime, though seemingly some members of his flock were inclined to defy his authority. It is said that when he first came to Elsecar his verger, 'Old Math Rush', went down on Monday mornings to Forge Lane, to chase up Irish labourers working at Elsecar Iron Works who had failed to attend Mass the previous day, in order to collect their church dues from them. The men, however, did not appreciate his visits, running and hiding while the harassed verger chased them and pleaded, 'The Father has to live.'

Surprisingly, Father Smith was a great friend of the Rev. Charles Molesworth Sharpe, a Low Church, much-loved Vicar of Elsecar whose incumbency, from 1888 until 1922, roughly overlapped his own. These two clerical bachelors visited each other on alternate Friday afternoons in order to play chess and take afternoon tea.

There were rumours in the town when Father Smith died that he had been buried with his boots on so that, at the General Resurrection, he would be among the first to rise.

Father Smith was succeeded by Father White, who in turn was followed by two Irish priests, Father Grogan and Father Quinn. Father Grogan became quite friendly with my parents through visiting my father's printing office. He could never read his own handwriting but my father, who had been trained to decipher all kinds of script, never experienced any trouble with it.

Throughout the 'twenties and 'thirties there was still a good deal of religious suspicion and intolerance, Catholics describing Protestants as 'heretics', Protestants accusing Catholics of being priest-ridden and idolatrous. Despite this antagonism, some Protestants always turned out to watch the Catholic processions which took place each year on the first Sunday evening in May and the Sunday after the Feast of Corpus Christi, following the curving route of Longfields Crescent. Marshalled by three men wearing crimson sashes, including Mr Thomas Doyle of the Gardeners' Arms and Mr Joseph Parr, the processions were impressive sights to watch. The centre of attraction was the May Queen, attended by her page and cushion bearer and dressed either in white or in pale blue, followed by maids-of-honour walking in pairs. After them came the adult congregation, singing 'Faith of our fathers'. Lastly, with a canopy held over his head, came the priest carrying the Host. In front of him walked little girls in white, kissing rose petals and strewing them in the road. As a child brought up in a very different tradition, I was at once puzzled and fascinated on the occasions when my mother could be persuaded to take me up to join the onlookers.

The Methodist Churches

Like most industrial areas in the North, Hoyland has a strong Methodist tradition. Barley Hall near Thorpe Hesley, two miles away, was among the earliest centres of Wesleyan preaching. When Mr John Johnson of Barley Hall moved to Hoyland in the mid-eighteenth century, living at Manor Farm off Market Street, he brought his faith with him. Services were held in the farmhouse until, for an outlay of £800, the building with the fortress-like façade now occupied by Charisma Antiques was constructed as a chapel on a site given by a later farmer, Mr William Gray. It is said to have been built in 1809, though a stone in its west-facing façade appears to bear the date 1800. It remained in use until 1975, when a new chapel was opened further along the street, made from Dr Wiggins' house and surgery.

Sometimes calling itself 'The Old Body' to distinguish itself from denominations founded more recently, Hoyland's Wesleyan congregation between the Wars was one of the most prosperous in the town and included such business families as Taylors and Goddards, the butchers, Fords the newsagents and ladies' outfitters, and Keys the estate agents.

The manse was the large, bay-windowed house in King Street whose garden adjoins the Miners' Welfare Hall. Here ministers and their families came and went at three-yearly intervals. The minister in the late 'twenties was named Parkinson, and had a daughter Margaret and twin sons who were called George and William. Among ministers who served during the 'thirties was the Rev. J. Edward Penna. The most memorable of them was, however, without doubt the Rev. Peter Hutchinson, a bachelor with a round, cheerful face and large white teeth who was looked after by his mother and sister. They had previously lived in the Shetlands, and Mrs Hutchinson told my mother one day what a pleasant change it was to live where there were trees and where the wind was not forever blowing.

In 1932 Mr Hutchinson founded the first Boy Scout Company in Hoyland, and thereafter he could frequently be seen wearing his 'dog collar' in conjunction with a scoutmaster's uniform. A member of the Company was James Marsh, who subsequently took a Degree at Oxford and ended his career as headmaster of a grammar school in the Manchester area. Another was Denis Mallison, destined to become a leading figure in South Yorkshire Scouting circles.

Not everyone, though, approved of the Scouts, some of Hoyland's Primitive Methodists fearing that the movement had military leanings. The Primitive Methodist Chapel, newer, larger, and more architecturally pretentious than the Wesleyan, had huge round-topped windows and, facing the street, an imposing-looking trio of double doors. It stood at what is now the junction of King Street and Southgate. Its foundation stone had been laid in 1880, on Monday, 14th June, the ceremony being followed by a public tea in the Mechanics' Hall. The manse, at the end of a narrow lane along which stood several other properties, was the solitary house of vermilion brick which now stands back from King Street just above the top of Millmount Road.

During the early 'twenties this chapel was so well attended that it could field both a football and a cricket team. In the 'thirties it was damaged by subsidence and had to be held together with timber balks and equally unsightly iron plates.

The United Methodist or 'New Connexion' Chapel, whose foundation stone was laid only four months after that of the Primitive Methodist, was at the other side of King Street, further down, between The Five Alls and Victoria Street. Although it, too, appeared to have been built strongly enough to last a thousand years, with an imposing row of entrance doors and round-topped windows set in chiselled stone, it was a smaller, homelier-looking place and was hemmed in by other properties, preventing it from being seen to advantage.

An organist during the inter-war period was Mr Walter Levitt, who lived with his wife and his two red-haired sons, Eric and Brian, in a house across the street.

There was also a 'New Connexion' chapel at Platts Common, standing to the right of the road as one approached the first houses in Wombwell Road from Market Street.

In addition there were two former chapels in inter-war Hoyland. One of these, the town's original Primitive Methodist Chapel, was in King Street, between Lowbridge's hairdresser's and the Turf Tavern. By the 'twenties it had been made into shops, one of them selling furniture, the other newspapers, tobacco and toys. The other chapel building, in Bethel Street, the original home of the 'New Connexion', was used during the 'thirties as a printing works.

In 1932 the Wesleyans, Primitive Methodists and United Methodists amalgamated, becoming known simply as Methodists, and so in Hoyland their places of worship were given distinguishing names. The Wesleyan Chapel on Market Street became St Paul's, the Primitive Methodist Chapel became known as Mount Tabor, and the United Methodist Chapel reverted to its original name, Bethel.

The highlight of each chapel's year was always its Anniversary, a festival in which the children took the centre of the stage. At special morning and evening services a visiting preacher gave the address, and Sunday school scholars sang special hymns of a simple, trusting and joyful kind, in which thanks for the beauty of nature often featured. There were violinists in the area who used always to attend on these occasions, helping free of charge with the accompaniment. (My self-effacing father was deeply touched when one year, after he had printed Mount Tabor's hymn sheets, he was invited to be the guest preacher − a request which he modestly declined.)

Though there was much real poverty in those days not only among the unemployed but also in the ranks of the lower-paid manual workers, care was taken, however poor a family might be, to send its children to the Anniversary looking a credit to everyone concerned, the small boys scrubbed and wearing their best suits, the girls wearing pretty new hats and dresses. The hats were often garlanded with flowers and ribbons. (A favourite hat of mine was cream-coloured straw, with daisies and pink rose buds round it. My mother always referred to it as my 'Anniversary' hat.)

Anniversaries, as befitted such happy occasions, took place in May and June, the months of sun, blossom and greenery, and were times for family reunions and visits from distant friends. With other Anniversaries being held by chapels in surrounding areas, it was important that each one should keep to the same Sunday in the month every year, so that dates did not clash.

With its augmented number of worshippers, an Anniversary was also a time for swelling chapel funds. There was friendly rivalry over who would take most in collections, especially between Mount Tabor and St Paul's. Despite having the more affluent congregation, St Paul's was usually the loser by the narrowest of margins.

Following the decline in church and chapel attendances during the years after the Second World War, Mount Tabor and Bethel were both closed in the early 'sixties and were demolished shortly afterwards, their congregations joining that of St Paul's and the old rivalries gradually fading.

Hill Street Congregational Chapel

Then as now, there was no Congregational place of worship in Hoyland, its Congregationalists or 'Independents' worshipping at Hill Street Chapel in Elsecar which, because 'Stubbin' is Hill Street's colloquial name, was usually known as 'Stubbin Chapel'. Opened in 1839, four years before Elsecar Parish Church and twenty years before the date on the front of Elsecar Wesleyan Reform Chapel, this was an oblong stone structure with double doors approached by a short flight of steps from the street and surmounted by a handsome Gothic window. The chapel stood where a car park has now been made. A double-fronted, bay-windowed stone house between it and the Hill Street Post Office once served as a minister's residence. At right-angles to this was the schoolroom, past which a narrow path led to the small, secluded graveyard with its blackened tombstones.

By the 'thirties the chapel had for a number of years had no minister resident in the village. Then in 1936 the Rev. Evan Llewellyn Lewis, a short, dark, genial Welshman, was appointed, being placed in charge both of Hill Street itself and of the Congregational Chapel at Wombwell. Mr Lewis and his tall, good-looking wife moved from Burnham-on-Crouch with their daughter Olwyn Madge (who took a Degree in English and for a while was a teacher at Doncaster) and their small son Keredig. They lived not at the Manse but in Armroyd Lane, where they stayed until 1946, when they returned to Essex.

It was on a visit to Hill Street Chapel during her youth that my mother saw a 'miracle' occur. Among the congregation there was a man who was paralysed and sitting in a wheelchair. During the sermon a whiff of smoke appeared, escaping through a grating. The cripple was the first to notice it. He leapt nimbly to his feet and was the leader of the exodus into the street.

Regular worshippers at Hill Street during the period between the World Wars included two families living in Barber Street. One of these was the Marches, two of whose members, Wilfred and Annie March, taught at Market Street and King Street respectively. The other was the Nobles, who moved there from

Elsecar in 1934. Miss Margaret Noble, now Mrs Peter Ashwell, is still a member of the congregation and plays her part in church activities, despite having gone to live at Upper Haugh.

The organist was Mr 'Billy' Solomon (his full Christian names were William Edward Thompson), who lies buried under the white marble angel near the tower of Elsecar Parish Church. His father, Mr Laban Solomon, still remembered in the village with esteem, composed hymn tunes and other sacred music and is buried under the kneeling angel at the end of the churchyard nearest to Wath Road. (At one time William Solomon, a Fellow and Bronze and Gold Medallist of the Victoria College of Music, was a member of an instrumental trio which was available for concerts and 'at homes'. He played the piano, Hervey Holden the violin and John Woodcock the 'cello.)

Like St Andrew's and Mount Tabor between the Wars, 'Stubbin Chapel' was affected by subsidence during the 'seventies. Said to be beyond economic repair, it was pulled down during that decade and was replaced with the present neat brick structure. The new chapel or church, as it is nowadays called, built on the site of the minister's house and opened in 1979, is linked with one at Herringthorpe with which it shares its present ministers.

The Salvation Army

Besides its church and chapel congregations, inter-war Hoyland had a large number of Salvation Army members. Their headquarters was a single-storey cottage, with one room on each side of a central door, on the site of the Festival of Britain Garden at the junction of Mell Avenue and Market Street. The cottage had once been a charity school maintained by Earl Fitzwilliam.

In its smart red-and-navy uniform, the Army held a Saturday evening service, spreading its message to late market shoppers, on the open space fronting the Strafford Arms. It also toured the town on Sunday evenings, playing and singing hymns at selected spots. One of my first recollections is of seeing the band, with its gleaming wind instruments and booming drum, grouped under a gas lamp at the end of a yard in Booth Street. Its visits were as much a part of

Sunday tea time as home-baked bread, fried ham and eggs and 'spice' cake eaten in a cosy gas-lit room with a blazing fire.

The Army also had a large Hoyland Common following. My father recalled how, during his childhood at Stead Lane, he had been roused on Sunday mornings by the fervent singing of hymns with such stirring openings and choruses as 'Oh, that will be glory for me', 'We'll journey together to Zion' and 'I believe we shall win' at its Citadel in nearby Chapel Street (sometimes, because of the corrugated iron used in its construction, irreverently referred to as 'The Tin Trunk'). It was also customary for the Hoyland Common Salvationists in those days to hold what they called 'ham, jam and glory teas'.

In Lent, Salvation Army members came round distributing 'self-denial' envelopes for householders of all denominations to place contributions in. Inevitably their zeal and earnestness and their skill at shaking the collecting box led to some unkind jokes, one jingle running:

> We've got an army, Salvation Army.
> It stands in the market place,
> Shouting 'Sinners, will you come?
> Put your money on the drum,
> We only need elevenpence-halfpenny for a bob.

Occasionally, too, children would sing, to a tune resembling the central theme of Beethoven's famous 'Egmont' overture:

> Sally Army sells fish,
> Three-halfpence a dish.
> Will you buy some?
> Will you try some?
> Sally Army sells fish.

The Bethany Mission

The Bethany Mission, with a form of worship plainer and simpler even than those of the various Methodist denominations, and a fundamentalist approach to the Scriptures, was founded by Mr

Charles A. Carney, a Sunderland man who, about the early 'twenties, came to Hoyland to work for Mr Herbert Edwin Key at his Estate Office on Market Street. For many years after its foundation, therefore, it was often referred to as 'Carney's Mission'. Its first minister was a tall man, Pastor Frank Dove. He married Mr Key's sister Alice and lived in a flat above the Estate Office. (Mr Key's other sister, Elizabeth, married Mr Harry Haywood, a credit draper who lived at Hemingfield and was the organist at Jump Wesleyan Reform Chapel.)

Until some years after the Second World War, when it moved to its present purpose-built premises at the bottom of High Croft, the Mission was housed in what were known as 'Woolley's Rooms'. These were first-floor rooms above two of the shops in West Street owned by the baker and confectioner Mr Albert Woolley, and formed part of a building owned in earlier years by a family of maltsters named Wigfield.

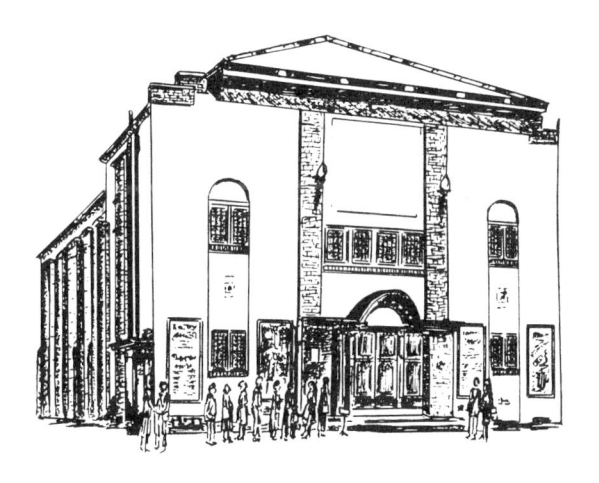

CHAPTER EIGHT

Sport and Entertainment

The Coming of the Radio

Like the rest of England, Hoyland in the 'twenties experienced a home entertainment revolution with the coming of the radio or 'wireless'. Even my father who, although a first-class printer and skilful amateur photographer, was never much of a home handyman, managed to build a set. Buying a blue-print which he taught himself to read, he constructed it in the evenings on a board when the table had been cleared after tea, assembling the bulky valves and coils and soldering in place the coloured wires linking up these components. He also learned to employ such alien-sounding terms as 'rheostat' and 'grid–bias'.

When the set was finished, a 'bakelite' board which he fitted at right-angles to the base hid the 'works' from view and held the tuning dial, which was several inches wide and was rotated with loud banshee squeals known as 'atmospherics' when one tried to tune in to a station.

Wireless aerials were long and cumbersome. Ours consisted of a wire trained through the hall and attached to an almost telegraph-sized pole in the far corner of the front garden. Since few Hoyland homes were wired for electricity, most Hoyland radios were battery-powered, needing both a large dry 'high tension' battery and a wet one known as the 'accumulator', the latter being a small, thick-walled glass tank filled with acid and with metal plates across it. Accumulators lasted only a week, and then needed re-charging. It was customary to have two of them, each with a luggage label tied to it bearing the owner's name, one in use, the other one away being charged. A charging service was provided both at George Neil's Aero Garage on Market Street and at Bircher's cycle and radio shop in King Street.

There was much competition in those early days to see whose home-made receiver could be tuned to the most impressive list of foreign stations. A name frequently heard was Hilversum, but each 'ham's' driving ambition appeared to be to obtain a whisper from Schenectady, on the east coast of the United States. One of the keenest of these early enthusiasts was Mr George Chambers of High Street, who would close his fish-and-chip shop late in the evening and then sit up until the early hours trying to tune in to some strangely-named station whose signal had hitherto eluded him. One of his main rivals was my Uncle Fred, who repaired boots and shoes in a shop across the street, on the site of the present Kwik Save supermarket.

My father eschewed this 'one-upmanship', his efforts being confined to contacting 2LO and 5XX, BBC stations. He and my mother liked to listen in the evenings to a comedian called Stainless Stephen and a pair of singers, Flotsam and Jetsam, the latter of whom reached incredibly deep basso-profundo notes. In the 'thirties, as the scope of programmes widened, they enjoyed the accounts of his north-country wanderings by a man with the pseudonym 'Harry Hopeful' and, though they found gardening a boring chore, they also liked to hear the friendly voice of Mr C.H. Middleton, whose helpful talks were entitled 'In your Garden'.

As she went about her work my mother liked listening to the Morning Service; my father, however, disliked what he called the BBC women singers' 'screeching' voices. Among the hymns they regularly sang were 'Ye watchers and ye holy ones', set to a tune composed by Gustav Holst, and 'Now thank we all our God' to the tune 'Nun Danket'. Being a toddler who was quick to memorize, I used to stomp round the house singing with fervour my own version of the latter hymn, including the outlandish phrase 'All plaisem samps to God'.

In retrospect, the secular music broadcast seems to have erred towards the highbrow. A man whose works were regularly 'plugged', and of whom my Uncle Fred spoke with great reverence, was the modern Hungarian composer Béla Bartók. I confused him with a soprano, Bella Bailey, whose silver tones my parents both admired and who later changed her name to Isobel.

At a more popular level, songs which were heard almost 'ad nauseam' included 'Myself when young' from the *Rubaiyat* of Omar Khayyam, those two favourites of the 'twenties, 'Bye-bye, blackbird' and 'When the red, red robin comes bob, bob, bobbin' along' and, moaned by a tenor, 'I wonder, I wonder, I wonder, I wonder how I look when I'm asleep'. (When this was suddenly dropped from the repertoire, my mother said drily, 'Somebody must have told him.')

We all three enjoyed the recitals of light music by the BBC organist, Reginald Foort and his successor, Sandy Macpherson. There were also regular short broadcasts on the 'mighty Wurlitzer' from such romantically-named cinemas as the Granada, Tooting and the Trocadero, Elephant and Castle. A favourite with listeners in the Hoyland area was Reginald Dixon, a native of High Green, playing the organ of the Tower Ballroom at Blackpool.

The Children's Hour, hosted by various 'aunties' and 'uncles', was another popular favourite from the start. In the early days there was a Radio Circle, like the children's clubs run by various newspapers, in which a child listener could be enrolled by paying a small fee. Members each received a round enamelled badge and, while their number was small enough to permit this, names were read out on their birthdays over the air, those of twins being followed by a jaunty 'Hullo, twins!'

Picture Palaces

For people who preferred going out to be entertained and liked this entertainment to be visual, the event of the 'twenties was the advent of the 'talkies', after a decade or more of silent films. Hoyland picturegoers had three venues to choose from: the Kino, the Cinema and the Electra Palace.

The Kino, on the corner of Broad Street, was originally called the Princess Theatre (a name still to be seen on its façade). It was constructed in 1893 by a local building firm, John Parr and Sons, and was owned at first by Mr William Ottley, my father's uncle, who until his death early in 1914 kept the drapery and millinery shop in King Street that was later run for many years by his widow. His son by a previous marriage, John Albert Ottley, a gifted pianist, played the piano at the Princess and, employing a professional pseudonym, was for some years the resident conductor of the Gleneagles Hotel Orchestra in Perthshire.

The Princess specialized in melodrama, staging such plays (many of them made famous by the great Sir Henry Irving) as *The Corsican Brothers*, *The Face at the Window* and *The Bells*. The actor who played all the leading rôles was a photographer, Roy Colville, noted for his pictures of the Hoyland district, whose West Bank studio, on his retirement, was bought by the late Mr Alfred Hoyland. Prices ranged from fifteen shillings for a box to ninepence for a seat downstairs in the pit and sixpence to sit in the gallery.

The Princess also staged variety shows. It was as a comedian billed in one of these that Fred Titcombe, who married Mrs Dewhirst, the widowed landlady of the Queen's Head, made his début in Hoyland. My father remembered an occasion when Mr Titcombe made a joke the point of which was lost on his audience. He immediately brought the house down, however, by solemnly exclaiming, 'Roars of silence!'

The Princess management seems to have been sensitive to changes in public taste and quick in its reactions. As early as 1902, only nine years after the theatre opened, short, silent motion pictures were being shown between the acts of plays. By the 'twenties live shows were no longer staged there, the Princess having in the meantime become what was popularly known as a 'picture palace'. Like the name of the Clothier's Arms at Elsecar, its new, Americanized-German name Kino, meaning a film-theatre, soon came also to denote a neighbouring bus-stop.

To meet the increasing public demand for films, the Hoyland Cinema was purpose-built in about 1920, between the market and the Strafford Arms, by a consortium of business men, the Hoyland Cinema Company. It was a two-storey, oblong, dark brick structure with a row of emergency exits down each side and, facing the street, a symmetrical stucco façade on which were boards displaying coloured 'stills' calling attention to the week's attractions. Inside, as at the Kino, stairs climbed tortuously from each side of the foyer to the circle or 'balcony'.

There were nevertheless some minor differences of interior décor. For instance, as befitted what had once been a Victorian theatre, the Kino's tip-up seats were upholstered in a garishly opulent-looking crimson plush; the Cinema's, though equally comfortable, were a restrainedly luxurious Prussian blue. The clock to the viewer's left of the Cinema screen carried a subtle form of advertising. Instead of numbers, its square face displayed the letters spelling the name 'Rowland Cross'.

Spacious and situated centrally, the Cinema was also an ideal venue if some outdoor gathering needed to be moved indoors when the weather proved inclement.

Its manager in the 'thirties, Mr Cecil Atkin, married Miss Annie Adlington, a box-office cashier, who was a sister-in-law of Mr Thomas Doyle, the landlord of the 'Gardeners'.

Newer than the Kino, older than the Cinema, the Electra Palace, built in 1914 and romantically named after Electra, the heroine of three Greek tragedies, was technically in Elsecar, not in Hoyland, being just over the boundary between the two. It had no circle and possessed the unusual feature of having some double or, as they were usually called, 'courters" seats towards the back of the auditorium.

Its manager when I was very young was the father of Mr Fred Wrightson (nicknamed 'Ferdie') who taught Standard 6 at King Street, a link between cinema and school that a former neighbour of mine had reason to regret. At the age of twelve, he and a friend visited the Electra and sat smoking cigarettes on the back row. The next morning, at school, they were charged with this offence and soundly beaten for it.

In the 'thirties, to sound glossier and more 'with-it', the Electra's name was changed to Futurist, as which it continued to be known until its closure during 1986. The single-storey building, repaired and re-furbished, has now become a video-games and pool hall, and has reverted to the name Electra Palace.

It was perhaps thanks to its more modest size and consequently lower overheads that the Futurist was able to stay open as a cinema, showing mostly sexy X-films and horror movies, for about twenty years after the Kino had become a bingo hall. For the Cinema there was no such reprieve. Likewise hit by falling attendances as television remorselessly usurped the 'big screen's' place, it closed completely in 1957. After a respite during which there were rumours that it was going to be made into a super-store which would replace the Co-op's various Hoyland shops, it was pulled down late in 1971 and its site was incorporated into that of the resuscitated Hoyland Market.

Throughout the years leading up to the Second World War, every week these three picture theatres each showed two programmes, one on Monday, Tuesday and Wednesday, the other on Thursday, Friday and Saturday. It was therefore possible for a Hoyland film 'buff' to see a different show each weekday night, without venturing out of the township. There were two screenings, the 'First House' and 'Second House', for either of which seats could be booked beforehand. At the Kino and Cinema, balcony seats cost the most. Those in the centre block were a shilling each; those in the two outer blocks were only ninepence. During the interval, when the lights came up, advertisements for local shops were screened, the usherettes paraded with ice-cream and sweets, and a male member of the staff paced the aisles pumping out disinfectant from a spray gun, like those which were once used for killing flies, to protect patrons from airborne bacteria.

Those were the years of the Hollywood 'greats', among whom were tall, rugged Gary Cooper, suavely handsome Clark Gable, tempestuous Joan Crawford, composedly beautiful Greta Garbo and blonde, elegantly-gowned Marlene Dietrich, after whom several baby girls born in Hoyland were named during the nineteen-thirties. Without doubt, however, the biggest crowd-puller and the one whose name was most widely copied was Shirley Temple, the singing, dancing child star with her dimples and tossing bubble curls, who appeared in such films as *Captain January* and *Baby Take a Bow*.

A minor sensation was caused during this period by the release and subsequent showing in the provinces of Korda's *The Private Life of Henry VIII*, with Scarborough's Charles Laughton in its title rôle, the first serious attempt to portray on the screen characters and events from English history. A film more directly linked with the Yorkshire coast was *Turn of the Tide*, set in Whitby and Robin Hood's Bay and based on Leo Walmsley's novel *Three Fevers*. It was not shown in Hoyland, but my father took me to see it one Saturday at the Empire in Wombwell. I also remember going with him to see two religious epics, *The Sign of the Cross* and *Ben Hur*, which drew packed houses at the Cinema.

In larger towns, the 'thirties were the heyday of the super cinema with its fitted carpets, glittering chandeliers and huge Wurlitzer organ. Though he might not be among those called upon to give quarter-hour broadcasts for the BBC, the musician who performed on one of these was certain to gain local recognition. The organist at the Rotherham Odeon was Mr Thomas Dando who, I recall, once gave a recital at the Hill Street Chapel. My father printed the programmes, and Mr Dando wrote direct to him naming the pieces he proposed to play. A young friend of ours was delighted when my father gave her the letter afterwards, bearing its unsolicited signature.

Another of these palatial cinemas built between the Wars was the Ritz in Peel Street, Barnsley, its site now that of Leo's supermarket. At one time the organist there was a local man, Mr Trevor Willetts, who came from Jump and for a brief period during the 'forties played the organ at St Andrew's.

'Feasts' and Fun Fairs

In those days when few people could afford to go on holiday, and tastes in entertainment were perhaps more undemanding than they are today, a highlight of the year for all age groups in Hoyland and the places round about was the visit of the fun fair, which was known by everybody as the 'feast', the reason being that most village fairs traced their origins to the celebrations once held in honour of the local church's saint's day.

Hoyland Feast was held in mid-summer on the Town Field, beside the Roman Catholic School in West Street. Hoyland Common Feast, which followed in July, its date like that of Tankersley Clyppings governed by the 'old calendar' observance of St Peter's Day, appropriately took place in a field adjacent to the ancient Cross Keys Inn, a hostelry which in its early years was owned by the churchwardens at Tankersley. (People of my parents' generation often remarked that, by the time Hoyland Common Feast arrived, there was an hour less daylight.)

Neither of these Feasts however could compare, either in size or in popularity, with that held at Elsecar a week after Whitsun, at the time of the patronal festival of Elsecar Church, which is dedicated to the Holy Trinity. Its site was the 'Crab Cloise' off Armroyd Lane, an area of rough grass dotted with hawthorns and presumably once with crab apple trees, crossed diagonally by a black cinder track leading towards the top end of the park, and bordered on its lower and upper sides by the cricket field and the one-acre strip alongside the Old Vicarage drive.

On Friday the coming of the Feast was heralded by the slow, rumbling approach of traction engines, smelling of oil and bright with polished brass, towing the 'feasties'' ornate caravans (how I always longed to live in one of them!) and huge container vans loaded with parts of roundabouts and stalls. The head of the Tuby family, which owned them, had at one time been the Mayor of Doncaster. In his honour one engine was named 'Ex-Mayor'. Another, said to be named after his wife, was 'Nora'. Through thick black cables snaking over the grass, the engines also powered the strings of bulbs garishly illuminating the field after nightfall.

By noon on Saturday all was set up in readiness to entertain the crowds which streamed down Armroyd and Fitzwilliam Street. At one time there were three sets of roundabouts. Nearest to the main gate were the flying chairs, which my mother would never allow me to ride on because, she said, they were too dangerous (and which I thought looked boring anyway). The carousel (known as the 'cocks and hens') comprised a ring of leggy ostriches and two inner rings of horses with glassy eyes, the harness painted on their wooden sides bearing such romantic names as 'Ivanhoe'. The carousel was my favourite. It circled round a lilting fairground organ with a row of pastel-painted figurines beating drums, tinkling silvery bells and clashing cymbals. The third roundabout was a slow, lumbering switch-back whose cars were hybrid monsters, colourfully scaled like dragons but shaped like whales, with seats of faded, red, moth-eaten plush and with brass rails for passengers to hold on to during their undulating ride.

Sedate and old-fashioned the switch-back may have been, but the Feast never seemed quite the same again after the year in which it failed to appear and its place was usurped by something called Noah's Ark, where patrons rode on small wooden animals fixed to a gently rising and falling floor, while a loudspeaker blared such ephemerally popular tunes as 'Olga Polovski's a beautiful spy' and 'I'll tell the tale of the "Nancy Lee" '. Equally uninteresting-looking, to my young eyes, was the set of dodg'em cars which made its appearance at roughly the same time.

Other attractions usually included a cakewalk, twin steam-powered swing-boats pothering black smoke, and a children's roundabout turned with a wheel like that of an old-fashioned mangle. There were also what some people brusquely dismissed as the 'catch-penny' shows: coconut shies in which the coconuts were rumoured to be glued to their sawdust-filled cups, shooting galleries and round 'roll-em-in' stalls, where most of the prizes displayed were cheap vases or huge cuddly dolls that nobody ever appeared to win.

The path from the smaller of the two field gates was lined with the vendors of brandy snaps, whelks and stewed peas. I longed to sample the two latter, but my mother forbade this on hygienic grounds, saying that the spoons and saucers they were eaten from were not washed clean in between customers by their peremptory dipping in bowls of water which gradually came to resemble thin soup. Outside the gate a man was always standing selling paper canaries tied to sticks. They were magenta, sulphur yellow or royal blue, and made a 'chirring' sound when the sticks were swished.

Feast weekend, like chapel Anniversary time, was an occasion for family gatherings and for friends who lived away to come visiting. In readiness to feed them ham was boiled, tongues were pressed, 'spice cake' was baked and, on the day itself, trifles were made and dishes of cucumber and onion prepared. My mother's parents lived in Armroyd Lane and always asked me, with two older cousins from Rawmarsh, to tea on Feast Saturday. My grandparents' drive, during May and June, was bordered by regimented rows of tulips – yellow, pink, red, or striped in scarlet and white like café awnings. To this day, whenever I see massed tulips in bloom, I hear the sounds and smell the oil and steam of Elsecar feast field.

As soon as we arrived we would persuade some adult (usually kind, patient Aunt Alice) to escort us, clutching our pocket money, down to the field. Sometimes, if we pleaded long and hard enough, a short evening visit too would be allowed, when the crowds were denser and the sounds more strident. Usually, however, this visit was confined to walking round and watching wistfully. Children's afternoon rides had cost a penny each; now cards hung on the roundabouts saying 'All Classes Twopence'. The rides were noticeably shorter, too.

To children, Feast Sunday was an anti-climax. The fun fair was closed, its roundabouts and stalls shrouded in tarpaulins. This was the day of the 'Hospital Sing', with afternoon and evening services held in neighbouring Elsecar Park. Clergy from various churches led the prayers, a local band accompanied the singing of well-known hymns, preferably with sonorous tunes, and a speaker (usually a matron or consultant) from a Sheffield or Barnsley hospital gave the address. The collections taken, like the proceeds of a flag day held on Feast Saturday, were used to buy extra comforts for the in-patients in local hospitals.

The Feast re-opened on the Monday evening, giving those of us at Ecclesfield Grammar School a reason for pleading to be excused our homework (as we did when Marshalls' Feast came to Chapeltown), but was truly a skeleton of its former self, with roundabouts and stalls stripped to their frameworks in preparation for packing and moving on.

Not long after the nationalization of coal on 1st January, 1947, the National Coal Board took over and re-named the Elsecar Cricket Club neighbouring the Crab Field and proceeded, to the anger and dismay of people in both Elsecar and Hoyland, to annex the latter to the cricket field, surrounding both with a high concrete fence. (Mr D.P. Beattie, from his retirement in London, threatened to tear this offending barrier down when he next came to see his Hoyland friends. He was prevented from making this gesture by his untimely death soon afterwards.)

For a few years after being expelled from its traditional home, the Feast was held instead on the 'Furnace Hills' approached along Forge Lane, ground which was both uneven and out-of-the-way. Then it moved to a field on Distillery Side which was rented by Elsecar Parish Church. After the church ceased to rent the field and so was unable to lend it, the Feast stopped coming and a village tradition regrettably died out.

A great deal of excitement was aroused in Hoyland when, one summer in the mid-thirties, a circus spent a week on the Town Field. The performances it gave were well patronized. My mother and I went there one sunny evening. Among the people I remember seeing were the Rev. Ian Moffat and his wife, both obviously enjoying the spectacle. For some reason, though, this proved to be just a 'one-off' occasion. (Perhaps the circus was only filling in time between other, more important appearances.) Whatever the reason, the clowns, elephants and prancing horses did not return the following year to entertain us.

Hiking, Biking and Other Outdoor Activities

The 'thirties brought a craze for open-air exercise comparable with the present vogue enjoyed by jogging. It became the done thing for the young (and sometimes less young) to don shorts, heavy boots and open-necked shirts, leave the drab towns with their poverty behind and stride out towards the open country on a hike, which may perhaps best be defined as a cross between a country ramble and a route march. There was even a jaunty little song being sung and whistled which began, 'I'm happy when I'm hiking, hiking all the day.'

It was during this decade that, to meet the needs of long-distance hikers venturing too far to be able to return to their own beds, but unable to afford the luxury of sleeping at guest houses or country pubs, the Youth Hostels Association was especially active converting old buildings up and down the land into places offering a cheap night's lodging to the bona-fide walker.

The craze caught on in Hoyland as it did elsewhere. A weedy youth who used to bring our milk, and looked hardly strong enough to lift the can, proudly sported on his coat lapel a badge emblazoned with the word 'Hiker'. Each Whit Monday the young members of the congregation at the John Knowles Memorial Church went hiking together to Kinder Scout, near Edale. A certain miner at Elsecar Main, nevertheless, doubted the wisdom of this kind of pastime. Asked one day, when he went to collect his pay, 'Are you going hiking this Whitsun?' he promptly answered, 'Not likely. I went hiking at Easter and I've done nothing but hike [hawk and spit] ever since.'

This was also a great time for cycling clubs whose members, by purchasing £3 bikes on the instalment system, could exercise equally healthily but were able to travel farther and faster. They included the Hoyland Clarion Cycling Club which, like so many other sporting groups, had its headquarters at a local pub.

For a brief period between the Wars, organized roller skating had a following in Hoyland. One of its organizers and keenest exponents was Mr George Neil of the Aero Garage. This activity usually took place indoors, in a hall at Hoyland Common. One light evening, however, a roller skating race took place from Allott's Corner to the Milton Hall. I remember standing at the top of Booth Street and seeing the competitors go skimming by. (The fact that the race, downhill most of the way, could be held without risk of serious accidents is an indication of how slower and sparser Hoyland traffic was then than it is today.) The winner was a young woman named Smith whose parents kept the Crown Inn at Elsecar.

A traditional north-country sport still being practised in interwar Hoyland was knur-and-spell, which basically consists of seeing which player can knock a large white marble, known as a 'common pot knur', the farthest, using a specially-shaped stick or 'spell'. When walking home on Saturday afternoons after visiting my grandparents in Armroyd, I have seen men playing this game on the Council Fields, the area of rough grass which in those days extended from Millhouses Street to George Street. (Indeed, the sight became as much a part of late Saturday afternoons in my young mind as was eating tea to the accompaniment of Football League results heard on the radio.)

Knur-and-spell competitions were held from time to time.

Only knurs of a certain size were allowed, and sums of money were bet on the contestants. My father usually printed the posters. He himself took no interest in these contests but, though only small and slight, his Great-Uncle John Ottley, who lived at Harley and of whom I have heard him speak many times, is reputed to have been one of the finest knur-and-spell players Yorkshire has ever known. Sadly, I never met this talented sportsman. Before my days he came to an untimely end at Worsbrough crossing when, having stood waiting for a train to pass, he stepped into the path of another one approaching unseen along the other line.

Music and Dancing

One of my earliest recollections is of a dull, grey, drizzly winter's afternoon when, bored and restless, I was standing on a stool staring out of the living-room window. I wished fervently that something nice would happen. Then suddenly it did. From the end of the street came a rainbow-coloured shower of notes played by the barrel organ which, like the barm man and itinerant greengrocers, came on its round each week. The local name for it, tinglairy, had a charmingly onomatopoeic sound.

The man pushing it and turning the handle to produce the music is a shadowy figure in my memory. I am told, however, that he was a disabled ex-serviceman called Charlie Marples and that he lived in George Street.

The mood of the 'twenties was one of light-hearted reaction after the gloom and horror of the First World War. This was the decade of the jaunty Charleston, as characteristic of the times as were cloche hats, dropped waistlines and pointed-toed, ankle-strap shoes. One of my father's assistants, Miss Hilda Jones, who lived on Reform Row at Elsecar, taught me when I was about three to sing:

> Let's all go to Mary's house, to Mary's house, to Mary's house.
> Let's all go to Mary's house and have a real fine time.

> Her Pa and Ma are full of pep,
> You ought to see the old man step.
> He does the Charleston fine.

and:

> My girl's got red hair, got red hair, got red hair.
> My girl's got red hair, lovely ginger hair.

As she went about her jobs, perhaps folding cards or working the small treadle-operated press, Hilda often sang another hit, 'Ain't she sweet?', of which I am irreverently reminded when I hear parts of Widor's much-acclaimed Organ Toccata.

When the Charleston was danced to a gramophone, this would be the old-fashioned, scratchy, wind-up kind, probably with the sound transmitted through a convolvulus-shaped horn. (My parents remembered the days when the records had been not disc-shaped but cylindrical like jam jars.)

The jazz-crazy 'thirties were the age of the 'big bands', whose sound was dominated by the saxophone, the names of such band leaders as Jack Hilton, Ambrose and Roy Fox becoming household words. On the 'wireless' there were regular broadcasts by Henry Hall's BBC Dance Orchestra, which faded out with a cheerful signature tune entitled 'Here's to the next time'. Matching the mood of the moment, Mrs Slowen of King Street sold squares of marble cake, topped with pink, brown and yellow feather icing, on which she conferred the topical name 'jazz'.

The popularity of ballroom dancing received a boost from such films as *Top Hat*, starring the lithe Ginger Rogers and Fred Astaire. A great deal of my father's time was spent printing posters for dances in the Hoyland area, where the music was usually supplied by either Ron Belk's or Bob Lomas's band. A favourite venue was the Milton Hall (originally called the Market Hall, since it was built in 1870 to house an indoor market, but re-named after the Fitzwilliams had repaired and renovated it in the early 'thirties). Another favourite spot for dances was the Church of England or 'Slosh' School at Tankersley.

Most of the popular songs of this period had romantic words and memorable tunes, which one could not resist whistling or singing. Those I clearly recall fifty years on include: 'Twas on the Isle of Capri', 'The merry-go-round broke down', 'Twas one night when the moon was so mellow', 'Little old lady passing by', 'South of the border down Mexico way', 'Smoke gets in your eyes' and 'Music, maestro, please'. The tune which really swept the country, however, towards the end of the decade, was 'The Lambeth Walk' from the former Wakefield organist Noel Gay's musical *Me and My Girl*.

The 'thirties also saw a sudden craze for buying piano accordions on the 'never', instruments optimistic buyers often found more difficult to play than they had assumed. Indirectly, a young man whom my parents knew met his death through aspiring to buy one. He wrote off for an illustrated catalogue which his mother, hoping to thwart his ambition, burned. In angry reaction on discovering this he left home and enlisted in the Royal Navy, which at that time was recruiting avidly with the aid of the slogan 'Join the Navy and See the World'. (A cynical song blaring out that year from the loudspeakers at Elsecar Feast began, 'We joined the Navy to see the world. And what did we see? We saw the sea.') In the War which broke out shortly afterwards, when he could have been in a 'reserved' civilian job, he was killed on active service.

Holidays and Excursions

Holidays with pay did not become statutary until 1938. Until then Hoyland workers who 'went away' each year were mainly professional or self-employed. Most chose easily-accessible coastal resorts, Scarborough, Bridlington and Cleethorpes to the east, Morecambe, Blackpool and Southport to the west. (For some reason Morecambe was always a favourite with Methodist families.) The minority of holiday-makers travelling to such distant resorts as Bournemouth and Torquay were generally looked on as snobs.

SPORT AND ENTERTAINMENT

In the late 'twenties and early 'thirties my parents and I spent an annual fortnight at Scarborough, except for the year when business was so bad that we could only afford a week at Cleethorpes. We did not stay at a guest house or hotel, which would have seemed an unnecessary extravagance but, like many other families in those days, rented 'apartments' in a private house. When I was very young we stayed with a widow, a tall, genteel woman with a mass of white hair who, despite having three daughters out at work, welcomed the extra money to put towards the rates on her large house near Dean Road Cemetery. In later years our landlady was a spinster whose father had captained a sailing ship an oil painting of which, becalmed permanently on a sea the colour of green table jelly, hung over my bed in one of her fusty-smelling bedrooms. The house had dusty-looking venetian blinds, a cracked wash-basin, heavy mahogany furniture and chocolate-coloured paint. For all that, it was our holiday home, and we cheerfully put up with its shortcomings.

Each day started with a visit to the butcher, the baker, the grocer and the greengrocer (or instead of the butcher the fishmonger, with his striped apron and straw 'boater' hat), to buy food which the landlady then cooked for us while we enjoyed the attractions of Peasholm Park, lazed on the sands or visited the harbour, where my father liked to photograph the shipping. With a child's perversity, I much preferred the Bramble Jelly and Golden Shred we ate at Scarborough, storing the jars in a capacious sideboard, to my mother's home-made strawberry-and-gooseberry jam and mouth-watering three-fruits marmalade.

When in 1935, to my dismay, my parents chose to visit Whitby instead, still staying with a private family, we were venturing into unknown territory. When, that same year, the aunt and uncle from Rawmarsh whose children always came to Elsecar Feast purchased a large black Austin Westminster and decided to drive up to Scotland in it, staying at Oban and exploring the hills and glens, this seemed the height of luxury and romance. When elderly, bearded Mr William Firth, a partner in the firm of C. Firth and Sons, plumbers, electricians and decorators, went on a cruise to the Canary Islands and called one evening at our house to tell us the tale of his experiences afloat, he was treated like a traveller back from Mars. (He stayed talking until four the following morning, when one of his two sisters came seeking him.)

Most Hoyland people's holidays were restricted to a few excursions or 'day trips' each year. As a 'thank-you' for their unpaid services, churches treated their choristers to an annual 'choir trip', usually to Scarborough, Blackpool or Bridlington, hiring Mr Ernest Tipler's motor coach or a coach supplied by the Yorkshire Traction Company. For members of the choir the trip was free. If there were any seats to spare, however, members of the congregation and other friends could pay to occupy them. It was customary too, as it is today, for working men's clubs to give their members' children an annual seaside outing.

My mother, who grew up at Elsecar, remembered how she looked forward each year to going with various brothers and sisters on the Rechabites' outing to Cleethorpes. Though the Independent Order of Rechabites is a friendly society with teetotal ideals, the number of families whose children were taken on this trip suggests, in view of the many hostelries at that time thriving in Elsecar, that not all its members strictly adhered to its views on abstinence. On the Saturday in question, special trains were run from the Great Central goods station. Movable steps were used, there being no platforms, to enable passengers to climb aboard. The return fare for an adult was one-and-three (one shilling and three pence). That for a child was proportionately less.

Another excursion to Cleethorpes from Wath Road goods station was run each year until the Second World War by the Old Horse Party, a mumming group which, besides the Old Horse itself, included such bucolic characters as the Farrier, the Gardener's Son and the Smiling Young Man, each introduced by an accordion player singing a suitable piece of doggerel verse. The group toured the village and its pubs at Christmas and was also sometimes invited to Wentworth House, to perform in front of Earl and Countess Fitzwilliam and the members of their Christmas house party. The outing on which the proceeds of its efforts were spent was for local children who would nowadays be classified as 'underprivileged', but in those days were described Dickensianly as 'crippled, fatherless and poor'.

In 1939 this excursion had to be cancelled. It was arranged for Saturday, 2nd September, by which time the country was already mobilizing and all available rolling stock was needed to move troops and to evacuate city children to safer areas. I particularly remember this because members of the 'Busy Bees', a girls' sewing party at St Andrew's Church with which my mother was associated, had been going to have an outing to Cleethorpes too, in a coach attached to the end of the children's train.

Some employers, among them the Urban District Council, treated their workers to an annual day out. They also included the Seventh Earl Fitzwilliam, who laid on an excursion every year for his Elsecar Main and 'New Yard' employees. One year during the 'thirties this took the form of a railway excursion to Liverpool. My mother and one of her two younger sisters, Aunt Alice (the one who escorted my cousins and me to the Feast), were delighted when they managed to obtain two tickets, one from my grandfather, another from one of his workmates who, like him, was not very interested in 'gadding off'. Met at Liverpool by a paper firm's 'rep' who lived there and called on my father from time to time, and knew people who could pull the requisite strings, they had the fascinating experience of being escorted over a liner scheduled to sail later that day.

For younger members of the community there was the occasional school outing, though these were less numerous than they are today. In 1934 Ecclesfield Grammar School, whose catchment area Hoyland was in, organized a train trip to York featuring as its highlights visits to the Minster and Rowntree's chocolate works. I did not go, but went the following year with a similar party to Liverpool. There we rode on the overhead railway, looked over a small passenger/cargo ship, crossed by ferry to Lever's Port Sunlight works (where we saw them boiling large vats of soap and were served inedibly greasy mutton for lunch) and ate our sandwich tea at Liverpool Zoo – a crowded schedule which left us no time for an intended visit to the Cathedral, at that time in the final stages of construction.

Towering above all other Hoyland excursions, however, was 'Beattie's Big Trip' which ran to Blackpool Illuminations each autumn from Elsecar and Hoyland LMS, leaving on a weekday morning and coming back the following day during the small hours, the 'razmataz' including streamers, balloons, free sweets and, to ensure that everything went with a swing, the genial, forceful personality of Mr Douglas P. Beattie himself, as organizer and master of ceremonies.

A youth working for the Maypole Dairy Company, Reginald Thornsby, was given the day off from his shop work to travel aboard the special train, where he gave out advertising novelties to children being taken on the trip, most of whom, since this was mid-week, had presumably not yet attained school age. (To a child who was attending King Street School, it was tantalizing to stand in the yard at playtime and watch the maroon-coloured carriages slowly pull in to a platform packed solid with waiting trippers, a prisoner yearning to accompany them. In retrospect the majority seem to have been middle-aged women about to embark on what for many of them was no doubt the highlight of an uneventful year.)

These memories are substantiated by a photograph, loaned to me recently, taken by Mr Roy Colville. It shows Mr Beattie on the station platform behind a banner with the inscription 'Beattie's Big Trip', flanked by serried rows of people most of whom are women in the costume of the 'twenties.

Aristocratic Occasions

On the last day of 1931 William Henry Laurence Peter Fitzwilliam, Viscount Milton, the Seventh Earl Fitzwilliam's son and heir, celebrated his twenty-first birthday. This coming-of-age was an occasion for lavish and joyful celebrations in Wentworth Park, which I am told included a firework display and the roasting of an ox.

In April 1933, the Earl's workmen at Elsecar were taken like the rest of his employees by chartered ship to Dublin, to see Lord Milton married in St Patrick's, the Church of Ireland Cathedral where Jonathan Swift, the author of *Gulliver's Travels*, was once Dean. The bride, Miss Olive Dorothea Plunkett (the daughter of a Church of Ireland bishop who was related to the Guinnesses, from one of whom he inherited great wealth), caused a minor sensation by being married not in traditional white but in ice blue, a colour very fashionable that year, different shades of which were worn by her twelve bridesmaids.

Besides attending the 'Lordy's' son's wedding, this outing gave many of the participants a chance they would otherwise never have had to explore the attractions of Dublin itself, with its eighteenth-century squares and terraces, its famous quays bordering the Liffey and, linked indirectly with the festivities, the Guinness brewery.

During the inter-war period, the Fitzwilliams still owned many houses, farms and shops in the Hoyland area. Most of their Elsecar property, including the now-renovated Reform and Station Rows, had been purpose-built to house mining families. Their Hoyland property, more scattered and varied, included large detached houses and some shops, some rumoured to have been cunningly acquired by getting illiterate owners to sign them over in return for repairs that they could not have found the money to undertake themselves.

Rents for Fitzwilliam properties were paid half-yearly, in November and in May, at the Estate Office at Wentworth House. Two consecutive rent days were held each time, the first for farmers, shopkeepers and people occupying other sizeable properties, the second for those in workmen's cottages. Having paid his rent, each tenant was entitled to partake of the rent dinner which was laid on at the Estate's expense — a 'thank-you' and also an arrangement which, before Wentworth was served by buses, had ensured that those who had come long distances on foot were not obliged to walk back home hungry.

Within living memory, Wentworth rent dinners had been sumptuous repasts of roast beef and vegetables, followed in November by Christmas pudding with custard sauce and in May by rice pudding laced with currants. A strictly limited allowance of beer was available to those who wanted it.

Like most free handouts, however, the dinners were abused by a greedy minority. Numerous tales were once in circulation about the way in which some folk behaved at them. When passed the potatoes, one old woman declared sharply that what she wanted was not 'taties' but more meat – she could get all the 'taties' she required at home. Another had made herself a special apron on which was sewn an outsize pocket in which she was able to smuggle home slices of beef. A leading citizen of Hoyland was once caught slipping a hunk of Christmas pudding into his pocket. The equally respected neighbour accompanying him promptly poured a jug of custard over it, remarking, 'Tha mud as weel he' this an' all.'

Largely to end such abuses as these, the rent dinner of the 'thirties had become a simple meal of pickles and cold meat. About 1935 even this was stopped, the 'thank-you' which replaced it taking the form of half-a-crown (twelve-and-a-half new pence).

Royal Occasions

In Hoyland as throughout the rest of the kingdom, the excitement grew almost hysterical when on 29th November, 1934, Prince George, recently created Duke of Kent (a title held by his great-great grandfather) married Princess Marina of Greece. Television was in its experimental stage and was not destined to come north for many years, but people gathered round their wireless sets to hear the sound broadcast from Westminster Abbey, outside which the commentator was Howard Marshall, whose name was normally associated with commentaries on Test Matches. Schoolchildren were given a day's holiday to celebrate the event.

The Princess's name, in newspapers and journals, was frequently prefixed with 'the beautiful', and 'Marina blue' (a variety of turquoise) and Marina-style pill-box hats and envelope handbags were a 'must' for young women, in all walks of life, wishing to look chic and appear fashion-conscious.

When on 6th November the following year the Duke of Gloucester, back from an Australian tour, married Lady Alice Montagu-Douglas-Scott, the petite, pretty bride was overshadowed by the adulation surrounding the previous year's new Duchess. The occasion was further muted by the fact that, because Lady Alice's father had recently died, the wedding took place privately and was not broadcast, although pictures of the happy couple standing with the King and Queen on the Palace balcony, the bride wearing a gown designed by the then unknown young man Norman Hartnell, appeared in the following morning's newspapers. We children had breathed a sigh of relief on learning that, despite the curtailed ceremonial, we were still to be given the day's holiday we had been promised.

Six months earlier, in May 1935, bearded, patriarchal-looking King George V had celebrated his Silver Jubilee. Though there was no television on which to view the procession to St Paul's for the Thanksgiving Service, people opening their newspapers the following day could see pictures of him and his regal-looking consort, Queen Mary, driving in an open carriage followed by another in which rode the 'Little Princesses', Elizabeth and Margaret Rose of York (at that time their Majesties' only grandchildren with the exception of the Harewood boys), accompanying their parents and in hats and coats which, the captions informed us, were rose pink. Princess Elizabeth, next in succession to the throne after her 'Uncle David' and her father, had been a focus of interest ever since her birth in April 1926. (For my eighth birthday my parents gave me a 'Princess Elizabeth' doll, with a head of bright yellow curls and white frilly dress, but unhappily it had to be left behind, for fear of transmitting infection, when I came home from Kendray Hospital after being treated for diphtheria.)

Despite the fact that the Depression had reached its nadir and there was grim, grinding poverty everywhere, which might have bred resentment of Royal pomp, the spontaneous loyalty which came welling up on the occasion of King George's Jubilee seems in retrospect to have been more heartfelt than the 'superstar' veneration directed towards present-day Royalty. Perhaps in part it had been prompted by the simple sincerity of the Christmas broadcasts the King inaugurated in 1932. Also there was relief that, despite his premature ageing, his lung troubles of the late 'twenties appeared to have been overcome.

Perhaps, too, people were ready to seize any excuse to put their cares behind them and celebrate. In Hoyland red, white and blue bunting decked streets and homes. My parents purchased a large Union Jack which, as we had no flag pole to fly it from, was hung 'Barbara Frietchie' style from an attic window high in the gable end. Travelling by special train that spring to Liverpool with the school party from Ecclesfield, I noticed the profusion of flags and bunting hung like washing across the drab 'Coronation Streets' of the Lancashire slums through which we passed.

At the end of our tour of Port Sunlight we were given medallions of pale green 'Vinolia' soap, embossed with the profiles of the King and Queen. The West Riding County Council gave its schoolchildren a fountain pen and propelling pencil each, in a suitably designed presentation box — a useful though not a durable memento.

On Jubilee Day itself, Monday, 6th May, Hoyland's United Thanksgiving Service was held on the Town Field off West Street. The procession from the town centre was led by the Salvation Army Band, which also accompanied the singing of the 'Battle Hymn of the Republic', at that time starting to enjoy a vogue (at Ecclesfield it was often our assembly hymn), though the wording of the title made it seem perhaps an odd choice for a Royal occasion. The choice of both band and music prompted the caustic-tongued Rev. H.A. Crowther-Alwyn, Vicar of St Andrew's and a High Churchman, to write scathingly in his Parish Magazine about being asked to walk to the 'football field' behind the Salvation Army Band playing 'John Brown's Body'.

Since that year's Urban District Council Chairman was Councillor John Leo Joyce, a Roman Catholic, there was much speculation in Protestant circles as to whether his confessor would allow him to take part in the service. In the event, Councillor Joyce did attend. He also lit a celebration bonfire at Hoyland Law Stand after dark that evening. Piled almost as high as the Stand itself and consisting of old colliery tubs or 'corves', it burned from ten o'clock that Monday night until two the following morning.

Relief at the King's seeming recovery was short-lived. Barely eight months later George V was dead. On the evening of 20th January, 1936, I was allowed to stay up later than usual and, gathering round the sitting-room loudspeaker, my parents and I listened with disbelief as the Chief Announcer, Stuart Hibberd, said in hushed tones, 'The King's life is passing peacefully to its close.' (Mr Hibberd always read the News 'breathily', which prompted my Aunt Alice to remark, 'The Chief Announcer lost his breath the night the King died, and has never got it back.')

The grief caused by the King's passing was as sincere as the joy which had greeted his Jubilee. There was no need for any Court pronouncement to tell the country mourning should be worn. My father and other men put on black ties in a spontaneous gesture of respect. At St Peter's, Hoyland's original Parish Church, which my parents and I attended at that time, a memorial service was held at which worshippers were handed officially-issued service papers. I remember the hushed, solemn atmosphere in the packed church as the Rev. Ian Moffat led the prayers, and the emotional moment when, at the end of this act of homage, the organist started to play Handel's 'Dead March in Saul'.

Life, however, continues, and the death of a monarch means that a Coronation is imminent. Therefore, no sooner were the black ties off than Jack Kennerley, our elderly neighbour in Green Street, a man not known for spending lavishly, started rummaging behind Rowland Watson's fruit shop when it had closed each Friday and Saturday, looking in discarded boxes for papers which had wrapped apples, oranges, peaches or pears. These he painstakingly made into bunting which, when the time came, was stretched across the street from the row of three cottages in which he lived to the sycamore trees bordering Rowland Cross's garden.

In Hoyland as throughout the rest of the country and Empire, the Abdication of King Edward VIII left public opinion sharply divided. Once the shock waves it generated had subsided, however, the build-up to his brother's Coronation was as enthusiastic as had been that towards his father's Jubilee. A member of Hoyland's Coronation Committee, and the man in the forefront of its preparations, was that great organizer, Mr D.P. Beattie. It was at Mr Beattie's instigation that a competition was held to choose for the town a Coronation Queen. Competitors had to be aged eighteen, and were asked to send their portraits to the *Express*. Several photographs were published every week, together with a form on which readers could vote for the girl they considered the most suitable. There was also a contest to select two attendants, one of whom must be fourteen and the other rather younger.

Tension mounted as the closing date drew near. There were rumours that one Hoyland business couple were buying up spare copies of the *Express* and sending in the forms which they contained, to provide their daughter with additional votes. The winner was chosen, at a dance in the Milton Hall, from a short list made up of those girls who had won the highest number of votes. She proved to be a plump girl with dark, curly hair, the daughter of Mr 'Teddy' Williamson, the conductor of the Elsecar Band. The senior attendant was Miss Alice Mary Ward, a pale girl with clear-cut features and straight, light brown hair who was a fellow-pupil of mine at Ecclesfield. The junior attendant was Miss Rita Meadows, a small child with blue eyes and golden curls. On the morning of Coronation Day, Wednesday, 12th May, wearing their white ceremonial dresses, the three made an attractive tableau riding in procession on a decorated float.

Hoyland's decorations were even more lavish than those put up for the Silver Jubilee two years earlier. The Town Hall façade was draped with huge Union Jacks, and lamp standards were hung with long, decorative pennants. The Coronation Service was broadcast, as Princess Marina's wedding had been. (Interest in what the Princess would be wearing was as great as that in the gold-embroidered robes Norman Hartnell had designed for the Queen Consort.) Listening to it my father was reminded of how, as a boy aged eleven in August 1902, he took part in the singing of

'Zadok the Priest' by St Peter's Church choir, whose choirmaster he said was Mr Joseph Laver, to celebrate the Coronation of King Edward VII and Queen Alexandra.

Since the day was cool and showery, Hoyland's own service to mark the occasion took place not in the open air, but in the comfortable, spacious Cinema. It was conducted by the Vicar of Hoyland, the Rev. Ian Moffat – one of his last public appearances before moving later in 1937 to Mirfield.

Various mementos were distributed. The West Riding County Council gave each schoolchild an inscribed teaspoon packed, as the Silver Jubilee writing sets had been, in a decorative box. On the occasion of the Jubilee, the Barnsley British Co-operative Society had given each of its members a caddy of tea, with King George in naval uniform on one side and on the other Queen Mary in a turquoise gown, each framed in a border of silver and pale blue. As Coronation souvenirs, members were given glass tumblers engraved with the heads of the new King and Queen, and filled with either lemon curd or raspberry jam.

As an epilogue to Hoyland's celebrations, the official Coronation medal allocated to each administrative area was presented to Mr John R. Shephard, who had been responsible for the excellent street decorations. Bureaucracy being its rigid self, however, no official recognition was given to Mr Beattie, whose tireless work and organizing skill had done so much to ensure the social success of the occasion.

CHAPTER NINE

Medicine and Health

BETWEEN THE WARS, before the inception of the National Health Service, medical practices were still bought and sold, or passed down from one generation to the next. General practice in Hoyland for much of that time was associated with four families: the Allotts, Ritchies, Wigginses and Faircloughs.

Until his death towards the end of the 'twenties, Dr Wordsworth Leach Allott, a member of an old South Yorkshire family, lived and conducted his practice at Fieldhead (which shares its name with a gentleman's residence in Charlotte Brontë's *Shirley*), the rambling, mellow-looking house in West Street opposite the new Telephone Exchange.

MEDICINE AND HEALTH

An old man with a white, patriarchal beard, he was Hoyland's Medical Officer of Health, a position he had held since 1891, and Public Vaccinator. (In those days it was still compulsory to have infants vaccinated against smallpox, unless the parents signed a form declaring their objection on grounds of conscience to this procedure.) The Public Vaccinator's services were free. A snag to using those of Dr Allott, however, was that to ensure the effectiveness of the dose he still made four scratches on the baby's arm, whereas his younger colleagues made only one, leaving unsightly scars which, in later years, were especially unwelcome on girl patients who wished to wear sleeveless dresses.

'Old' Dr Allott died suddenly of a stroke in 1927. I was almost certainly the last patient to see him, though the occasion was a purely social one. My mother and I met the doctor going in at his gate one afternoon when we were on our way to my uncle's at West Bank. I proudly showed him a miniature loaf tin that I had been given when we called at Garner's hardware shop in High Street. He died the next day and, like a number of other prominent Hoyland people about that time, was buried at Wentworth. His widow and spinster daughter, Miss May Allott (so named because her birthday was in May), moved into a smaller house and his son, Dr Horace Rhodes Leach Allott, took up residence at Fieldhead with his family.

Dr Horace Allott was a tall, stern-looking man with strong features and horn-rimmed spectacles. When he visited me during childhood illnesses, he always wore a thick tweed overcoat and smelled incongruously of some kind of cologne. Distressed already by the tension in the house when it proved necessary to send for him, I was terrified both by his deep bass voice and by his heavy footfalls on the stairs and landing.

Like his father before him, Dr Horace Allott was the town's Medical Officer of Health. So was his daughter, Dr Joy Sinclair Leach Allott, who succeeded him at Fieldhead early in the 'forties. The Allotts also had a Hoyland Common practice, in Sheffield Road near Allott's Corner which, incidentally, takes its name not from them but from another family, Charles Allott and Sons who, earlier this century, owned grocery and drapery stores both there and on the corner of Hill Street and Church Street at Elsecar. This practice, run by Dr Horace Allott during his father's lifetime, was taken over by his son, Dr Eric Sinclair Leach Allott and his daughter-in-law, Dr Marie, after their marriage in 1944.

When 'Dr Joy', as everybody called her, moved about 1963 to take up an appointment at Sidmouth, where she had spent many holidays as a child, she was succeeded at the Fieldhead practice by Dr Harry Gray, after whose tragic death in 1972 it was assigned to Dr Agarwal, who now runs it from the Hoyland Health Centre. After 'Dr Eric and Dr Marie' chose to retire prematurely, the Hoyland Common practice passed through several hands, including those of an Irish doctor and his wife, before being combined with the Hoyland practice run by Dr Donald James Fairclough and his partners.

The Allotts were a family of churchgoers. Dr Horace's wife, Mrs Ethel Gabrielle Allott, had a sister who was married to a clergyman, the Rev. Theodore Henry Egbert Japing, a graduate of Durham University, who was appointed to St Polycarp's at Malin Bridge in Sheffield. Mrs Allott herself was for a time a churchwarden at St Andrew's, a paragraph in a national newspaper claiming that she was the first woman ever to hold such office. Later the Allotts worshipped at St Peter's, where for many years Mrs Allott supplied and arranged the altar flowers for major festivals.

A sidelight on the changing living standards of professional people since the Second World War is provided by the fact that, at Fieldhead, Dr Joy Allott was able to keep two resident maidservants, Elsie and Mary, a part-time sewing maid, and a gardener-handyman, Colin Jackson, to run her establishment and relieve her of distracting household worries. (In Mr Jackson's time, the land which is now the Belmont Club car park was part of the grounds of Fieldhead, and comprised an immaculately-kept gravel drive surrounding a circular flower-bed which in summer was ablaze with brilliant colour.)

Dr William Ritchie, a Scotsman, had come to Hoyland towards the end of Queen Victoria's reign, living at the house now known as Riversdale situated at the corner of Market Street and Duke Street. The small room with the blocked-up doorway facing Duke Street was built for his use as a surgery.

Among the homely wisdom credited to him is the saying that 'If you leave a cold, it will go on for a week. If you treat it, it will only last seven days.' He was equally down-to-earth on the best way of serving cucumber: 'Slice it thinly and then place it in a dish, salt and pepper it, cover it with vinegar – and throw it out of the window.'

By the 'twenties William Ritchie was growing old. He died in October 1930, aged eighty-one. One of his sons, Dr Horatio Nelson Ritchie, however, practised at Hoyland Common, in the house on the corner of Watson Street that is now a wood-carver's. He was noted for his conscientiousness and, before 'casual' shoes became popular, is said to have worn elastic-sided boots which could be pulled on quickly and easily if he was called to a night emergency.

At one time he was assisted in running the practice by Dr Brian Rawlin, a grandson of Mr Joshua Rawlin of Glebe Farm, a man who had the distinction of serving as a churchwarden at Tankersley for fifty years. On leaving Hoyland Common, Dr Rawlin was in practice at Dinnington and South Anston until his death in the late 'seventies. His son, Dr Michael Rawlin, succeeded him there.

Dr 'Raysher' Ritchie, as most people called him, died prematurely in the mid-thirties, an event which caused a feeling of great loss in the community. He was buried near the south-east corner of the original churchyard at Tankersley, the inscription on his tombstone describing him, in the phrase the Scriptures apply to St Luke, as 'a beloved physician'. There is also a memorial window to him, in which the same words are included, in the south wall of Tankersley Church between the main door and the tower. A grey granite obelisk to other Ritchies including the old doctor and his wife, the words on one side of it barely legible, stands to the left of the path from the upper gateway of St Peter's Churchyard in Hawshaw Lane.

Dr Ritchie's successor at Hoyland Common was a Jewish

physician, Dr Philip Lewis, who after the War took into partnership Dr Shaw, a Pole who had married an Englishwoman, become naturalized and taken an English surname. He in turn was joined there by Dr Mir, who now runs the practice from Hoyland Health Centre together with Dr Marshall.

Dr Barclay Wiggins, Sr., a tall, lanky Scotsman, came to Hoyland in the eighteen-nineties as a young assistant to Dr William Ritchie. One of his first duties was to attend the birth of one of my mother's friends born during that decade. Deciding to launch out independently, he subsequently purchased Ivy House, a gloomy-looking place behind a high stone wall between Dr Ritchie's garden and Tithe Laithe. Having put up his brass plate, he enlarged the premises extensively and it is rumoured, being a good Scot, expressed indignant surprise when his rateable value increased in consequence.

During the 'twenties Dr Wiggins' only child, Dr Barclay Wiggins, Jr., a man noted for his blunt outspokenness, qualified and joined his father in the practice. In the 'thirties they took on a young assistant, Dr John Aiken McEwen, a graduate of Glasgow University, a move which proved very popular with their patients. Like the Glasgow-trained veterinary surgeon in the James Herriot books, Dr McEwen at first lived 'over the shop', marrying and setting up house with his bride in a small flat over the surgery, to which a homely touch was added by a cage-bird in the large window facing the street. In the Second World War, Dr McEwen served with the Forces, and his wife rejoined her Scottish family. When the War ended they returned to Hoyland and the Wiggins, Wiggins and McEwen partnership took shape.

The Wiggins practice always seems to have attracted a considerable number of its patients from Jump, which has never had a resident physician. One reason perhaps was the accessibility of the Market Street surgery, easily reached by the path up the hill, known as Jump Fields, which formed the grazing land of nearby Manor Farm.

One of Hoyland's best-known, most respected citizens, distinctively dressed during the summer months in dark grey trousers and cream linen coat, the elder Dr Wiggins died in his nineties during the long cold spell at the beginning of 1963. A few years later his son, who lived with his wife and family at Kirby Lane, the road which links Thorpe Hesley and Hood Hill, retired prematurely owing to ill health. In the early 'seventies Dr McEwen, too, retired from general practice. Their successor, Dr Bhartia, runs the practice from the Hoyland Health Centre, and Ivy House has been converted into a Methodist church with a minister's flat and rooms for social functions.

The Fairclough family, the only member of this medical quartet still to be represented in the town, was the most recent of the four to arrive there. This happened when Dr James Herbert Fairclough, whose father was a schoolmaster near Louth, came to Elsecar after the First World War with his Wentworth-born wife Wilhelmena MacDonald Fairclough, who had trained as a nurse and whose family came from the Border country of Scotland, and opened a small surgery in Church Street, next door to the boys' school.
About 1930 the Faircloughs moved to Walderslade, the large house opposite the Miners' Welfare where their son, Dr Donald James Fairclough, now practises along with his four partners. There, though afflicted with a slight stammer, Dr Fairclough applied himself energetically not only to running his medical practice but to the organization of such activities as the Elsecar Midland Musical Festival (to which he gave the Donald and Christine Cup, named after his two children), the Chrysanthemum Society and, during the Second World War, the National Savings Movement. For this he organized concerts at which he got nationally-known celebrities to appear. To help to boost savings in the Hoyland area, he also coined such pithy slogans as 'Don't Ruhr if you are too late' and (after the famous Dambusters Raid) 'Don't damn his bombs; bomb his dams.'

Dr Fairclough died a number of years ago, while only in his sixties. However, a link with those days is maintained not only by the continuing practice of medicine at Walderslade but by Dr

Donald Fairclough's involvement in the social activities his father supported.

Walderslade itself has an interesting history. It was built at the start of the century by a master builder, Thomas Playford Hague whose initials, with the date 1904, can be seen inscribed over the blocked-up gateway facing Millhouses Street, and was named after a village down in Kent where his daughter Ena, a delicate child, spent a holiday which greatly improved her health. Mr Hague, who also built Vernon Cottages (at first one house), named after his eldest son Vernon, moved to Bridlington and from Bridlington to Scalby where another son, who died at Pickering in 1986 at the age of eighty-nine, was for thirty years a member of the now-defunct Scalby Urban District Council.

Previous doctors to practise at Walderslade, after the Hagues left there, were Dr Lawrence and Dr Fisher, the second of whom moved to Nether Edge in Sheffield. Another physician in that area earlier this century was Dr Abbott, who lived at the black-and-white bungalow, formerly the Roman Catholic Presbytery, on the corner of St Helen's Street and Hill Street and whose name appears on a programme in my possession, dated 1911, alongside that of Earl Fitzwilliam as a Patron of the Elsecar Cricket Club.

Seeing the Doctor

During the inter-war years, before the coming of the National Health Service, one was either a private or a 'panel' patient. The private patient paid about half-a-crown for visiting the doctor's surgery, and slightly more for a house call. The typical 'panel' patient was a manual worker (the self-employed, people in certain official jobs and white-collar workers with over £250 a year were not covered by the scheme) who, in return for buying a weekly insurance stamp, qualified not only to receive an Old Age Pension and Sickness and Unemployment Benefit, but also to obtain free treatment from any doctor who agreed to accept him on to his list or 'panel'.

Since this scheme was the brain-child of David Lloyd George, the Liberal politician, panel patients were usually called 'Lloyd George' patients, just as being off work on sick pay was known as being 'on the Lloyd George'. When it was introduced in 1911, doctors welcomed it as guaranteeing them a steady even though a modest income. (My mother recalled how one doctor, in those early days, proudly pointed out to her his brand-new car, calling it 'a present from Mr Lloyd George.')

This two-tier system had its drawbacks, however. Only the insured worker himself was on the panel. If his wife or one of his children fell ill, he had to pay for their treatment privately – which inevitably led to allegations that some doctors cared less conscientiously for the breadwinner himself than for his family.

At the same time, most doctors found the need to employ a man who went from house to house to collect the fees some private patients owed them, literally at the rate of sixpence a week, and at least one Hoyland doctor's receptionist kept beside her a list of patients to whom credit must not in any circumstances be allowed.

The range of drugs and treatments at that time was far narrower than it is nowadays. Most medicines prescribed were in liquid form, and to my recollection most tasted bitter and (presumably to make them look attractive) many were coloured a bright cherry red. Panel patients were given prescriptions to take to their chemists. For private patients medicines were supplied by the doctor himself and mixed at his surgery by a dispenser, who doubled as a receptionist. (At Fieldhead this was Mrs Allott herself, a tall woman with a commanding presence who in earlier years had been a ward sister at the Royal Hospital.)

Going into Hospital

The two teaching hospitals in whose catchment area Hoyland found itself during the 'twenties and 'thirties were the Royal Hospital and Royal Infirmary in Sheffield, whose names were usually shortened to 'The Royal' and 'The Infirmary'. The former, opened in 1858 in West Street, on a cramped site surrounded by streets and shops, was originally a dispensary only, The Sheffield Public Hospital and Dispensary being the name by which it was once known. The latter, in the drab surroundings of Neepsend, dated from the late eighteenth century, when local philanthropists built it as a place for treating the 'sick poor'. (The Infirmary had once stood in a park, the intention being that the poor would benefit from being able to fill their lungs with fresh, clean air. Over a century later its main block, sash-windowed and classically proportioned, still retained a marked resemblance to a stately home, despite the disappearance of the park under the encroachment of slum property.)

Known as the 'voluntary' hospitals, 'The Royal' and 'The Infirmary' depended largely on fund-raising efforts of various kinds, including 'hospital sings' and sales of work. My parents remembered how, in their young days, people of social standing and ample means could make an annual subscription to one or both and in return get a number of 'recommends' entitling them to submit patients for treatment. One such subscriber was the Rev. Charles Molesworth Sharpe, Vicar of Elsecar from 1888 until 1922, whose stipend of £200 a year in those days permitted him to make this gesture. After the birth of her sixth and final child, my father's mother had a 'gathered' breast for which immediate surgery was needed. She felt indebted ever afterwards to Mr Steele, the Vicar of St Peter's, the church where she and her husband and family worshipped, for supplying the 'recommend' enabling her to be admitted to the Royal Infirmary.

Consultants, who were known as 'honoraries', gave their services in teaching hospital wards free of charge, relying for a living on pay-bed and nursing home patients. The general surgeon at 'The Royal' to whom the Allotts usually referred their cases was a Lancastrian, Mr Harold Blacow Yates, noted not only for his professional skill but for his disconcertingly rude remarks, especially to the 'difficult' or pretentious. Dr Fairclough sent his surgical cases to tall, urbane Mr Lytle of the Infirmary.

In the Sheffield area there was a scheme called the 'Penny in the Pound', a man who paid into this scheme each week a penny out of every pound he earned being entitled to free hospital residence for himself and his dependants. In-patients not covered by this insurance were, during their stay there, questioned searchingly by the hospital almoner about their means and consequent ability to pay. A number of my father's customers who had been 'hospitalized' afterwards indignantly told him stories of the arguments they had had with the person whose title they pronounced 'lady al-moaner'.

Beckett's Hospital in Barnsley, which was founded in 1865 and named after a linen manufacturing family which had given generously towards its construction was, like 'The Infirmary' and 'The Royal', largely dependent on legacies, subscriptions and gifts. Through not being a teaching hospital with consultants to give patients the benefit of their expertise, in Hoyland it was generally looked down on. Its subscribers included mine owners, and it was widely thought of as a place where miners had legs or fingers amputated, not always particularly skilfully, after sustaining injuries at work. (Some even went to the length of calling it 'The Butchers' Hospital'.)

A second general hospital in Barnsley was that forming part of the poor-law institution, commonly called the workhouse – a grim, prison-like building overlooking the town from high ground at the top of Gawber Road. Built originally for the treatment of sick paupers, though it also took some terminally-ill patients and others whom more prestigious hospitals preferred not to admit, in the 'thirties it was given the name 'St Helen's', in honour of the saint to whom Barnsley Parish Church was dedicated in medieval times, and upgraded into a general hospital. However, the prejudice against it lingered on and there was always an undeserved stigma attached to being treated or to dying in St Helen's.

In the late 'thirties there were plans afoot to replace Beckett's with a new, more commodious hospital building on the neighbouring extension to St Mary's Churchyard. Fortunately this scheme was postponed because of the War, and the churchyard extension was later converted into a pleasant and leafy town-centre park, those memorials still legible being kept and arranged in an orderly pattern alongside the paths. Under a new and better scheme the Barnsley District General Hospital, opened to patients in 1977, was erected in the more open, extensive grounds adjacent to St Helen's, which was bulldozed as part of this operation and of which no visible trace remains.

People living in the Hoyland area and wishing to have private in-patient treatment could go into a hospital pay-bed (the top floor of the Royal Hospital had a number of private rooms) or else into the Claremont Nursing Home, run by the Claremont Sisters, which at that time was a house in Claremont Crescent, near the site where the Royal Hallamshire came to be built. (For a few years after the new Claremont was opened at Sandygate in 1953, the old home was used as a pre-nursing school.)

The hospital room charge was £7 a week, including theatre fee, dressings and drugs. Claremont's charge, exclusive of these items, was seven guineas. Even though in those days the average workman's wage was only £3 or £4 a week, in 'real terms' these charges were far lower than the £100 a day or more being asked at most hospitals and nursing homes today. The surgeon's fee was thirty-five guineas for a major operation. The anaesthetist's was usually five.

Nurses and Midwives

Although before the National Health Service there were no Community Nurses whose services were available free to people ill at home, there were District Nurses whose main concern was with the poorer section of the community. There was also a Nursing Association in Hoyland which employed its own nurse, whose services could be used in return for an annual subscription. (The Secretary of the Association was Mrs Beardwood, whose husband, Mr Fred Beardwood, was a tailor carrying on his business at a council house near the War Memorial.)

Many people, however, who were bed-ridden in their own homes relied on unskilled, voluntary help. During November 1931 an elderly member of my family suffered a stroke which partially paralysed her. She lived until the following February and was buried on Shrove Tuesday. During her three months' illness she received regular visits from the family doctor, but for nursing she depended mainly on neighbours and relatives. (Today she would have been rushed into hospital, and might even have been placed in 'intensive care', as soon as her condition was diagnosed.)

Before the Second World War most infants were born at home, with a midwife present and the doctor called only if the birth proved slow or difficult. In my grandmothers' days the unofficial 'midwife' was usually the woman who lived next door, who herself had probably had several confinements. In the inter-war years a few women still officially practised without formal training or certificates. One of these, an old woman living at Jump who had delivered thirteen pairs of twins in that village, a fact reported in the national press, sometimes walked up to Hoyland past our house, always wearing a snowy white apron.

The trained midwives working in the Hoyland area included Miss Nora Walker of Skiers Hall, who during her professional career delivered nearly five thousand infants, sometimes walking in the middle of the night to places as far afield as Pilley 'Brickyard', and Mrs Harriett Ann Knowles of Cherry Tree Street (formerly Miss Harriett Ann Rushworth and the sister of Mr John Rushworth, the piano tuner).

'Mums' were immobilized for a fortnight after each birth, staying in bed and sometimes encased in stiff linen 'binders', thought to help them to get their figures back. During this time, shopping and household chores were shared by husbands, mothers and other relations.

The Hallamshire Maternity Home, to which many of Hoyland's mothers started to go (and whose first name had to be changed to Chapeltown after the Royal Hallamshire was built) and the Maternity Block at St Helen's (now replaced by the Gynaecology Department of the Barnsley District General Hospital) were both opened early in the nineteen-forties. Their beds were gratefully booked by servicemen's wives who, with husbands in the Forces and mothers, sisters and neighbours going out to work to advance the war effort, had no-one to look after them at home. (The lingering prejudice against St Helen's is illustrated by the fact that a family friend, telling my mother that a neighbour of hers had recently given birth to a baby boy there, added, 'He wasn't born in the workhouse, you know.') Mothers stayed there a fortnight, the same length of time that they had spent as invalids at home.

Before this, except for any private homes (there was one run by a Sister Pilley at Sheffield), the only 'lying-in' hospitals available to Hoyland mothers were the small Pindar Oaks Maternity Home in Barnsley, down a lane behind the Traction Company's sheds and, in Sheffield, the Jessop Hospital for Women.

To my mother and her friends, who had grown up in the long shadow of Victorian prudery, 'Jessop's' was a word to be uttered in whispers with an obvious air of refined distaste, first glancing over their shoulders to ascertain whether I or any other child present was listening. One reason for their attitude may have been that, though this institution did an excellent job of handling naturally complicated deliveries, it was also the place to which women, not all of them socially deprived, were rushed for emergency surgery following 'back-street' and self-induced abortions.

No-one used the word 'hysterectomy'. My mother, if she had to mention this operation, called it with obvious embarrassment 'a Jessop's job'. Most people just spoke, with a morbid relish, of 'having everything taken away'. As a child I was so conditioned by the way in which my elders used to speak the name that, if I met anyone called Jessop, I felt instinctively uneasy in their presence. I also used to spend hours wondering what the strange operation could have been that my Uncle Fred's wife's sister had undergone and to which people still alluded from time to time with so fascinating an air of secrecy.

Prevalent Illnesses

In Hoyland between the Wars there were still cases of pulmonary tuberculosis, whose name was usually shortened to T.B., and some children at school had ugly scars puckering their necks where tubercular glands had been removed. It was to stop the spread of tuberculosis of the bone, a condition caused by drinking infected milk, that the Sanitary Inspectors of those days kept so close a watch on local dairy herds.

There were no quick-acting anti-tubercular drugs. Sometimes sufferers went away for lengthy stays to sanatoria, usually built, like that near Grassington in Wharfedale, in country places whose air was thought to benefit the lungs. Sometimes they just grew steadily worse at home. Nor did 'consumption', another name for it, confine itself to the under-privileged. Jack Cross, the youngest son of Rowland Cross the King Street grocer, suffered from this disease and spent years living in a chalet in the grounds of his father's town-centre residence, Greenfield House, the air out in the garden being deemed to be better for a man in his condition than that indoors.

Young women in their twenties would appear to have been a group especially at risk. I have several times heard my mother say, when speaking of some married couple of her generation, 'Of course, she's his second wife. His first died of consumption. She had that typically flawless T.B. complexion.'

Naturally, if a large family was packed into a small two-up-and-two-down house and could not afford the kind of food it needed to build up its resistance to disease, more than one member was likely to succumb. This led to a commonly-held belief that 'consumption' went in families, and resulted not from exposure to infection but from some form of hereditary weakness.

There seem to have been fewer cancer cases in those days. Perhaps there were fewer carcinogens added to food, and less pollution in the atmosphere. Perhaps some cases were incorrectly diagnosed. Or perhaps the almost furtive secrecy surrounding cancer cases resulted in fewer of them ever being heard about.

There was no hospital such as Weston Park in the area specializing in the treatment of cancer patients, and there were no hospices such as St Luke's at Sheffield, or the St Peter's Hospice being planned for Barnsley, for the care of the terminally ill. Some cases were treated with radium, but more sophisticated practices such as chemotherapy were not yet known. Once diagnosed and operated on, usually with little hope of success, patients were sent home, many of them to die, treated with increasingly large doses of morphia. Patients were rarely told the truth about their illness. When their relatives were, it was tantamount to hearing that a loved one had been given a sentence of death.

There must also have been cases of leukaemia, but this was a disorder of which one never heard. Perhaps it was sometimes erroneously treated as severe anaemia, a disease from which several people my parents knew were reputed to have died during the 'thirties.

Then as now, there were periodic outbreaks of such childhood infections as whooping cough, chickenpox and measles, which were considered part of the common lot and against none of which any immunization yet existed. Measles and whooping cough sometimes proved fatal and could leave very unpleasant aftereffects, measles tending to damage the ears or eyes. Nevertheless some parents believed that, when one child in a family caught an infection, it was best to put the rest in the same room, or even to let them sleep in the same bed, 'so that they can all get it over together.'

Scarlet fever and diphtheria, abbreviated in Hoyland to 'fever' and 'dip', were taken a good deal more seriously. Once a child was found to have caught either of these, it was rushed in a jolting wooden ambulance (commonly known as the 'fever van') to Kendray Hospital on the outskirts of Barnsley or, during the later 'thirties, to Wath Wood. A member of the Sanitary Inspector's staff then came to fumigate the parents' home, sealing the fireplaces, windows and doors of rooms the child had recently been in and leaving sulphur candles burning in them, a process thought to kill lingering germs.

A stay at Kendray (six weeks for diphtheria and five for scarlet fever) was traumatic, incarcerated by a high boundary wall beyond which nothing could be glimpsed of the outside world but a few neighbouring council 'semis' and the tip of the conical spoil heap at Barnsley Main. There were single-storey ward blocks in the grounds – Lambert, Arnott and the oddly-shaped Round Block with its tall central chimney and small semi-circular wards for scarlet fever cases, and Long Block for cases of diphtheria. Each had two wards, a boys' ward and a girls', bleak and cheerless with black iron bedsteads, green paintwork and walls, and naked light bulbs under flat white shades. Also, near to the gates, there was Old Block where typhoid, still found in this country in those days, was treated.

With no antibiotics then available for combating infection, the diphtheria cure was a distressing series of 'anti-toxin' injections. It was held that poison engendered in the system by the presence of the diphtheria bacillus could permanently damage the patient's heart. To reduce heart strain diphtheria sufferers were kept flat on their backs for the first three weeks, without even a pillow and with little to do except stare at the ceiling.

Hospital food, as I discovered when taken to Kendray a few days before my eighth birthday, was boring and plain. Breakfast comprised mugs of sickly cocoa and 'doorsteps' spread sparingly with margarine. ('Crust' being marginally tastier than 'crumb', when the breakfast trolley came into the ward it was mobbed by those patients no longer bedfast, elbowing each other and shouting, 'Gi' me a cruss!') Lunch started with what restaurants and hotels impressively call 'consommé julienne', and ended prosaically with rice pudding. The main course was boiled potatoes, cabbage and mince or boiled potatoes, turnip and fried fish. Tea was more 'doorsteps', served with mugs of tea. Such luxuries as boiled eggs and fresh fruit were served only if a patient's visitors brought them. The eggs were boiled hard and served without cups – perhaps the reason for the hard boiling was to prevent runny yolks from being spilt on bedclothes.

No-one between the Wars yet realized the need for a sick child to see its mother as often as possible. Visiting times were a mere two hours a week, one on Wednesday afternoon and one on Saturday, which meant that parents living out of town had to travel on buses crowded with market shoppers or football fans. Visitors were not allowed inside the wards. Instead they stood in all weathers on wooden steps talking through the windows with the patients, whose beds were swung round to make conversation easier.

Fortunately, protective injections against diphtheria became available during the 'thirties and were offered not only to infants but to older children, immunizing sessions being held at schools for those not already rendered immune the hard way by having had this disease. Future generations of children were thus spared the ordeal of being snatched from their families to spend dreary weeks as 'dip' patients in 'fever' hospitals.

During the spring of 1931, an unusual epidemic visited some parts of the West Riding. The official name of this disease was, I am told, cerebro-spinal fever. In Hoyland, though, where several cases occurred, 'spotted fever' was the name that it was known by.

The health authorities were gravely concerned by this outbreak of a frequently fatal infection. To kill any germs to which they had been exposed, Hoyland people were asked to call at the Town Hall where, in a little room on the first floor, a boiler filled with a mixture of Izal and water gave off a cloud of pungent-smelling vapour. When my mother and I went shopping, we usually called and stood for a short time, inhaling deeply. There was often someone in there whom we knew. Indeed, calling at the Town Hall for disinfection became something of a social ritual.

Whether the Izal fumes did any good or whether, by crowding together in such a small space, we were simply putting ourselves more at risk, is a matter for conjecture. In Hoyland as elsewhere in the county, however, like most epidemics this one spent itself after a few anxious weeks and was soon forgotten.

Then as now, medical fads and fancies came and went. A belief widely held during the 'twenties and 'thirties was that tonsils, whether septic or not, were best removed. When I was due to see the school doctor, my mother would admonish me, 'Breathe through your nose, or they'll say you've got to have your tonsils out.' A family friend, widowed in the First World War, sent her two sons away to boarding school, to free herself to take full-time employment. She received a letter from the headmaster, some weeks before the start of their first term, saying that it was a school rule that all pupils should have tonsillectomies before their admission.

Similarly many adults were told by their doctors, 'You must have your teeth out; they're poisoning you,' although the teeth in question seemed quite sound.

Dentists and Dentistry

During the inter-war years, there were two dental surgeries in Hoyland. Mr Harold Harvey, who when he came there was newly qualified, practised at Hoyland House, a detached, double-fronted Market Street residence on the site which is now by a coincidence that of Harvey and Richardson's chemist's shop. Mr Harvey also had a surgery at his home, situated at Firs Hill in Sheffield.

In his spare time he grew yellow tomatoes which, as a child, I was surprised to find just as tasty as the more tempting-looking red ones. I have since learnt that their name was Golden Sunrise, and that they were a particular favourite with Victorian gardeners.

Mr Paul Horwich, a small, elderly Jew who wore glasses and had a little moustache, lived at Huddersfield but practised at Hoyland. His surgery was in West Street at Woodhouse, a farmhouse previously occupied by the Allen family and once owned by the Townends.

It was to Mr Horwich that I was taken, following a custom prevalent in those days, to have two milk teeth extracted and so leave room for my upper front teeth to develop straight. I am told I proved such an exemplary patient that, instead of charging my mother for this, the dentist gave me a sixpence.

The surgery in those days was in the room to the left of the entrance. To reach it from the waiting room, one had to walk along a dimly-lit corridor. The dentist's chair was upholstered in some kind of brightly-patterned carpeting material. The colour of the ruby red spittoon was appropriately close to that of blood, which presumably it was meant to camouflage. Children being treated were distracted by the presence of a small Scottish terrier, Kiltie, whose name I found puzzling, unable to see what connection there could be between it and the brand of shoes that I was wearing.

When about 1932 Mr Horwich retired he was followed by Mr Albert Vernon Yates, a tall man with fair, wavy hair who, except for a brief spell in the Royal Navy, was in Hoyland until shortly after the Second World War. Though no dogs ever appeared in his surgery, he was an official of the Hoyland and District Canine Society. His small, dark, pretty daughter Beryl was a pupil at King Street towards the end of my time there. After leaving school she became a hairdresser, and opened a salon in a cottage adjacent to the garden of Woodhouse.

Mr Yates' successor, Mr Middleton, a tall, heavily-built man with spectacles, became seriously ill and died after being in Hoyland for only a short time. His successor was Mr Rajah R. Nalliah who, though semi-retired, still lives and practises at the house to which he came some forty years since.

Though they had two local dentists to choose from, some Hoyland patients preferred to go to Mr Willie Thorne of Chapeltown, one reason being that he was said to be more willing to give gas for the extraction of a single tooth than were his Hoyland colleagues, a fact which greatly endeared him to schoolchildren. He was the father of Margaret Thorne, now Mrs Alexander, a dentist in partnership at Hoyland Common with her husband, Mr Stanley Alexander, and was the son-in-law of Mr Job Birkinshaw, who was for fifty-eight years the organist at St Peter's, Tankersley.

Within the memory of many people alive during my childhood, however, there had been no full-time dentist in the area. The printer my father was apprenticed to spoke of going for extractions to a man who came each Friday evening to a small terrace house on Market Street, just beyond Ryecroft Place. The front room became a makeshift surgery where the family living at the house sat round enjoying the free spectacle or, as he put it, 'staring like savages'.

For seeing the dentist during the inter-war years there was no cut-and-dried appointments system. Patients went either when driven by toothache or when they could raise the courage to do so. To avoid having to take time off work, those not impelled by pain usually chose Saturday afternoons, when waiting rooms were full of anxious faces watching for the white-coated receptionist to appear with her peremptory 'Next, please.'

Few people tried to keep their teeth for life or ever took the trouble to have them filled. One reason may have been that this procedure, done with a pedal-operated drill, was tedious and painful. Another reason was perhaps to economize. The charge for an extraction was half-a-crown. It cost three times that sum to have a filling. For whatever cause, most waited till their teeth were past repair and then had them removed in a series of sessions 'with the needle'. To ensure that the gums had stopped shrinking and to obtain a good fit, six months were allowed to elapse before dentures were fitted. There were thus always plenty of people to be seen in the town with lantern jaws and Punch-and-Judy profiles calling attention to their toothlessness.

Pharmacies

One of Hoyland's first recorded pharmacists was Mr 'Jossy' Willey, who is said also to have extracted teeth and whose shop was at No. 1 King Street, the premises on the corner of George Street to which the Globe Tea Company moved later. He died in May 1903 and is interred in the extension to St Peter's Churchyard, where his family plot, surrounded by rusting iron railings and marked by a tall, urn-topped obelisk, lies to the right of the path leading from the upper gateway.

Mr Willey's successor at the pharmacy was Mr John E. Matthew, who at one time had a shop in Elsecar, at No. 41 Church

Street. By 1911 he had moved his Hoyland shop to No. 26 King Street, where the preparations he advertised included two veterinary medicines, Matthew's Roup Pills for Fowls and Matthew's Pig Powders, which were no doubt much called for in those days when pigs were kept by numerous small households.

During the 'twenties and 'thirties this chemist's shop, situated between the Co-op butcher's and the Maypole Dairy Company, was run by tall, taciturn Mr Ernest Parkin, Sr. and possessed a number of traditional features. Two pharmacist's bottles, one filled with green fluid, the other with red, were displayed high in its window, and tiers of small, square mahogany drawers, inscribed with strange names in gold lettering, covered the lower half of the wall behind the counter. One which intrigued me as a child was 'myrrh', with its evocation of the Nativity story.

Until 1935, when he moved to Ipswich after marrying Miss Marion Hough, the King Street teacher, and settled there in business on his own, Mr Parkin's eldest son Arthur assisted him, besides practising at the same premises as an optician. The Parkins also had twin sons, Ernest and John, the first of whom worked with his father for a time, served with the Forces in the Second World War and took over the pharmacy in his own name in 1946. He stayed there for roughly a quarter of a century, until 1972, when the business was bought by Mr David Harvey, who is now one of the partners in the firm of Harvey and Richardson. Now the pharmacy has moved to Market Street, and the King Street premises are shared by a boutique and an insurance broker.

There were two other pharmacies in Hoyland during the Parkins' time. On the lower corner of Booth Street and King Street, with its door across the corner and a large clock dominating the wall behind the counter, was that owned by the Co-op. Like all Co-op shops, it was well patronized thanks to the dividend on purchases. There were some, however, who expressed the view that the drugs used there were inferior to those which were dispensed at Matthew's.

The manager during my early childhood was a stout man named Watts, who dressed for work in a grey warehouse coat. He did not live at the manager's house, the dark brick, double-fronted No. 3 Booth Street. This was occupied by Mrs Edith Grimes, an eccentric widow whose husband, whom I dimly recall as a tall man with glasses and a dark moustache, was a former pharmacist who had died in harness. (Mrs Grimes hit the local headlines briefly in the late 'thirties when, in a raffle at the Congregational Chapel, she won a handbag given by the Queen, the present Queen Mother.) Mr Watts' successor, Mr George Irvin Atkinson, moved from Hoyland to Barnsley to start his own business at a shop in Agnes Road.

Like most chemists, the Co-op sold various items not strictly associated with pharmacy. As a child, I was sent there from time to time to buy Old Calabar dog biscuits for our Labrador retriever. They were iron-hard and several inches square, with scraps of dark dried meat baked into them, and had to be smashed with a hammer before being put into her feeding bowl. The assistant must have cursed inwardly on seeing me, since they were kept upstairs and he had to walk along the shop and up a flight of stairs to weigh them.

Since it closed as a chemist's about 1970, the shop has served a number of purposes. For a short time it was a branch office of the Department of Health and Social Security. Today it is a ladies' hairdresser's.

The third pharmacy was some distance down the street in the first of the two single-storey shops, which have now been made into a hairdresser's, between Storrs' bakery and the Futurist. Its proprietor, tall, stout Mr George Young, who as a youth had worked for Mr Matthew, lived with his wife, their daughter Margaret and Arthur their son at No. 192 King Street, one of the houses at which for a time Miss Alice Emily Caws had her school.

Mr Young died prematurely during the 'forties. His widow ran the business for a time and then sold it to Mr Reginald F. Wainwright whose successor, Mr David John Richardson, closed this King Street shop and moved to Market Street, in partnership with Mr David Harvey, after the Duke Street Health Centre was built. The wheel came full circle when Harvey and Richardson, after Dr

Donald Fairclough and his partners moved back from the Health Centre to Walderslade, opened a branch next to Mr Richardson's old shop, in the premises which in pre-war years were Storrs' bakery.

Dr William Smith Booth

Among the patent medicines sold at Matthew's were Dr Booth's Gravel Pills, Tic and Neuralgia Powders, Lung and Chest Elixir, Nit Ointment and Parry (a liquid, said to contain paregoric, for soothing fractious infants).

Dr William Smith Booth, to whose formulae they were prepared, is first heard of in Hoyland in 1855. Called in his house deeds an apothecary, he purchased a triangular plot of land from two maltster brothers, Robert and William Wigfield, the grandsons of Joseph Wigfield, a nail merchant, whose names are frequently encountered in Hoyland records of those days. The land, which had previously been used as a garden, was situated in the Nether Field (a name dating from the days when villages had open fields cultivated in strips) and lay just to the north of the unpaved lane which was to become King Street.

On this site the doctor built Netherfield House, a detached, four-square residence of Blacker Hill sandstone, incorporating a surgery and waiting room and with accommodation for himself, his family and their servants. An interesting sidelight on Victorian hygiene is afforded by the fact that, despite being a purpose-built doctor's house with rooms ten feet high in order to ensure an ample supply of air, it had no bathroom. Its only water supply came from a well in a corner of the garden, whence it was piped to a pump on the stone sink in the large servants' kitchen. The only sanitation was an earth closet next to an ash pit at the far end of the yard.

With Hoyland's population expanding rapidly after the opening of the Milton Iron Works and that of the Hoyland and Elsecar (later the Hoyland Silkstone) Colliery, Dr Booth had chosen a propitious time to put up his brass plate there. Further proof of his business acumen is provided by the fact that, when a joiner fell behind with paying his bills, the doctor allowed him to work off the debt, no doubt several times over, by doing the new house's woodwork free of charge, including the window shutters, panelled doors and elaborately-turned staircase banisters.

A grandson of the doctor's, William Firth, a partner in the firm of C. Firth and Sons, whose mother's maiden name was Mary Booth, once told my father that his grandfather had a liking for gin, which as a child he was sent out to fetch, twopennyworth each time. The tale also survives of how one day the doctor, visiting a friend's for tea, lurched (perhaps under the influence of gin) against his hostess's wobbly round table, sending food and china crashing to the floor. These seem to be the only anecdotes extant about a man whom one instinctively knows to have been a 'character'.

His name is, nevertheless, perpetuated in that of Booth Street, developed along the eastern side of his land.

After Dr Booth's death in November 1880 the house was let to a succession of tenants and was then sold in 1897. It was bought by my father in 1939, and was later bequeathed to my mother, who in turn left it in her will to me.

CHAPTER TEN

Streets and Home Life

WHEN HOYLAND still lived mainly by agriculture, before the Milton Iron Works and later the Hoyland Silkstone Colliery changed its appearance and lifestyle, most of its homes were farms or cottages built along the level half-mile of Market Street, whose past importance is attested by the fact that people of my parents' generation called walking on that street 'going on the Town'.

In the inter-war period, just as today, most of Hoyland's public buildings could be found there. On the right, as one proceeded from 'Cross's Corner', were the Strafford Arms (now called The Beggar and the Gentleman), the Hoyland Cinema, the old Market Place, the 'Little Infants' School' (now St Andrew's Parish Hall) and, fifty yards further on, the Post Office. On the left were the National Provincial Bank, the old Wesleyan Chapel (now Charisma Antiques) and, some distance away, St Andrew's Church and the original Market Street or 'Board' School.

It was also a street of large and imposing houses. Highfield House, a few yards past the Post Office, was the home of Mr Harry Cecil Utley, a retired Elsecar Main Colliery cashier and amateur 'cellist whose son, Harry Utley, Jr., lived on there after his father's death till the 'seventies, when he and his wife moved to Hemingfield. In the first Mr Utley's days the grounds included not only a lawn, flower-beds and fruit trees but, at the back of the house, a crown bowling green in which he took a justifiable pride.

The next property beyond Highfield House, standing well back and known as The Meadow, was the home of grey-bearded Mr Luke Dickinson, who died in August 1935, and his son-in-law and daughter, Mr and Mrs James Taylor, whose butcher's shop is now the Hoyland office of Selway and Co., the estate agents. This house, with its range of outbuildings and adjacent pasture land, was clearly a place where small-scale farming and the slaughter of beasts for retail sale had been combined. In those days there was still a small shop to one side of the gate, with a shuttered window facing towards the street, from which freshly-killed meat had once been sold. (A similar shop, now put to another use, survives at Wentworth opposite the old churchyard.) This connection with the meat trade was maintained when, for some years after the Taylors left, The Meadow was owned by Mr Frederick Daniel Bean, the King Street and Platts Common pork butcher.

Bark House, the long, low residence behind the present Fire Station, was the home of Mr William ('Billy') Barber, an elderly character with a reputation for stinginess and dourness, whom my father nicknamed 'Old Sobersides' since he was very rarely known to smile, and from whom Barber Street has taken its name. Mr Barber died in 1933. Soon after the outbreak of the Second World War the house was acquired by a family named Watson, who turned the outbuildings into a pickle factory (which seemed something of a gamble at a time when the rationing of meat was imminent), selling their red cabbage, onions and piccalilli under the trade name 'Montagu Products'. The factory stayed in business for a while after the War ended; then it closed and Bark House reverted to being a private residence, which was modernized a few years ago and, seemingly as a pun on its name, now displays on its roof a dog-shaped weather-vane.

Last on that side of the road but by no means least, its spacious grounds at Hoyland Green extending from Jump Lane (now renamed Greenside) halfway to the junction of Market Street and Hawshaw Lane, was the town's most prestigious dwelling-house, Hoyland Hall which, with its wings rising to different heights, would have made a fitting home for the heroine of a nineteenth-century romantic novel. Thought to date from the late eighteenth century and to have been erected for a private owner, the Hall had associations for many years with the Hoyland district's heavy industry. For some years prior to 1841 it was the home of Henry Hartop, a partner at the Milton Iron Works who left to run the Works at Elsecar. Forty years later it was offered for sale as part of the estate of a descendant of William Vizard, the first owner of Hoyland Silkstone, and by the 'twenties of this century it had long served as the official residence of the Hoyland Silkstone Colliery manager. From Hoyland Silkstone's closure during that decade until some time after the Second World War, when it was used for educational purposes before being left to become partially derelict, the managers of Rockingham Colliery lived there. The first of these was Mr Gibson Reid who, after his retirement, managed a little drift mine of his own somewhere in the Wortley or Thurgoland area. His successor was Mr McNeil whose daughter Edith, a few years my junior, was at Ecclesfield Grammar School during part of the time I spent there.

On the far side of the street near the town centre, next to the former Post Office and where Harvey and Richardson's pharmacy now stands (and not to be confused with Hoyland Hall) was Hoyland House, a more modest stone-built structure with a small front garden and with two large square bays flanking a front door with a frosted pane. This house, used as a dental surgery by Mr Harold Harvey, was one of three Market Street properties which had medical or dental associations. Riversdale, the detached house on the corner of Duke Street, which during the inter-war years still retained its original sash windows, had in earlier years been the home and surgery of Dr William Ritchie. The doctor died in October 1930 and his wife Susannah in January 1943. In the house they left two of their daughters, Janey and Mary, genteel middle-aged spinsters who might have stepped from the pages of *Cranford*. Next door, at gloomy-looking Ivy House, with its fringed window blinds, heavy, dark green front door and high-walled garden with tall poplar trees (today transformed out of all recognition into a light, pleasant Methodist Church), lived and practised Dr Barclay Wiggins, Sr.

The stone-fronted house named Brentwood, on the corner of Spring Gardens, is of comparatively recent date. It was constructed about 1910 for Mr Herbert Garner, a tall, heavily-built High Street ironmonger and a founder-member of the John Knowles Church. After the sudden death of Mr Garner in 1932, his widow moved to a smaller house in West Street and Brentwood was sold to Mr David Clayton, the furniture dealer at No. 9 King Street. After the Claytons went to live in Barnsley, where they had another furniture and antique shop near to the traffic lights on Sheffield Road, the house was occupied for several years by a genial, rotund man named Silverwood, who owned and with his two brothers-in-law ran Hoyland's three picture houses, the Kino, Cinema and Futurist, and who pioneered the sale there of ice lollies (especially popular while sweets were rationed), to which he gave the descriptive name 'fruiticles'.

Between Brentwood and the east end of St Andrew's Church there was a property known as Kirk Farm, a charming house built end-on to the road, from which a small paddock separated it, which looked as if it had been spirited to Hoyland from some peaceful corner of the Yorkshire Dales. Between the Wars it was the residence of a brother and sister, Charles and Jessie Guest, both of them teachers at Market Street School. Not long after the end of the Second World War, six council houses were built on the paddock (some of the first of Hoyland's post-war homes), and the farmhouse itself was pulled down some years later, its site becoming that of the St Andrew's Centre.

The pleasant, almost rural atmosphere exuded by Market

Street was further enhanced by the original St Andrew's Vicarage, donated to the church by Earl Fitzwilliam, who also gave the land the church stands on. (Some people still alive during my childhood always referred to it as 'Clifton Villa', since it had earlier been the residence of Luke and Peggy Clifton, who lie buried with some of their children who died young, including their twin sons Mark and Luke, near the Main Street wall of Wentworth old churchyard.)

Although small by vicarage standards, it had character and stood in sizeable grounds, with a long lawn sloping towards the street in front, a vegetable garden approached through a stone arch behind and, at the back of the church, a large orchard. In the yard were two bothy-style cottages, each of which had one room up and one room down, built as homes for a gardener and a coachman.

Like The Meadow, the house on the corner of Mell Avenue which has recently been given a 'face-lift' bore signs of being erected as the home of a butcher-cum-smallholder. In the interwar years it was occupied by the butcher Mr Thomas Frederick Guest, who also had a Platts Common shop and was a brother of Charles and Jessie Guest, the teachers. At that time a shop and a large slaughter-house stood at right-angles to the house end and the pavement.

Mr Guest's wife, formerly Miss Gertrude Joll, who achieved the distinction of living to the age of a hundred, dying on 19th June, 1985, was a sister of Mr Ernest Joll, the china shop proprietor. The Guests' twin sons, George Donald and William Edward, qualified in pharmacy and accountancy respectively. 'Eddie' Guest married Miss Jean Cooper, the elder daughter of Mr and Mrs Harry Cooper, the High Street drapers and outfitters, who resided at Cloughlands in South View Road.

The old house with long-and-short stonework round its windows standing back from the road, its grounds adjoining those of Market Street School, was the family home of the Hagues, who for several generations were one of Hoyland's most reliable and respected building firms. Its occupants during my childhood were Mr and Mrs Arthur Hague, the son and daughter-in-law of Mr Mark Hague, and their sons James and Harold.

Interesting though these Market Street houses are, by far the most historically important of the buildings associated with that area are two pulled down several decades ago, Manor Farm and the Tithe Barn.

The barn was situated in Tithe Laithe, on the plot of land now occupied by Westcroft. ('Laith' is an old Norse word, meaning a barn, brought to the North of England by the Vikings and still occasionally to be heard there. On bitter days in winter, for example, when draughts crept round our door and window frames, my mother was frequently heard to say, 'It's like sitting in a laith.') When Hoyland formed part of the parish of Wath-upon-Dearne, it was built for storing the tenth part or 'tithe' of each Hoyland farmer's produce due from him to the Vicar of Wath. In the late eighteenth century, however, even before the Tithe Commutation Acts replaced such payments in kind with fixed money charges, it had been made into four cottages, though the massive stone arch once surmounting its great double doors was still clearly visible in the long wall facing towards the street.

A few years after the end of the Second World War, at a time when many old houses were being pulled down, the Hoyland Nether Urban District Council demolished the cottages as slum property. If only they had survived a few years more into this conservation-conscious age, their fate might have been very different.

Manor Farm, a large, gaunt-looking house of dark-coloured stone standing on the site that is now occupied by the misleadingly-named Manor House Close, had religious connections of a different kind, having been closely associated with the rise of Methodism in the town from the time when, in the mid-eighteenth century, Mr John Johnson of Barley Hall (an early Methodist stronghold) came to live there. From then until 1809, when Hoyland's original Wesleyan Chapel was built on land given by Mr

William Gray, a successor of Mr Johnson's at the farm, prayer meetings used to take place in the farmhouse. Also, according to tradition, John Wesley preached there and scratched his name on one of the window panes.

A late Victorian occupant of Manor Farm was Mr James Duke Gray (presumably a descendant of William Gray), who seems to have been a memorable character, since he was still being talked of during my childhood, one of the sayings attributed to him being 'There's nowt i' this world like a cup o' good tea.' He had also obviously been looked up to. Nobody called him 'James Gray' or 'Old Jimmy Gray'. He was always given his full set of names, prefixed by the title 'Mister'. His simple headstone can be seen in St Peter's Churchyard.

By the 'twenties, however, the farm was being run by another Methodist, Mr Edwin Fisher, who was a brother of Norman Fisher, the Market Street draper and tobacconist. In 1930 Edwin Fisher suffered a tragic loss when his elder son Albert Lister, aged twenty-four, was working on a farm in North Dakota, where he had gone with his friend Reginald Hirst Allen, the youngest son of George Hirst Allen, the grocer, at a time when North America was luring young people disillusioned with post-war Britain. While cleaning out a well, he was overcome and killed by poisonous gas. A great sensation was caused in Hoyland when his body, embalmed and dressed in his best Sunday suit, was brought home in an American-style casket for burial in Kirk Balk Cemetery.

The Fishers' farm labourer, William Fitzjohn, who came from Cambridgeshire, was a tall man with a large grey moustache, whose stoop may have been the result of bending over the handles of the horse-drawn plough. His wife Louisa, a plump, homely woman, hailed from the Huddersfield area and spoke with a West Yorkshire accent, always for instance calling the oven 'th' ooven'. She was a devout Methodist and a member of the Chapel sisterhood. With their son Arthur, who worked in the building trade and married in the 'thirties, they lived in the low-ceilinged farm cottage, with its living room and scullery downstairs and two bedrooms (one leading out of the other) above, behind the Market Place. At one end of the sizeable garden they kept a few fowls. As a child I was sent there on Saturday mornings for eggs. Mrs Fitzjohn sold them by the shillingsworth, as was customary in those days, the number varying from nine in late spring, when the hens were laying well, to six or less during the winter months.

In 1929 the Fishers moved to Hardwick Lane Farm at Aston, near Sheffield. Another link with Hoyland was forged, though, when their son George Edmund, who still farms at Aston, married Miss Mary Joll, the third daughter of Ernest Joll, the King Street china salesman. Manor Farm's tenancy was then taken over by Mr Thomas Lodge who with his wife, four sons and four daughters had previously been living at Jump Farm, a building standing back from Greenside Lane, with four huge ash trees guarding its approach, on the site now occupied by Parkersell. Following an old country tradition, Lodges moved into the house on New Year's Day and took over the land attached to it on 1st May. Mr Lodge's brother, William Henry Lodge (known by his neighbours' children as 'Nunc' Lodge), farmed at Upper Hoyland Hall, and a link with the Fishers was created when Norman Fisher, whose first wife had died, married Miss Daisy Lodge, one of William Henry's daughters.

About this time Mr Fitzjohn retired, going first to Cherry Tree Street and then to Hill Crest. The work of ploughing, harrowing, sowing and reaping Manor Farm's arable fields in the ensuing years fell to Mr Lodge's two eldest sons, Thomas and Clifford who, when the farm was taken by the Council for building land after the Second World War, moved to the Old Hall Farm at Tankersley and Spring Wood Farm down Stead Lane respectively.

Being too big for even a large family's needs, the farmhouse had at some time in the past been divided into two. The part of it facing towards Market Street, behind the two tall poplars which still stand guarding the entrance to Manor House Close, was occupied by Mr and Mrs Alfred Vaines, a middle-aged couple often seen walking out accompanied by their well-fed spaniel dog. Mr Vaines was a colliery fan man. A further Methodist connection lay in the fact that Mrs Vaines' sister Miss Hilda Smith, who lived with them, was a worshipper at the Wesleyan Chapel a short distance away.

The farm buildings, grouped round a yard to the east of the house, had several unusual features. The barn roof was supported by huge tree trunks roughly hewn into shape with an adze. Situated in the stackyard behind the barn, and covered by a half-octagonal roof, was a piece of archaic machinery known as a 'gin race'. Designed rather like a supermarket turnstile, it had four sections in each of which a horse could be harnessed. As the horses plodded round, their movement worked threshing machinery in the barn itself. By my early years, however, the gin race had fallen into disuse, and a threshing machine contractor was hired whose arrival was signalled when, some autumn morning, glancing from our kitchen window towards the farm, one saw clouds of smoke and heard machinery whirring, an experience which always aroused in me a feeling of irrational excitement.

The farmland, which was owned by Earl Fitzwilliam, covered roughly the same area as is occupied today by the Greenfield Estate, stretching from behind the house and yard to Greenside Lane, bordering the valley locally called Jump Pit, and abutted on by the ends of old Cherrytree Street, old Barber Street, Bethel Street (most of which has now been pulled down) and Booth Street. The steep section below the farmhouse was rough pasture and was used solely for grazing cows, in those days mainly brown-and-white shorthorns. It was traversed by an eroded path from the stackyard corner to a 'go-through' leading into Greenside Lane. In Hoyland this part was known as 'Jump Fields'; conversely, it was 'Hoyland Fields' to Jump people. The rest of the fields, one of which contained an old air shaft which was fenced in by a high, square brick wall, were arable, being planted in rotation with wheat, oats, potatoes and turnips. Access for carts and waggons was provided by a track which ran parallel to Market Street, skirting the garden wall of Greenfield House (this stretch was always known as the 'Field Top'), and then turned at right-angles and descended towards the hedge forming the boundary with Jump Pit.

STREETS AND HOME LIFE

Besides its gentlemen's residences, Market Street during the 'twenties and 'thirties still had a number of old cottages, some of them once the homes of nail-makers. Stone-built and with low ceilings and solid floors, they were mostly grouped in yards and short terraces. Behind Hoyland House there was Waterton's Yard, named after a nail-making family; off Tithe Laithe there was Wood's Yard. There were cottages up curiously-named Little Leeds, which once possessed a nail forge, while across the street behind the Post Office, almost forming a separate hamlet, was a group with the charmingly rustic name Ryecroft. Royston Hill till the late 'thirties was a short street of small terrace homes and opened off Market Street, opposite its junction with Greenside Lane. When some of these were threatened with demolition their owner, William Allen the architect, gave them for a peppercorn rent to the Boy Scouts, who converted them into the present Scout Hall.

King Street

The King Street area, unlike Market Street, is able to boast few buildings of great age or architectural interest. There were still people living in my childhood who recalled the days when it was just a lane, unpaved and for much of its length not built along.

Between the two World Wars, just as today, the section from the Town Hall to Barber Street held the town centre's longest stretch of shops. Meanwhile, nevertheless, it has undergone great changes. Three beer houses (the original Turf Tavern, The Five Alls and the Rock Inn) have disappeared, as have the Mount Tabor and Bethel Chapels. New shops with flats above them have replaced some which pre-dated Queen Victoria's reign, between the corner of Market Street and Green Street, and a clean sweep has been made of most of the homes and also of a number of little shops that once bordered the road between the end of Bethel Street and Barber Street.

The stretch of King Street below Barber Street looked much the same in the 'twenties and 'thirties as now. On the right, between No. 103 and the King Fish Bar (in those days Mr and

Mrs Fred Sabin's fish-and-chip shop), was a small wooden shop occupied by a cobbler named Wright, who lived at Birdwell and whose little daughter, Margaret, was a pupil at King Street School. The shop at the corner of Gill Street sold groceries and sweets. It was run by Mrs Ibbotson, the wife of Herbert Ibbotson, one of the town's door-to-door greengrocers.

Until the new Methodist Church and Flat were opened in 1975, the large stone house just below Noble Street was the Methodist (formerly the Wesleyan) Manse. Below this was the County Library housed, just as it was destined to remain until early April 1987, on the first floor of the Miners' Welfare Hall, which had been built in 1924. In the early 'thirties the Librarian was a tall, stooping man with a white moustache, who lived in a shabby-looking old house above the entrance to Sebastopol. His successor, still remembered by many borrowers, was Alwyn Whittlestone of Elsecar, a small man who worked in a grey warehouse coat and held and voiced profoundly Socialist views. Also, each week a baby clinic used to be held on the ground floor of the 'Welfare'.

Across the street above High Cottages was a small wooden shop, painted dark green, where a family called Whittlestone sold greengroceries. No. 174, a short distance below and now made into a private residence, was the Britannic Assurance Company's Hoyland office.

In some of the little streets leading off King Street, however, more notable changes have taken place. Green Street, marked on my house deeds of 1855 as an 'occupation road', was a cul-de-sac ending at the stone wall which now separates its made and unmade sections. To the left of this wall a flight of worn stone steps, two on the upper side, three on the lower, gave pedestrians access to the 'Field Top', the cart track bordering the land of Manor Farm which provided a short cut to Market Street, particularly to the Post Office, for the people of Booth, Bethel and Barber Streets. (My mother told how, in their early married days, she and my father were wakened each Monday morning by the sound of clogs clattering over the steps as people from Jump came to

Guest's or Naylor's pawn shop, to pawn Sunday suits until the following weekend.)

To the left of the street, its grounds stretching as far as the Cinema and the old Market Place, was Greenfield House, built by the Knowles family in about 1880 and during the period between the Wars the home of Rowland Cross, the grocer. A handsome building of dressed Brighouse stone, with a glass sun parlour along one side and an ornamental dormer in its roof, it faced on to a large lawn whose centrepiece was a white marble fountain. (One of my earliest memories is of standing at an upstairs window in Netherfield House and watching the wedding photographs being taken, between the fountain and the sun parlour, when one of Rowland Cross's daughters, Miss Gladys Cross, married a young man named Uttley from Harley.)

Screened from the lawn by a summer-house and greenhouse was a large vegetable garden, bordered on its street side by sycamore trees whose boughs provided places to which to attach bunting at Coronation and Jubilee time and the largest of which, opposite our house, I fancifully called 'our apple tree'. The gardener for a time during the inter-war years was George Newstead, who lived conveniently near in Booth Street and, being a native of East Anglia, was spoken of by the nickname 'Norfolk George'.

After Rowland Cross's death during the 'thirties, his widow Elizabeth Cross remained in residence at Greenfield. After she died in 1945 at a time when, though the price of 'semis' was soaring, large properties were tending to hang fire, the house was sold, reputedly for £800, to Samuel Smith's Brewery Company of Tadcaster, which in 1960 erected the new 'Turf' (now The Kestrel) on the vegetable garden. After being let to a succession of tenants who had come into the district at the time when open-cast coal was being mined at Wentworth the old house, stranded in its remnant of garden, was pulled down in November 1965.

On the other side of Green Street, behind the Co-op drapery store (now a furniture shop), was the Co-op reading room, much frequented by certain senior citizens. This two-storey brick structure, with its outside staircase ascending from the yard behind the shop, had a rather dingy and run-down appearance. A mysterious-looking door facing the street seemed never to be opened.

Next, at an angle to the unmade road, came the row of three cottages with no back doors owned by Mr John E. Matthew, the pharmacist. In No. 1 lived one of the town's eccentrics, 'Saddler Jack' Kennerley. In No. 3 during the 'twenties lived the lamplighter George Worthy and his family. In No. 5 lived Mr and Mrs Owen Hazell and their son Jack. Mrs Hazell was Mrs Kennerley's niece. Both Mr and Mrs Hazell worshipped at the John Knowles Church, where Mrs Hazell was at one time the magazine secretary. Lastly, occupying the corner site between Booth Street and the 'Field Top', there was Netherfield House, built by Dr William Smith Booth, where my parents set up home after their marriage in August 1920.

Booth Street itself, named in the doctor's honour, had been built piecemeal and was mainly a street of small homes, some of them in pairs, others in short terraces, some built of brick but most of local sandstone. The oak tree at its junction with Green Street was in the garden of No. 31, a semi-detached cottage, facing Jump, with a porch resembling a weather-house. Here lived Miss Lydia Ramsey, a slight, elderly woman with glasses who had been companion-housekeeper to Mrs Bartlett, founder and benefactor of the John Knowles Church. Next door lived Mr and Mrs Walter Shepherd, who were the caretakers at King Street School, together with Fred their son.

A peculiarity of Booth Street was that it contained back-to-back properties. (Although there were a few at Elsecar, they were not characteristic of the area.) There were ten of them built end-on to the street, where Mr P.W. Shaw has his building yard, and designed on an ingenious principle whereby the attic staircase of each house fitted over the main stairs of that behind it. In these cramped homes, with one room to each floor, large, cheerful families were born and raised; everyone knew and helped everyone else, and friends and relatives from miles away were housed and entertained at holiday periods. (My mother often jokingly remarked that the walls were obviously made of elastic.)

There were always plenty of children in the street, toddlers who played on the pavements but never seemed any the worse for the tumbles they took and older ones who strayed further afield, causing mums in overalls to call stridently from entry ends before meals and at bed time.

Booth Street's informal friendliness reached its peak on the evening of November 5th each year, young and old gathering round a bonfire in 'Parr's Yard', behind a row of four terrace houses owned by the local building firm, John Parr and Sons, two of whose members, Herbert Parr and his half-brother Ernest, lived at Nos. 25 and 23, across the street from us. Each child took its own fireworks. Mine usually consisted of Catherine wheels, chrysanthemum fountains, snow-storms and other pretty and quiet ones. I recall the panic, however, when one year a boy produced a 'Devil among the Tailors', which exploded and threw jumping crackers out, sending the assembled company scurrying for shelter.

More sombre memories dating from the 'thirties concern the deaths of two women living in the street. According to a custom which in those days was still occasionally being observed, on the day of each funeral the open coffin was placed on trestles outside the home of the deceased, to give passers-by a final glimpse of her and also a chance to pay their last respects.

Though Booth Street may have lacked social pretensions, it still had a rather more prosperous air than neighbouring Bethel Street, whose drab two-up-and-two-down terraces opened off narrow pavements. The communal yard between one of these and the cart track leading down from the 'Field Top' was always strewn with litter and tin cans. My father nicknamed it 'Salmon Tin Row', remembering how during his childhood days salmon had been one of the earliest and most popular tinned foods to reach the shops. (Since it had been so cheap, he always used to call it 'poor man's friend'.)

This street also boasted two larger buildings. A detached stone residence behind Parr's Yard had in living memory been a lodging house kept by the Smiths, a family some of whose members ran

Hoyland businesses between the Wars. Across the road, nearer to King Street, was a former chapel used for a few years during the 'thirties as a printing works. It was from this original Bethel Chapel, erected about 1860, that the street had taken its incongruously biblical name, a name which was perhaps the reason why this part of Hoyland at one time enjoyed the sobriquet 'The Holy Land'.

It was there and in similar streets on the same side of King Street that, during this period, many of Hoyland's low-income families lived. Victoria Street (on one corner of which stood the Queen's Head), Rock Mount (branching off above Goddard's, now Hague's, butcher's shop) and Elizabeth Street (at right-angles to Rock Mount and running almost parallel to King Street) likewise consisted of small terrace homes, most of which had been built of stone quarried locally. They were pulled down under a slum clearance programme implemented by the Urban District Council towards the end of its lifetime.

It was on the other side of the main road that the town's most memorably named street was to be found. Built by Mr George Dawes in the eighteen-fifties to house some of his workmen at the Milton Iron Works, it was called Sebastopol in memory of the siege of the port of Sebastopol on the Black Sea coast during the Crimean War. (Similarly, various pubs and terraces were given the name 'Alma' in honour of a French and British victory over the Russians which was gained beside the river of that name.) Yet, despite its patriotic origin, the word sometimes led to confusion. The story is told of how a young woman who came to stay with some relatives who lived there received a letter which had been addressed 'c/o Sir Baster Poole'. In conversation, its four syllables were usually shortened to 't'Pool'.

The 'Pool' plunged steeply towards Millhouses Street from between two shops (Humphrey's bakery, later Green's fish-and-chip shop, and a small general store) facing the 'Queen's'. Its six terraces of rough, dark-coloured brick had iron-framed windows and stood, fish-bone style, at right-angles to the roadway. The bottom two enjoyed an open view over their front gardens and the 'Cinder Hills' towards the Elsecar Reservoir and Wentworth.

Grown shabby and with rather a raffish reputation, Sebastopol survived for decades after the Iron Works closed in the early eighteen-eighties. Like Victoria Street, Elizabeth Street and Rock Mount, it was demolished and its tenants were re-housed some time between 1960 and 1974.

Milton Road

Until the present steep, wide Milton Road was constructed about 1930, this main road out of Hoyland towards the south, linking it with the old Barnsley to Sheffield turnpike, was the gentle curve kinder to draught horses whose weathered surface, littered with loose stones, loops from the top to the bottom of the hill.

Adjacent to the then unspoilt countryside of Spring Wood and the Cloughs, with panoramic views towards Wentworth and with amenities comprising three small shops, a 'chippy', a wall post-box and two pubs (the 'Furnace' and the now-unlicensed 'Forge'), Milton (few people added the word 'Road') appeared at the time at which I first recall it almost to constitute a separate village. Some people clearly thought of it that way. There is at least one stone in St Peter's Churchyard on which the deceased is described not as 'of Hoyland' or 'of this parish' but simply as 'of Milton'.

The three ponds which had supplied water to the Iron Works (two at the Furnace Inn side of the road, one at the other) were not yet landscaped, the environment not being thought of then as of much consequence; nevertheless, they had already become a favourite haunt of anglers. Beyond them rose the green hump of Primrose Hill, crowned with the long, low, rural-looking house in which Mr Reuben Simpson, under-manager of the drift mine near Spring Wood, lived with his devoutly Methodist wife, their son George Harry and their daughter Connie. The hill itself was as countrified as its name. The Simpsons kept bees and sold honey from them and, in a field nearby, Tom Cutts the coal leader pastured his cart horse, Bob.

To the left, as one proceeded down Milton Road, there were no buildings between Syddenrath (the home of Mr Morton Davy, a partner in the firm of J. Davy & Co. Ltd., the ironfounders) and Millhouses Street at the hill foot until, during the early 'thirties, the old people's bungalows in Milton Crescent and along Millhouses Street itself were built. Above them were a number of allotment gardens. The land between Milton Crescent and Gill Street, on which Sebastopol spread apron-wise, comprised a triangular acre or so of rough grass, stretching from George Street to Millhouses Street and with a path running down either side, known as the 'Council Fields' (some people still called it the 'Local Board Fields') and, fenced off from this by wooden railings, more allotments.

Opposite the bottom of the Council Fields and end-on to Millhouses Street was a tall building which had been made into two cottages, but had originally been a corn mill. (They were the houses the street took its name from.)

West Street

West Street, formerly known as Finkle Street, a name found elsewhere in this part of Yorkshire, at the start of the 'twenties still possessed several noteworthy features. Beyond the Old Post Office Buildings, which stood partly in West Street, partly in Milton Road, were two of the yards, Naylor's and Belmont, which once formed an architectural feature of Hoyland. They were separated by a large, dingy-looking building owned by the baker and confectioner, Mr Albert Woolley. On the ground floor of this there were three shops. The accommodation above the two larger ones, 'Woolley's Rooms', for many years housed the Bethany Mission. It had also once been a Liberal Club.

My parents told of how a revivalist preacher once held an open-air meeting in Naylor's Yard, where he told his listeners unequivocally, 'You people of Naylor's Yard will all go to Hell.' Some absent-minded member of his audience responded with a fervent 'Praise the Lord!'

Belmont Yard, which led to the old Belmont Club, had in

earlier years been the site of a malt kiln owned by the Wigfield brothers, Robert and William, from whom William Smith Booth in 1855 purchased the land he built Netherfield House on. (In the days when most households brewed their own beer, the maltster's seems to have been a common trade in this part of South Yorkshire. Kilns are also known to have existed at Rawmarsh and Thorpe Hesley.) The Wigfields had nail-making connections, too, and from contemporary records seem to have taken an active part in Hoyland's social life.

At the start of the 'twenties there were no other buildings on that side above Fieldhead, home of the Allott family, three generations of which were doctors in the town, until one reached St Helen's Catholic School, except the two shops (now converted into houses) below the gateway into the Town Field. The first shop was a butcher's. The second was a grocery and sweet shop run by Mr George Eaden, whose son Eric became a professional violinist and at the start of his career played in the Municipal Orchestra at Whitby.

Above the school and the site of St Helen's Church (not completed until 1929) were the old council yard and, between this and Brooke Street, a short row of cottages on the corner of which was a small grocery and general store run by Mrs E. Burgin, the mother-in-law of George Chambers, the High Street fish-and-chip shop and off-licence proprietor. (Like many grocers, Mrs Burgin also sold patent medicines, those which she used to advertise including a useful-sounding specific, 'No-Ake' powders.)

Opposite the yard and driveway of Fieldhead, above Councillor Nathaniel Mell's property, stood Maltkiln Terrace, which derived its name from the fact that the kiln the Wigfields used to own was almost across the street from it. The Terrace's best-known inhabitant, a man on whose services many relied, was Herbert Horner, whose earlier life had overtones of both *The Water Babies* and *Oliver Twist*, since he grew up in the workhouse and was then apprenticed to a chimney-sweep named Tonks. His house, one of the middle two in the row, intrigued me when I called there with my mother to bespeak his professional services since (perhaps converted from some other use) its living kitchen was two storeys high and open to the rafters.

It cost a shilling to have a chimney swept (a procedure usually carried out before and after winter with its roaring fires) and meant getting up at an ungodly hour and shivering in an unheated, gas-lit room which was shrouded in dust sheets against the all-pervading soot. The occasion had its compensations, however. For entertainment value, Mr Horner was difficult to beat. An undistinguished-looking little man, he told stories as he screwed his rods together and skilfully eased them into the flue, usually about neighbours' quarrels from which he had emerged the undisputed victor.

On one occasion he claimed to have caught a neighbour called Mary helping herself to his sons' bonfire wood, and to have chased her screaming round the yard with a piece of bramble, which he called a 'breer', while her craven 'common-law husband' cowered indoors.

Some years earlier Mr Horner had lived in Sebastopol where, he recounted with obvious relish, he and an old woman who lived nearby had urged a girl whose husband bullied and beat her to ambush him armed with a broom one Saturday when, having spent half his wage packet on drink, he came swaggering home belatedly from the 'Queen's'. She had done so and the resulting blow to the braggart's head had left him lying unconscious in the yard, presumed dead by uncaring passers-by, till nightfall.

Mr Horner was also a fruitful source of mispronunciations and malapropisms. To quote two examples, concrete in his parlance became 'corncreech', and he scornfully dismissed a certain jumped-up nobody as not having a 'Bo-peep' (meaning bawbee) in his pocket.

The recital over and the chimney swept, the soot was gathered up into a sheet, which was then knotted like the spotted handkerchief Dick Whittington carries in pantomimes, and was taken on the 'Field Top' to be emptied on the edge of one of Manor Farm's arable fields, where it was said to benefit the soil.

STREETS AND HOME LIFE

Woodhouse, former home of the Allen family and one of Hoyland's oldest properties, with its links with the Townends and traces of pre-Georgian windows, was no longer a farmhouse but had become a dental surgery, and Longfields Crescent had been built on part of its land. However, in the 'twenties there were still fields across the road from it, with a farm gate where Valley Way now begins and, at the top side of this, an iron pump.

This land was farmed by Mr Wilson Lodge, a gruff, unkempt elderly bachelor, the uncle of Thomas Lodge of Manor Farm and his brother, William Henry Lodge of Upper Hoyland. His home was the farm cottage at Woodhouse which stood, with its door opening on to the street, below the dental surgery's front garden. (The long building with its end towards the road above the garden of No. 55 was once the Allens' barn, and that house itself was made out of another farm building. The Woodhouse stackyard used to extend as far as the end of the path which links West Street and Croft Road.)

Another of Hoyland's eccentrics, Mr Lodge once visited his solicitors, one of Barnsley's most prestigious legal firms, and demanded brusquely to see the senior partner. Invited to take a seat, he sprawled in a chair, in cow-redolent leggings and boots, produced a bag of plums from his jacket pocket and proceeded to eat them, spitting the stones in the general direction of the waiting-room fireplace. Like many farmers, he objected strongly when daylight saving was first introduced during 1916, blaming its instigator, Mr David Lloyd George, for its unsettling effect on his stock and declaring, 'There'll be no good done in this country while ever that little Welshman's alive.'

For a few years after Mr Lodge's death, Mr Henry (always known as 'Harry') Hall of Rose Cottage in Duke Street (a member of the greengrocery family of that name) kept several cows in one of the West Street fields, driving them home for milking twice a day through the centre of the town, a much safer procedure in the 'thirties, when traffic was lighter, than it would be now.

Housing and Building Projects

Until some years after the Second World War, when many rented homes were pulled down as slums (a process which had started in the 'thirties) and rent control and rising costs drove landlords to sell others when tenants left or died, a lot of Hoyland people still lived in houses rented from private owners.

A typical rented home between the Wars was a two-up-and-two-down terrace house, built of local brick from Shortwood or Skiers Spring, or else of stone from Birdwell or Blacker Hill. (Even if the back and ends of the row were brick, the front was often stone, 'stone-fronted' being a 'status symbol' to which attention was drawn if the property came up for sale.) The roofing material used for such terraces was always slate, though stone tiles had been used on older buildings in the area. Windows were usually four-paned sash. Doors were four-panelled, and were often painted brown and grained to make them look like polished wood. (The only other colour then thought suitable for painting outside woodwork was dark green.) Coal and keeping cellars and attics were commonplace, whilst some slightly more 'up-market' terraces had 'off-shot' sculleries, which in later years were able to have bathrooms built over them.

Amenities were primitive. The only source of water in the house was often a cold tap on a stone sink, water being heated in a side boiler (filled and emptied with an enamelled 'lading' can) incorporated in the kitchen range, whose black iron surface was polished each week with a substance called 'black lead'. (To avoid the need to have two fires in winter, some Hoyland homes had a second range in the front room, or 'room' as it was almost always called, the name being a relic of the days when kitchen and parlour were known as 'house and room'.) In the kitchen corner, between range and sink, there was often a 'set pot' (a built-in copper with a fire door below) for boiling clothes on wash-days.

The only bath was a zinc one used on the hearth and usually brought out once a week, the children queuing, the youngest first, to use the same water. The lavatory, probably shared with at least one neighbour and with a newspaper as a toilet roll, was at the far side of the communal yard — hence the Hoyland euphemism 'going down t' yard' for having one's bowels moved.

Some property owners were local people. Their terraces were often known by their names. In King Street, between Barber Street and Rock Mount, there was and still is stone-fronted 'Joll's Row', built by the family of which Ernest Joll, the china shop proprietor, was a member. A superior red-brick terrace in High Croft, owned by the Kellys of Cherry Tree House and demolished when the new Town Hall was built, was similarly known as 'Kelly's Row'. Some owners were shadowy figures who lived elsewhere, had no contact with their tenants and were often not even known to any of them by name.

The usual rent for a 'two-up-and-two-down' was from seven shillings and sixpence to ten shillings a week — trivial by the standards of today, but in those days a sizeable portion of a workman's weekly wage. Most people who owned a number of properties, or who lived out of the district, used to place their rent collection in the hands of Key's Estate Office on Market Street, between Joseph Smith's (now Farrar's) off-licence and George Neil's bicycle and radio shop. Its proprietor, Herbert Edwin Key, who was born at Jump and married a Whitby woman, as a compliment to whom he called his house on the corner of Tithe Laithe 'Streonshalh', was a small man with a very deep voice who always wore heavy boots, deported himself with great dignity, was a Wesleyan lay preacher and had a street, Key Avenue, named after him. He was helped by his son, Alan Skelton Key who died, one of Hoyland's best-known citizens, during December 1986. The actual rent collection, however, was done by Mr Charles A. Carney, who went round for this purpose in a car, taking note at the same time of any repairs the properties required, and who is also remembered in Hoyland as the founder of the Bethany Mission. Besides managing properties, the Estate Office gave advice on insurance and taxation matters and ran a Yorkshire Penny Bank agency.

Hoyland terraces were built to be let for gain, many of them during Queen Victoria's reign. The first years of the present century brought a fashion for building terrace-style homes in pairs, one for the owner and his family and the other to be let 'to pay the rates'. Such houses can be found in Cherry Tree Street and in 'old' Barber Street, all of them joined on to or built very close to other properties. Because one was meant for its owner's use they were usually well and substantially built and most still survive, transformed with 'picture' windows, stylish doors, bathrooms, indoor sanitation and new heating systems.

The two great changes to affect Hoyland's appearance between 1920 and 1940 were the disappearance of acres of farmland under council and privately-owned estates where each house, having a front and back garden, took up more space than earlier terrace-style homes had done, and the widespread rejection of stone as a building material in favour of more garish-looking brick.

The first council homes were built along one side of the short length of West Street stretching from Church View to the Law Foot (a spot which at that time boasted a small duck pond) and along either side of Fearnley Road (which was named after neighbouring Fearnley Farm), a new thoroughfare providing a short cut from West Bank to Hoyland Lane End. Among the first tenants to settle there during the summer of 1921 were Mr and Mrs Lawrence McNulty, Mr McNulty, who worked in the building trade, helping to construct the house they moved into and a few years later the new St Helen's Church. They were still there when Mr McNulty died in February 1986, and Mrs McNulty still resides there, which can surely claim to be a record for a council tenancy.

Similar houses followed in Longfields Crescent, West Street and Headlands Road (the latter named after the strips of land plough-horses turn on at the ends of a field). They promptly acquired and for decades retained the popular appellation 'The New Buildings'. Designed by Mr William Allen, the architect of the Miners' Welfare and the John Knowles Church, they were mostly in pairs and terraces of four and laid out on an enlightened principle whereby some had their kitchens facing towards the street, others their sitting rooms, to ensure that the latter got the maximum possible amount of sunshine. The initial rent for a house in a block of four was nine shillings a week. The semi-detached were larger, and their rents correspondingly higher.

Some corners had been cut in their construction. For instance, the kitchen walls were unplastered brick. Nevertheless, surrounded by gardens and with fitted baths, they must have seemed highly desirable to couples brought up in cramped terraces, with their lack of amenities, and setting up house when peace was restored after the First World War. (Some people, indeed, pronounced them too advanced, a great-aunt of mine from Hoyland Common expressing doubts on the hygiene of having a lavatory – she used the old-fashioned word 'closet' – indoors, even though it was only just inside, across the vestibule from the back door.)

Encouraged by an Act of Parliament, passed in 1923, offering State help to local authorities embarking on housing projects, the Council started a Hoyland Common estate about 1927, building Springfield Road parallel to Fearnley Road on land which had formed part of a little farm run by an elderly man named John Wood, whose family had been there for generations and from whom my father's parents in Stead Lane at one time bought their milk. (The farmhouse and adjacent outbuildings, together with a neighbouring cottage where Mr Wood's brother, Charles Wood, lived, survived until the start of the 'seventies, when they were demolished to provide a site for the new Police Station.)

About the same time, similar council homes were built at Elsecar, on the north side of Cobcar Lane and along an extension to Strafford Avenue, the 'model village' built for Fitzwilliam tenants and designed by the Wentworth architect, Herbert Smith.

Although semi-detached, these new houses shared a drawback with the smaller-type 'New Buildings', one which was a feature of Hoyland council homes constructed prior to the Second World War – to reach the stairs from the kitchen, tenants had to walk through the 'front room'. Some superior 'parlour-type' houses however were built, with three downstairs rooms opening off a hall, on Mount Crescent and the adjacent part of Hawshaw Lane, the latter ones enjoying the bonus of sweeping views across open country towards Ward Green and Worsbrough.

Despite all this building, there was a call for still more council houses as the worst of the town's old properties were pulled down, condemned as unfit for human habitation, leaving their tenants in need of re-housing. In the late 'thirties, barely a decade after the completion of the Springfield Road project, the Royston Hill Estate took shape on fields, between Longfields Crescent and Hawshaw Lane, crossed by a footpath where Croft Road now runs, thus converting the entire rectangle bounded by Hawshaw Lane, Market Street, West Street and Kirk Balk into a built-up area.

At that time 'Coronation fever' was in the air. Consequently, whereas Longfields Crescent and Fearnley Road had been named after the areas where they were built, most of the new streets were given names with Royal associations. They were Coronation Road itself, Crown Street (to which families from the back-to-back houses which had formed a distinctive feature of Booth Street were moved), Edward Street (the name was not changed when Edward VIII abdicated and was succeeded by George VI, whose name could not have been used in any case because Hoyland already had a George Street) and, honouring the entire Royal family, Windsor Street.

Among the exceptions was Clark Street, which was named after Councillor George Clark, a long-serving member for St Peter's Ward. Similarly Wilkinson Road at Elsecar, on another late-thirties estate, took its name from Councillor Albert Edward Wilkinson. The custom of naming streets after councillors persisted when council building was resumed after the Second World War, Mell Avenue, Eaden Crescent and Tomlinson Road (left derelict when its 'pre-fabs' were pulled down but now partially built on again) being named after Councillor Nathaniel Mell, Councillors John and Dennis Eaden and County Councillor (later Sir Thomas) Tomlinson respectively.

The late 'thirties also saw the building of the Hill Crest bungalows at Hoyland Common, the houses on the east side of Stead Lane and those along the section of Skiers View Road between Stead Lane and Hill Crest, thus forming another built-up rectangle, in this case one bounded by Skiers View Road, Fearnley Road, Hoyland Road and Stead Lane.

The inter-war years also brought a proliferation of houses built by owner-occupiers. The first sites to be developed in the 'twenties were Armroyd Lane (promptly, owing to its 'up-market' tone, nicknamed by Mr D.P. Beattie 'Peacock Lane') and the short stretch of Broad Carr Road between Kitty Hague Lane and Milton.

These Armroyd plots were sold by Earl Fitzwilliam at £2 per foot of frontage, and were hedged around with restrictions about the size and type of house that could be built on them and its distance from the lane and from its neighbours. Most of the first houses built were detached ones and, within these limitations, were designed to meet their owners' wishes. Some were built of soft local brick protected with a coat of 'pebble dash'. Some were deliberately kept small to qualify for a State subsidy paid under an Act passed in 1919 to individuals building themselves homes which reached a specified standard but did not exceed a certain cost. (They must, however, have cost at least £600, the minimum or 'tie' value specified by Earl Fitzwilliam when the land was sold.) They were always spoken of as 'subsidy' houses, usually in a patronizing tone.

Those who moved to Armroyd Lane and Broad Carr Road were mainly professional and white-collar workers, a high proportion of whom were school-teachers. In Armroyd lived Mr Henry (usually called 'Harry') Burton, headmaster of the Elsecar Church of England Boys' School and organist at Elsecar Parish Church; Miss Sarah Lister, the headmistress of Park Street Infants' School at Wombwell; and, living next to each other in a pair of 'semis' constructed rather later than the other new houses in the lane, Mrs Doris Hague, headmistress of the Elsecar Church of England Infants' School, and Miss Gwen Parkin, who was headmistress of the 'Little Infants' School' and later of West Street Infants' School at Hoyland. In Broad Carr Road, in two adjoining houses, lived Mr Raymond Belk, who taught first at Elsecar, then at Kirk Balk, and his sister-in-law Miss Blanche Booth, the headmistress of Elsecar Girls' School.

In both roads there were also officials from Elsecar Main. In Armroyd lived Mr Richard J. Polden, the time-keeper (who was also an Urban District Councillor) and Mr George Jackson, the pit cashier. Mr Jackson lived in one of four semi-detached staff houses built of Conisbrough brick by John Parr and Sons for Earl Fitzwilliam's Colliery Company. The families living in the other three were named Butterworth, Fletcher and Everett. In Broad Carr Road lived Mr William Hicks, a clerk in the wages department based at the 'New Yard', and Mr William Jackson, brother of George, whose job was to record the movement of railway waggons into and out of the colliery yard. (It was 'Billy' Hicks who, after he moved from a rented house in Church Street, summed up the joys of being an owner-occupier by remarking to my parents, 'I can't go complaining to the landlord now when anything goes wrong; I *am* the landlord.')

The inter-war years also saw the rise of the speculator builder, supplying homes not to rent but for purchasing, in the Hoyland area. An early estate to be developed was The Croft at Elsecar, built on what was previously a football field by Mr Walter Chadwick, a joiner and undertaker in Armroyd Lane and founder of the firm his son Mr Godfrey Chadwick now runs as W. Chadwick and Son. A Croft 'semi' cost about £450. Those who ventured to buy were frequently the butt of envious and spiteful remarks concerning their ability to pay, some people even going so far as to name the development 'Pinch Belly Avenue'.

Another joiner and undertaker who during this period ventured into building, though on a rather more limited scale, was Percy W. Mell of West Street, the elder son of Councillor Nathaniel Mell. In 1934 he built the eight privately-owned semi-detached homes which are at the King Street end of Barber Street. He also built the six at the corner of Market Street and Greenside (then always referred to as Jump) Lane.

The town's most prolific builder of houses for sale during this time was, however, Mr Charles Darwin (a scion not of the famous naturalist but of a local family), who in the 'thirties built most of Clough and South View Roads, and also Valley Way.

Marrying and Setting Up House

Despite the continuous building, public and private, throughout the 'twenties and 'thirties, Hoyland in those days seemed to suffer from a perennial housing shortage. This shortage, coupled with a reluctance to live with in-laws or in 'rooms', appears to have been one of the reasons why people tended to marry later then than their grandchildren do. One often heard some engaged couple say, 'We've got a house; we can get married now.'

Although hire-purchase firms were starting up in neighbouring towns like Barnsley and Rotherham, it was also still customary for couples to wait till they had saved up to buy furniture. The bride's own contribution towards the new home was her 'bottom drawer' or 'hope chest', which included towels, pillow cases, tablecloths and other essential items of household linen. To marry without an adequate 'bottom drawer' was considered to carry a social stigma. (Speaking of an acquaintance who tended to give herself airs, my mother was once heard to remark, 'She may think herself important nowadays, but when they were married she hadn't even got any sheets.')

The professions operated a 'marriage bar' and all women, no matter what their jobs, were expected to stop work on marrying. It was therefore also desirable to wait till the man was earning enough to keep them both. (I once asked my mother how much a young couple required in order to be able to set up house. She replied, 'On £2 a week they can get by; on £3 a week they can manage all right; and on £4 a week they are really comfortable.')

Owing to the uncertainties of the Depression, teachers, civil servants and others who enjoyed permanent, pensionable jobs were regarded with envy, even by the self-employed, though King Street teachers sometimes in my hearing spoke of themselves as being underpaid. Each September, my mother supplied the altar flowers at St Peter's Church two Sundays in succession, buying sixpennyworth of asters from an old man who grew them on his allotment, which was near the Council Fields. One Friday, when she and I had collected them, we met a headmaster's wife who cheerfully exclaimed, 'You've got your bouquet!' 'Yes,' my mother replied defensively, 'We're taking them to church. They don't look much, but there isn't much to spare for church flowers nowadays.' 'Come now,' the teacher's wife said with a laugh, 'Don't tell me that you're poor.' My mother turned to me angrily as soon as we were out of earshot. 'It's all right for Mrs So-and-So to laugh,' she fumed, 'but your father isn't paid like *her* husband. *He* hasn't got a regular £5-a-week job.'

Nearly everybody married in church or chapel. Register office weddings were contracted mostly by couples one or both of whom was divorced, who were not only frowned on by the Church but generally regarded as sinners in danger of eternal punishment. For those wishing to avoid the trouble and expense of a full dress, fully-choral ceremony, there was in those days what was always known as the 'eight o'clock' wedding, held as its name implies at 8.00 a.m., the earliest time at which a marriage is legal. For this the bridegroom wore his best lounge suit and the bride a new hat and coat or new two-piece, with a spray of flowers pinned to it. The guest list was restricted to a few close friends and a meal (literally a 'wedding breakfast') was later held at the bride's parents' home.

Few people married on a Saturday, which was a working day like any other. Besides, there was a rhyme in circulation which ran:

> Monday for health, Tuesday for wealth,
> Wednesday the best day of all;
> Thursday for losses, Friday for crosses
> And Saturday no luck at all.

Even where the ceremony was full-scale, the bride of the bright, brittle 'twenties was apt to choose a lace-trimmed, mid-calf dress in trendy beige instead of the traditional white gown and veil, partnering it with a sweeping-brimmed 'cloche' hat and carrying a huge round bouquet, for which red or pink roses or carnations were the favourite flowers, with heavy, trailing fronds of greenery. A popular material for bridesmaids' dresses was brightly-coloured floral crêpe-de-chine. Then as now, trends were set by the rich and famous. As a child bridesmaid at the age of five, I wore a winged Dutch bonnet of silver lace similar to those the attendants had worn at the wedding of Lord Louis Mountbatten and Miss Edwina Ashley in 1922. Wedding cakes were usually round, ornate and covered in delicate basketwork.

It was customary for the bride who could afford it, once settled in her new house, to employ some form of domestic help, even though she herself was at home all day. A familiar figure at that time was the 'day girl' who, though she did not actually live in, spent the whole day at her employer's house, arriving at eight in the morning and staying on until five or six in the afternoon. In return she received breakfast, lunch and high tea and was paid ten shillings a week — fifty pence in the currency of today, but worth much more in real terms when one has made allowance for inflation.

My maternal grandmother in Armroyd Lane always employed a 'day girl', as did the neighbours on each side of her, whilst Aunt Edith, whose husband was under-manager at the New Stubbin Colliery near Rawmarsh, and who was noted for her excellent food and easy-going personality, had a waiting list of young women eager to work there when the current 'day girl' left on marrying. My mother never employed a full-time girl, but had someone to 'help with the rough' on Fridays and to give her a hand at spring-cleaning time. She also sent the washing out each week. (Some women still supplemented their incomes by taking washing in.) I believe the charge for this was half-a-crown, as two shillings and sixpence (now twelve-and-a-half pence) was then called.

Although before the introduction of smoke-free zones, especially when Hoyland Silkstone's chimneys were belching smoke and the town was much grimier than it is today, some of the housework done in my childhood seems to have been unnecessary. Perhaps women with no jobs outside their homes felt a driving need to 'justify their existence'. I remember how every day after lunch, when I was very small, my mother would tuck me under her left arm and, with a duster in her other hand, go through the motions of cleaning non-existent dust from both our staircases, including their ornately-turned banisters. I also recollect the scorn with which she and her friends greeted the news, not long before the Second World War, that an acquaintance had acquired a washing machine — the old-fashioned kind with a hand-operated wringer.

'What a dirty, lazy way of doing things! How will she get her wristbands and collars clean?' was their concerted reaction.

Besides those who took jobs locally as 'day girls', there were still young women in the 'twenties and 'thirties who went away from Hoyland 'into service'. A place where maid-servants were much in demand was Salendine Nook, Huddersfield, where wealthy textile factory owners lived. Other girls migrated to the 'mill district', as West Yorkshire was usually called, to become operatives in the mills themselves.

However, though 'service' and factory work were better paid, shop work was considered more ladylike, and there was a cachet to working in a clothes shop, especially Storey and Cooper's in High Street, Butterfield and Massie's in Barnsley and Walsh's, Coles and other large Sheffield stores. The weekly wage was about half-a-crown, and parents were sometimes heard to complain that it did not cover lunches and bus or train fares. Nonetheless the prestige was sufficient to ensure that such shops never suffered a 'womanpower' shortage.

Personal Services

Another job with genteel connotations was ladies' hairdressing. Immediately after the First World War, when as a symbol of emancipation women started to have plaits and buns cut off, hairstyles were short, straight and somewhat severe, the favourite ones being the bob and shingle. By the 'thirties, however, the permanent wave had become fashionable. Being 'permed' took a whole morning or afternoon, and involved having strands of hair connected to an electrically-operated machine which 'baked' them. An alternative was the Marcel or water wave, quicker, cheaper, short-lasting, but suitable for a 'one-off' occasion. Styles (copied from those of the Hollywood film stars) were monotonous and unimaginative, usually embodying unnatural-looking 'corrugated-iron' waves.

Hoyland town centre had four ladies' hairdressers. At the West Street end of the Old Post Office Buildings, in a shop approached up a steep flight of steps, was Mrs Bessie Fletcher. In King Street, next to Maltby's greengrocery shop, there was Miss Nellie Barker. Further down the street was Miss Madge Hastie who, as Mrs Henfrey, still lives on Market Street at Fairfield, the house built by her parents about sixty years ago. Miss Hastie started in premises between the Maypole Dairy Company and the top of Booth Street and then moved to a shop across the road (formerly Ernest Joll's china shop and then briefly Rowland Watson's greengrocery and fish shop) next door to the butcher's run by her father and, after his death, by her brother Reginald. The fourth salon was that opened in the 'thirties by the Barnsley British Co-operative Society on the first floor of its drapery store at the corner of Green Street.

The best-known gentlemen's hairdresser in Hoyland between the Wars and for years afterwards was Mr Harold Oxspring Lowbridge (universally known by the nickname 'Tal'), who was in business at No. 5 King Street. His shop displayed a red-and-white barber's pole, and on its frontage could be read the words 'Estate Hairdresser'. Mr Lowbridge, who retired in the nineteen-seventies and can still be seen out shopping in the town, as sprightly and as talkative as ever, succeeded his father, Mr William Thomas Lowbridge. His widowed mother lived next to the shop at No. 7 where she could often be seen, matriarchal-looking in a long black dress, sitting in the doorway on a straight-backed chair, watching the world go by. (The elder Mr Lowbridge once helped to save the old 'Turf' when it was being threatened with closure. Asked the reason for his objection to this course at the hearing to decide the tavern's fate, he replied succinctly, 'Because I should have to go further for my beer,' omitting to add that the distance involved would be the extra few yards to the 'Strafford' or the 'Gardeners'.)

Mr Reginald Whittlestone did his hairdressing at No. 50 King

Street, next door to Frank Clarkson's greengrocery shop, and lived in one of a pair of old stone-built semi-detached houses across the way, standing back next to the Mount Tabor Chapel. His successor 'Peter', a grandson of Councillor John Eaden and a nephew of Councillor Dennis Eaden, has now been in business at that address for over a quarter of a century.

There was also a gentlemen's hairdresser's on the corner of Belmont Yard, in the smallest of the three shops which were owned by Albert Woolley.

Another Hoyland hairdresser between the Wars and a man who, like the chimney-sweep Herbert Horner, was a great purveyor of anecdotes in which he usually played the leading rôle, was Henry Stanley Lockwood Beaumont, who lived in a caravan, which he called 'the waggon', on the east side of Upper Hoyland Road. Mr Beaumont, whose family had its roots in the Huddersfield area, trimmed men's, women's and children's hair, visiting his customers in their own homes at irregular, unpredictable intervals. He had been badly wounded in the First World War, dressed untidily and walked with the aid of two sticks, one of which he was later able to discard. In pre-war days he had been a wig–maker with the Carl Rosa Opera Company, whose itinerary included opera houses in Spain and Italy, and his reminiscences were set in such places as Naples, Madrid and La Scala, Milan.

In those days when boots and shoes were meant to last and the cost of repairs was comparatively small, it unquestionably made better sense to mend than to discard them. Consequently, Hoyland managed to support several boot and shoe repairers. At No. 7 High Street, between the Gardeners' Arms and Milton Road, was my father's elder brother, Uncle Fred (his full name was Frederick William), who in his youth had been apprenticed to an elderly cobbler in Stead Lane called Denton. A small man who worked in a black apron, he was a counter-tenor in the choir at St Peter's and, as he bent busily over his last, sang snatches from old songs of which his favourite was 'The Rose of Tralee'. Like my father, he was a keen photographer and had had a number of prints exhibited.

STREETS AND HOME LIFE

With Uncle Fred and his wife, in the rambling house attached to the shop, lived her two bachelor brothers. The younger of them, Thomas Cutts, was a cheerful man who owned a horse and cart and earned his living as a coal leader. The elder, Albert, a tall, heavily-built, round-faced man with a moustache, had lost a leg during the First World War and went about on crutches. During the Second World War he was employed as a telephonist at the headquarters of the Hoyland Home Guard in a gardener's cottage, owned by Dr Wiggins, across Duke Street from the side gates of Ivy House. (In post-war years the cottage was used for a time as a surgery by Dr Agarwal.)

Mr John (usually known as 'Jack') Bradley was a First World War veteran who, until about the end of the 'twenties, repaired boots and shoes in a small lock-up shop just above the entrance to Sebastopol. Mr Bradley, who employed two men from Jump, then moved to the shop on the top corner of Booth Street and King Street, when it was repaired after being gutted by fire while it was a pork butcher's. Later still, after Mr Bradley retired, the shop was run first by one of his daughters and her husband, then by his eldest son, as an ironmongery and hardware store, and earned the affectionate nickname 'Little Woolworth's' because of the excellent variety of household objects (some not easily obtainable elsewhere) that could be bought there.

In the narrow shop across the street from Bradley's that is now the Abbey Veterinary Clinic there was another boot and shoe repairer. During the 'twenties this was a Mr Carr. He was succeeded by a Mr Warren, whose successor Mr Davies still worked there until quite recently. Further down King Street, opposite 'Joll's Row', where a concrete bus shelter has now been built, was the small wooden shop occupied by Mr Wright, the boot and shoe repairer from Birdwell. Next to the National Provincial Bank till the mid-thirties was Mr Ernest Welburn.

Though these businesses are only memories, the small shop in West Street that was once John Manley's is still open, its present proprietor displaying a board calling attention to his 'while-u-wait' shoe care service.

A customer this would have attracted was an Irish labourer

who once called at my Uncle Fred's. Sitting on the counter, he removed his boots and asked to have them mended immediately.

'I have another pair,' he confided cheerfully, 'but I'm afraid that at present they're in pawn.'

Index

Abbott, Dr, 200
Accounts Department, Town Hall, 15, 148
Adamson, Mr, colliery owner, 88
Aeroplanes, 'thirties models, 123
Agarwal, Dr, 196, 251
Ainsworth, Jessie, ladies and children's outfitter, 56
Air Race, England to Australia, 124
Alexander, Stanley and Margaret, dental surgeons, 212
Alexander's dental surgery, 29
Allen, George Hirst, grocer, 26, 36-7, 51, 98, 103, 224
Allen, Mr & Mrs Reginald Hirst, tobacconists, 51, 224
Allen, Councillor William, architect, 8-9, 36, 103, 155, 227, 240
Allott, Charles & Sons, grocers and drapers, 195-6
Allott, Drs Eric Sinclair Leach and Marie, 196
Allott, Mrs Ethel Gabrielle, 196, 201
Allott, Dr Horace Rhodes Leach, 195
Allott, Dr Joy Sinclair Leach, 85, 147-8, 196
Allott, Dr Wordsworth Leach, 194-5
Anniversaries, chapel, 39, 98, 161-162, 176
Ardron, Edwin, colliery winder, 85
Armistice Day, observance in schools, 130
Armroyd Lane, new houses in, 243-4
Ashton, Frank, painter and decorator, 103, 129
Ashton, Herbert, King Street schoolteacher, 103, 129, 141
Ashton, Tommy, 77
Atkin, Cecil, Cinema manager, 171
Atkinson, George Irvin, Co-op pharmacist, 215

Baker, Miss, King Street teacher, 127
Bakers' shops, 49-51
Ball Inn, 24, 28, 71
Ballroom dancing in Hoyland area, 181
Bank clerks, conditions of service, 31
Banking services, 29-31
Barber, William, occupant of Bark House, 219
Barclay's Bank, 30, 68
Barge families, 122

Bark House, 219-20
Barker, Miss Nellie, ladies' hairdresser, 249
Barley Hall, centre of Methodism, 159, 223
Barnsley District General Hospital, 106, 204, 205
Barnsley Girls' High School, 134, 139, 140
Barnsley Holgate Grammar School, 139, 140
Bartlett, Mrs Elizabeth, 84, 154-5, 230
Baxter and Weekley, welding engineers, 82
Bean, Frederick Daniel, pork butcher, 43, 219
Beattie, Douglas Porteous, clothier, 16, 26, 58-60, 61, 72, 120, 137, 177, 186, 192, 193, 243
Beattie family, members of, 59
'Beattie's Big Trip', 59, 186
'Beattie's Box', 26
Beaumont, Henry Stanley Lockwood, itinerant hairdresser, 250
Beckett's Hospital, Barnsley, 203
Bedford Brothers, char-a-banc proprietors, 114
Beer House Act, 73
Beggar and Gentleman, The, old name revived, 76
'Belchers' Club', 77
Belisha beacons, introduction of, 120
Belk, Raymond, Elsecar teacher, 141, 243
Belk, Ron, dance band leader, 181
Bell Ground, 79
Bell Ground House, 28, 88
Bellamy's Corner Boot Store, 29
Belmont Club, 77, 196, 234
Bennett, Rev. Charles William, Vicar of St Peter's, 154
Benson, 'Billy', Globe Tea Co. manager, 34
Bethany Mission, 165-6, 234, 239
Bethel Chapel, 72, 161, 162, 227
Bhartia, Dr, 199
Bicycles, price of, 121
Bircher, Arthur, cycle and radio shop proprietor, 120-1, 168
Birkinshaw, Harry, club steward, 77
Birkinshaw, Job, church organist, 212
Blacker Hill sandstone, 93, 216
'Bobbies' Dance', 22

Booth, Miss Blanche, Elsecar headmistress, 243
Booth, Dr William Smith, 84, 94, 100, 216-7, 230, 235
Dr Booth's patent remedies, 216
Booth's clothing factory, 75, 78
Bott, Mr, pork butcher, 16, 43
Boy Scouts, 160, 227
Brack, Betty, death of while a King Street pupil, 132
Bradley, John, boot and shoe repairer, 251
Braham, Mrs Effie, King Street teacher, 127, 129
Bread, home baking of, 50, 93
Brentwood, Market Street, 221
Brewery companies, 73, 74, 76, 229
Broad Carr Road, building of new houses in, 243-244
Brooke, Miss Edith, King Street schoolteacher, 36, 128
Brooke, Miss Ivy, Co-op tailoress, 58
Brooke, Ralph, headmaster, 36
Brooke, Wilton, grocer, 35-6, 98, 128
Brough's grocery store, 37
Brown, Mrs, King Street teacher, 128
'Bull muck' used as coal substitute, 90
'Bun and Milk Club', 23
Burdin, Betty, death of while a King Street pupil, 132, 140
Burdin, Samuel, colliery deputy, 87, 140
Burglaries, spate of in 'thirties, 24-25
Burkinshaw, Councillor Frank, 9
Burkinshaw, Councillor Mary, 9
Burtoft, Rupert, verger at St Peter's, 150
Burton, Henry, Elsecar headmaster and church organist, 243
Bus fares, 32, 116
Bus routes, operators on, 115
Bus stops, 4, 75, 171
Butchers' shops, conditions in, 41
Butterworth, Councillor Leonard, 10
Butterworth, Tommy, Assistant Rating Officer, 15
Buxton, Hugh, King Street headmaster, 30, 126-7
Buxton, Mrs, 126, 127

Cancer, attitudes towards and treatment of, 207-8
Carney, Charles, A., rent collector and founder of Bethany Mission, 165-6, 239
'Cat and Dog Pond', 14, 80
Caws, Miss Alice Emily, 76, 141-3, 215; pupils concerts, 143
'Caxton Press', 100, 161

Cerebro-spinal fever, 1931 outbreak of, 210
Chadwick, Dennis Edmund, Council Estates Surveyor, 15, 142
Chambers, George, fish-and-chip shop and off-licence proprietor, 168
Chandler, Francis Frank, 'Hoyland's Hero', 84
Chandler, Francis George, 84
Chant, Labrador retriever, 23, 43, 215
Chappell, Norman, lay reader, 15, 148
Char-a-bancs, 113-4
Charleston, popularity of in 'twenties, 180-1
Childhood infections, attitudes towards, 208
Children in hospital, attitudes towards, 209
Chimneys, sweeping of, 236
'Choir trips', 184
Cigarette cards, 52
Cigarettes, price of, 52
'Cinder Hills', 14, 233
Cinema, 66, 170, 171, 172, 173, 193, 218
Circus, visit of, 178
Claremont Nursing Home, 204
Clark, Councillor George, 10, 242
Clark (or Clarke), Dr., colliery owner, 88
Clarkson, Frank, greengrocer, 46, 74, 250
Clayton, Arthur, local historian, 128
Clayton, David, furniture shop proprietor, 62, 99, 221
Cleethorpes, Rechabites and children's outings to, 184-5
Clothier's Arms, 75
Clothing shops, 54-60
Coal, nationalization of, 177
Cochrane, Richard Harry, fishmonger, 47-8
Coggan, William, school attendance officer, 132
Colville, Roy, photographer and actor, 170, 186
Colville's tobacco and grocery store, 29
Confinements, home, 205
Conservative Club, 77
Cook family, joiners and undertakers, 9
Cook, Councillor Edwin, 9
Cooper, Harry, 16, 56, 222
Cooper, Miss Jean, 222
Cooper, Mrs Jessie, 56, 57
Co-op boot and shoe shop, 49, 54; butcher's shop, 43, 214; dividend, 39-40, 214; drapery store, 54-5, 229, 249; grocery assistants, 39; grocery store, 38-40; pharmacy, 16, 214-5; queuing at grocery branch, 40; reading room, 229; tailoring department, 57-8; 'tinning' department, 57
Copley, Harold, Co-op grocery manager, 38-9, 55
Cordeaux, Rev. J., Vicar of St Peter's, 145

INDEX

Corn mill, former, in Millhouses Street, 234
Coronation Queen, competition to choose Hoyland a, 192
Coronation souvenirs, 193
Costello, Miss, St Helen's teacher, 138
Coulson brothers, painters and decorators, 11, 101, 104
Coulson, Councillor William Simister, 10-11
Council estates, development of, 240-2
'Council Fields', 179, 234, 245
Councillors, naming of streets after, 242
County Library, 228
County Minor Scholarship, 138-9
Crabb, Councillor William Frederick, 7, 11, 48
Crab Field or 'Crab Cloise', 174, 177
Crabtree, Fred, fishmonger, 48
Crimean War, 81, 232
Cross, Miss Gladys, 47, 229
Cross, Jack, 207
Cross, Rowland, grocer, 3, 33-4, 42, 47, 74, 75, 191, 207, 229
Cross, William Barber, son of Rowland, 34
Cross Keys Inn, 174
Crown Garage (former smithy), 10
Crowther-Alwyn, Rev. Harold Augustus, Vicar of St Andrew's, 151-3, 190
Crowther-Alwyn, family, members of the, 152-3
Cutts, Albert, disabled World War One veteran, 251
Cutts, Arthur, butcher, 70
Cutts, Ephraim, grocer, 70
Cutts, Miss Lilian, schoolteacher, 70
Cutts, Manasseh, licensee, 70
Cutts, Thomas, coal leader, 70, 112, 251, 233
Cycling clubs, 179

Dales, Police Sergeant, 22
Danks, William George, Sanitary Inspector, 12-13
Davy's Foundry, 82
Dawes, George, ironmaster, 81, 232
'Day girls', employment of, 247
Dearne and Dove Canal, 83, 121-2
Dearne valley water, properties of, 20
Dearne Valley Water Board, 19-21
De La Salle College, 138
Dental charges, 213; surgeries, organization of, 213
Dentists and dentistry, 211-213
Depression of the 'thirties, 40, 46, 77, 116, 189, 245
Dewhirst, Mark, grocer and member of Cinema staff, 72
Dewhirst, Reginald, colliery electrician and grocer, 72

Dewsbury, Albert, Council Housing Manager, 15
DHSS, Hoyland offices of, 157, 215
Dickinson, Luke, occupant of The Meadow, 219
Diphtheria and scarlet fever, treatment of, 208, 209; development of immunisation against, 210
Dixon, Brian, newsagent, 62
Domesday Survey, Hoyland mentioned in, 1
Dove, Pastor Frank, 166
Dovecliffe Station, 107-8
Doyle, Thomas, greengrocer and licensee, 47, 73, 112, 159, 171
Driving test, institution of, 119
'Ducket' waste water closet, 13
Dunn, Mrs, firewood seller, 112
Dunstone, Harry, newsagent and violinist, 62
Dyson, Mr, off-licence proprietor, 52

Eaden, Councillor Dennis, 11-12, 242, 250
Eaden, Eric, professional violinist, 235
Eaden, George, grocer, 235
Eaden, Councillor John, 11, 242, 250
Earth closets, 6, 21, 95, 216
Ebblethwaite, William, pawnbroker, 43
Ecclesfield Grammar School, 9, 139, 177, 185, 190
Eddy, Miss, Infants' School teacher, 135
Edward VIII, abdication of, 191-2, 242
Eggs, buying and pickling of, 94, 225
Elizabeth, Princess, popular interest in, 189
Ellaway, Alfred, newsagent, 62
Elsecar, development of, 3
'Elsecar-by-the-Sea', 123
Elsecar Cricket Field, 132, 175, 177
Elsecar Feast, 53, 174-8, 182
Elsecar Forge, 80, 82, 158, 220
Elsecar goods station, 88
Elsecar, Hoyland and Wentworth Gas Co., 7, 17-18
Elsecar Main colliery, 9, 31, 85-7, 88, 126, 156, 179, 185, 219, part-time working at, 86; winding accident, 87
Elsecar Midland Musical Festival, 55, 134, 199
Elsecar Parish Church, 163, 164, 174, 177-8, 243
Elsecar Park, 5, 123, 177
Elsecar Reservoir, 122
Excursions, works, 185; school, 185, 190

Fads, medical, 210
Fairclough, Dr Donald James, 196, 199-200, 215
Fairclough, Dr James Herbert, 87, 199

Fairclough, Mrs Wilhelmena MacDonald, 199
Fairground attractions, 175-6; traction engines, 175
Fat, attitudes towards eating, 49, 50
Fawcett, George, Jr., 58
Fawcett, George, Sr., licensee, 58, 73
Fawcett, Mrs Mary, Market Street teacher and deputy head, 58, 134
'Feast', origin of the name, 174
'Feasts' and fun fairs, 174-8
Fieldhead, home of the Allotts, 194, 195, 201, 235
'Field Top', 52, 226, 228, 231, 236
Fincken, Christopher W., colliery manager and Local Board Chairman, 84
Fire Service, 16-17; station and brigade, 16; buzzer, installation of, 16
Fires, chimney, 16
First World War, food shortages in, 38
Firth, C. & Sons, plumbers and decorators, 17, 72, 100-102, 121, 216
Firth family, members of, 100-102
Firth, William, partner in C. Firth & Sons, 100, 137, 183, 217
Fish-and-chip shops, 48
Fish and chips, attitudes towards, 49; price of, 48
Fisher, Dr, 200
Fisher, Albert Lister, tragic death of, 224
Fisher, Edwin, farmer, 51, 64, 224
Fisher, George Edmund, farmer, 225
Fisher, Norman, draper and tobacconist, 25, 51, 57, 224, 225
Fitzjohn, William, farm worker, 224, 225
Fitzwilliam, Earl, 2, 85, 86, 88, 91, 135, 136, 146, 150, 164, 185, 186, 200, 222, 226, 243
Fitzwilliam Estate, properties owned by, 187
Five Alls, The, 74, 75, 161, 227
Fleetwood, George, blacksmith, 112
Fletcher, Mrs Bessie, ladies' hairdresser, 249
Fletcher, Moses, Old Eccles Cake Shop, 58-9, 137
Fletcher, Thomas Rawling, St Peter's School headmaster, 137
Fogg, Mrs, grocer, 46
Food, Ministry of, 36, 41
Food Office, 11
Football hooliganism, 71
Footrill Cottages, 87, 88
Ford, Fred, newsagent, 56, 61
Ford and Marsland, ladies outfitters, 56, 61
Forge Inn, 70, 233
Fozzard sisters, drapery assistants, 57
Free Church of England, 154
Funeral cards, 99; observances, 149, 231

Funerals, horses used at, 113
Furnace Inn, 70, 233
Futurist (Electra Palace), 70, 129, 172

Gallon's grocery store, 37
Gardeners' Arms, 47, 72, 159, 171
Garner, Herbert, ironmonger, 28, 45, 61, 156, 221
Garnett, Albert, verger at St Peter's, 35, 150
Gas and electricity services, 17-19
Gas appliances, 18; mantles, 17; fitters, 18; showroom, 18, 120; street lighting, 18-19
Gate Inn, 25, 70, 72
George V, King, Silver Jubilee, 189-191, 192
George V, King, death of, 191
George VI, King, coronation of, 192-3, 242
'Gin race' at Manor Farm, 226
Glebe Farm, Tankersley, 65, 197
Globe Tea Company, 22, 34-5, 213
Goddard, Edwin, butcher, 43, 159
Goddard, Harry, butcher, 43
Gramophones, early types of, 181
Gray, James Duke, farmer and 'character', 224
Gray, William, farmer and donor of chapel site, 159, 224
Green, Stanley, printer, 100
Greenfield Cottage, 55, 84
Greenfield Estate, 226
Greenfield House, 47, 74, 207, 226, 229
Greengroceries, varieties on sale, 44
Greengrocers' shops, 44-47
Grimes, Mrs Edith, 58, 215
Grimes, Walter, Co-op tailoring manager, 58
Groceries, changed methods of retailing, 33
Grocers' shops, 33-40
Grogan, Father, Roman Catholic Priest, 158
Guest, Mrs, butcher, 42
Guest, Charles Stuart, Market Street teacher, 134, 221, 222
Guest, Christopher, butcher, 42
Guest, George Donald and William Edward, 222
Guest, Mrs Gertrude, centenarian, 222
Guest, Miss Jessie, Market Street headmistress, 134, 221, 222
Guest, John & Sons, pawnbrokers, 58
Guest, Thomas Frederick, butcher, 42, 222

Hague, David, butcher, 27, 43
Hague, Mrs Doris, headmistress of Elsecar Church of England Infants' School, 40, 135, 243
Hague, Councillor Herbert, 12
Hague, Miss Irene, Infants' School teacher, 135
Hague, John, builder, 3

# INDEX

Hague, Mark and family, builders, 223
Hague, Thomas Playford, builder, 200
Hague, William, butcher, 43, 74
Hairdressers, ladies', 248-9
Hall, Miss Dorcas, draper, 43, 45
Hall, Frank, greengrocer, 45
Hall, Mr and Mrs George, greengrocers, 45, 156
Hall, Mr and Mrs Henry, greengrocers, 45, 237
Hall, John and Frank, greengrocers, 45
Hall, Miss Linda, dressmaker, 21
Hallamshire Maternity Home, opening of, 205
Hartley, Edmund R., gas showroom manager, 18
Hartop, Henry, iron works partner, 220
Harvey, David, pharmacist, 214, 215
Harvey, Harold, dental surgeon, 211, 220
Harvey and Richardson, pharmacists, 49, 211, 214, 215, 220
Hastie, Henry Vincent, butcher, 34, 42
Hastie, Miss Madge, ladies' hairdresser, 249
Hastie, Reginald, butcher, 43, 249
Hawksworth, Mrs Winifride, teacher, 138
Haywood, Ernal, church organist, 156
Haywood, Frank, checkweighman and churchwarden, 156
Haywood, Harry, credit draper, 96, 166
Hazell, Mr and Mrs Owen, 157, 230
Health Centre, 196, 198, 199, 215, 216
Hendy, Reginald W., railway van driver, 111
Hermon, the Rev. Mr, Rector of John Knowles', 155
Hickman family, association with Band, 75-6
Hickey, Miss, St Helen's School teacher, 138
Hicks, William, colliery wages clerk, 244
High Hoyland, need to avoid confusion with, 2
Hiking, 'thirties craze for, 178-9
Hill Crest bungalows, 15, 242
Hill Street Congregational Chapel, 8, 163-4, 174, 215; 'miracle' witnessed at, 163
'Hindenberg', German airship, 123
Hinton family, bus proprietors, 76, 114
Hinton, Reginald, licensee, 76
Hirst, Edgar, printer, 62, 84, 94-97, 156, 212
Hodgson, 'Tommy', bus driver, 114-5
Holdsworth, Mr, St Peter's School headmaster, 137
Holiday resorts, popular, 182
Holidays with pay made compulsory, 182
Holly House, 57, 88, 154
Hollywood 'Greats', 173
'Holy Land, The', 232
Horner, Herbert, chimney-sweep, 235-6, 250
Horrox, Councillor Reginald Edward, colliery manager, 9-10

Horwich, Paul, dental surgeon, 211, 212
Hospital charges, 204; consultants, 202; 'recommends', 202
'Hospital Sing', 177
Hough, Miss Marion, King Street teacher, 128-9, 152, 214
Houlton, Councillor Vincent James, school headmaster, 10, 138
Houses, back-to-back, Booth Street, 230, 242
Howard, Maurice, accountant and lay reader, 135
Hoyland, Alfred, photographer, 170
Hoyland Brick Company, 92-93
Hoyland 'Chapel', 2, 145, 147, 150
Hoyland Common, development of, 3; Feast, 174; market, 113
Hoyland and District Canine Society, 212
Hoyland Express, 121, 192
Hoyland Feast, 174
Hoyland Hall, 84, 85
Hoyland Home Guard, 92, 251
Hoyland House, 211, 220
Hoyland Law, meaning of the name, 149
Hoyland Law Stand, 20, 92, 136, 141, 190
Hoyland, Medieval history of, 2; origins of the name; population statistics of, 2
Hoyland Nether Working Men's Club, 77
Hoyland Silkstone Colliery, 20, 69, 82-85, 89, 122, 216, 218, 220, 247; explosion, 85
Hoyland Town Football Club, 71
Hoyland Town Silver Prize Band, 75
Hoyland and Wombwell Advertiser, 97
Humphrey, Harold, baker, 49, 232
Hurst, the Rev. Alan Greaves, Vicar of St Andrew's, 153
Hutchinson, the Rev. Peter, Wesleyan Minister and Scoutmaster, 160
Hymns sung in school, 130

Ibbotson, Herbert, travelling greengrocer, 47, 112, 228
Ice-cream vendors, 53
Illnesses, prevalent, 206-211
Iron Industry, 79-82
Iron ore, mining of, 79-80
Ivy House, former residence of Dr Barclay Wiggins, Sr., 221

Jackson, George, colliery cashier, 244
James, Edwin, draper, 61
Jazz, popularity of in 'thirties, 181
Jessop Hospital for Women, Sheffield, 206
'J.K.s', concert party, 156
John Knowles Memorial Church, 5, 33, 84, 116, 154-7, 178, 221, 230, 240

Johnson, Amy, pioneer aviator, 123-4
Johnson, 'Jimmy', railway van driver, 111
Johnson, John, Methodist pioneer, 159, 223
Joll, Ernest, china chop proprietor, 46, 222, 225, 239
Jones, Charles, Rating Officer, 14
Jones, Miss Hilda, 103, 180-1
Jones, Mrs Margaret, baker, 50
Jones, R., ladies' and gentlemen's tailor, 44
Joyce, Councillor John Leo, 10, 11, 190
Jump, building of church and terraces at, 81
Jump Farm, 225
'Jump Fields', 90, 123, 198, 226
Jump Red Lion Football Club, 71

Kay, Herbert, Water Board Inspector, 21
Keir brothers, potters, 93-4
Kelly, Mr Frederick, pupil at original St Helen's School, 138
Kendray Hospital, 189, 208-10
Kennerley, 'Saddler Jack', 90, 191, 230
Kent, Duke of, 77, 188
Kenworthy Brothers, motor coach proprietors, 7
Kestrel, The, 74, 229
Key, Herbert Edwin, 7, 30, 166, 239
Key's Estate Office, 59, 166, 239
King, Christopher, Co-op drapery manager, 55
King, Dorothy, 55
King, Miss Ivy M., pianist and conductor, 55, 120
King Street School, 50, 124, 125-32, 136, 137, 138, 139, 141, 186
Kino, 170, 171, 172, 173
'Kipper Pit', 87-8
Kirk Balk Cemetery, 22, 126, 134, 149, 224
Kirk Balk School, 121, 140-1
Kirk Farm, Market Street, 221
Knowles, Mrs Harriett Ann, trained midwife, 205
Knowles, John, 33, 154, 155
Knowles, Mrs Martha, 3-4, 33, 150, 154
Knur-and-Spell, 23, 179-180

Labour Exchange, 60, 156
Laister, Councillor Albert, 9
'Lanky Row', 83
Law, Mrs Doreen, ladies' and children's outfitter, 56, 102
Law Foot, 149, 150, 240
Law Hill, 137, 149
Lawrence, Dr, 200
Lax's Foundry, 82
Layte, Maurice, newsagent, 62-3

Lax, Mrs Beatrice May, Market Street teacher, 134
Lazenby, Mr, colliery manager, 84
Lessons, Police Sergeant Alfred, 22
Levitt, Walter, organist at Bethel (United Methodist) Chapel, 161
Lewis, Rev. Evan Llewellyn, Congregational Minister, 163
Lewis family, members of, 163
Lewis, Dr Philip, 147, 198
Lidgett ('Pill Box') Colliery, 88
Limb, T. & Son, plumbers, 104
Lister, Miss Sarah, headmistress at Wombwell, 243
'Little Infants' School', 51, 135-6, 150, 218, 243
Liturgical changes at St Andrew's, 152-3; at St Peter's, 148
Liversedge, Isaac, Co-op boot shop manager, 54
Lloyd George, David, 200-1, 237
Local Board, formation of, 3; replacement of, 5; further references to, 11, 84
Lodge, Clifford, farmer, 225
Lodge, Thomas, Jr., farmer, 225
Lodge, Thomas, Sr., farmer, 64, 225, 237
Lodge, William Henry, farmer, 57, 225, 237
Lodge, Wilson, West Street smallholder, 237
Lomas, Bob, dance band leader, 181
Lowbridge, Harold Oxspring ('Tal'), gentlemen's hairdresser, 249
Linn, John, bank manager, 29

McEwen, Dr John Aiken, 198-9
McNeil, Mr, colliery manager, 220
McNulty, Lawrence, builder, 240
McNulty, Mr and Mrs Lawrence, early council tenants, 240
McPartlain, Miss Margaret Mary, Market Street teacher, 134
McPartlain, Paul, plasterer, 134
Magson, Mrs Kathleen, West Street headmistress, 21, 136
Mail coaches, Leeds to London, 25, 105-6
Maltby, Miss Bessie, greengrocer, 43, 46
Maltby, Mr and Mrs Weadon, greengrocers, 45-6, 156
Maltby, Victor, 46, 156
Maltkiln Terrace, 28, 235-6
Manchester, Sheffield and Lincolnshire (later LNER) branch line, 83, 92, 106-8, 110
Manley, John, boot and shoe repairer, 251
Manor Farm, 51, 52, 64, 90, 112, 124, 159, 223-6, 228, 236, 237
March, Annie, King Street schoolteacher, 107, 129, 133, 141, 163

INDEX 259

March, Wilfred, Market Street schoolteacher, 107, 133, 163
Margarine, suspicions of, 33, 38
Marina, Princess, 77, 188, 192
Market, Hoyland, 66-68, 218; butchers' stalls in, 66-7; closure and revival of, 68, 172; opening of, 66
Market Street 'Board' School, 42, 132-4, 137, 219
Marsden, Mrs Kate, greengrocer, 45
Marsh, Frank, garage proprietor and coal leader, 120
Marsh, Police Sergeant, 22
Marshall and Mir, Drs, 198
Marshall, Mrs, postmistress, 25
Marshall family, members of, 26
Matthew, Jon E., pharmacist, 213-4, 215, 230
Matthew's veterinary medicines, 214
Marvin, Police Constable, 23
May, Miss, Kirk Balk headmistress, 140
Maypole Dairy Company, 37-8, 42, 43, 186, 214, 249
Meadow, The, Market Street, 219, 222
Meat, considered essential to a man's diet, 40-1; inspection of, 13; wartime allocation of, 42
Meat and poultry, kinds available, 41-2
Medical Officer of Health's Report, 14, 69
Medicines, dispensing of, 201
Melia's grocery store, 37, 57
Mell, Councillor Nathaniel, 7-8, 235, 242, 244
Mell, Percy Wilfrid, 8, 244
Mell family, members of, 8
Methodist church, new, 159, 199, 221, 228
Methodist churches, amalgamation of, 161
Middleton, Mr, dental surgeon, 212
Midland (LMS) Railway branch line, 80, 83, 88, 108-9, 110, 125, 129, 139, 157, 186
Midland Railway mineral line from Wharncliffe Silkstone, 110
Midwives, unqualified, 205
Miles, Albert, travelling greengrocer, 47, 112
Miles, Fred, greengrocer, 47, 77
'Militiamen', 118
Milk, method of delivering, 65-6; sampling of, 13; vendors, 64-5
Mills, Mrs Irene, lecturer and church organist, 154
Milton Hall, 22, 116, 179, 181, 192
Milton House, 81
Milton Iron Works, 69, 70, 80-1, 82, 216, 218, 220, 232, 233
Milton Ponds, 70, 80, 233
Milton Pottery, 93-4

Milton Road, route of changed, 15, 233; Victorian postbox in, 25, 233
Milton, Viscount, coming-of-age of, 186; wedding of, 186-7
Miners' strike, 1926, 89-91; social effects of, 90-1
Miners' Welfare Hall, 99, 160, 228, 240
Mines and mineworkers, 82-92
Mining subsidence, 20, 114, 122, 151, 164
Moffat, Rev. Ian, Vicar of St Peter's 78, 119, 146-7, 178, 191, 193
Moffat, Mrs Margaret Mary, 146
Moffat family, members of, 146-7
'Montagu Products', pickle factory, 219
Monk Bretton Priory, 79
Moody, Brightmoor, coal leader, 112
Motor cars, coming of, 34, 119; ownership of, 32, 119
Motor cycle combinations, 121
Motor cyclists, prosecuted for excessive noise, 24, 121
Mount Tabor Chapel, 100, 160-161, 162, 164, 227, 250
Moxon, Councillor Claude, 9
Moxon, Councillor Herbert Clarence, 9

Nail-making industry, 80, 227, 235
Nalliah, Rajah R., dental surgeon, 212
National Coal Board, 31, 177
National Health Service, 194, 200, 204
National Provincial Bank, 29-30, 31, 219, 251
National Registration, 14
National Savings Movement, 199
Neil, George and Sons, Aero garage and cycle shop, 120, 168, 179
Netherfield House, 84, 94-5, 100, 216-7, 229, 230, 235
'New Buildings', development of the, 240-1
'New Connexion' chapel, original, 100, 232
'New Connexion' chapel, Platts Common, 83, 161
Newstead, 'Norfolk George', gardener, 229
New Stubbin Colliery, 85, 247
Newton Chambers and Company, 84, 85
Newsagents and Stationers, 60-4
Newspapers and periodicals, 63-4
'New Yard', 31, 244
Noble, Miss Margaret (Mrs Ashwell), 163-4
Notre Dame High School, 138
Nurses, District, 204
Nursing Association, Hoyland, 204

'Old Gedney', 83
Old Horse Party, 184
Old Post Office Buildings, 25, 48, 56, 61, 62, 120, 234, 249

260 WHILE MARTHA TOLD THE HOURS

Organists, cinema, 169, 173-4
O'Sullivan, Miss, St Helen's School teacher, 138
Ottley, Cecil, master printer and author's father, 6, 23, 26, 28, 34, 41, 50, 52, 62, 67, 71, 72, 83, 90, 94-100, 104, 106, 108, 111, 112, 136, 137, 144, 146, 162, 165, 167-8, 169, 171, 173, 192-3, 217, 230, 231
Ottley, Elizabeth, author's mother, 17, 22, 24, 41, 50, 53, 54, 57, 58, 67, 71, 86, 94, 98-9, 109, 112, 124, 138, 142, 144, 162, 169, 176, 184, 185, 206, 210, 217, 230, 245-246
Ottley, Florence Cocker, draper and milliner, 55-6, 61, 62, 73
Ottley, Frederick William, boot and shoe repairer, 23, 26, 70, 112, 168, 169, 250-1, 252
Ottley, George, colliery 'contractor', 89
Ottley, John, knur-and-spell champion, 180
Ottley, John Albert, pianist and orchestral conductor, 56, 170
Ottley, Sarah, wife of George, 9
Ottley, Walter, death of, 89
Ottley, Councillor William, 6, 56, 170
Owner-occupiers, building of homes for, 243-4

'Panel' and private patients, 200-1
Parish magazines, 71, 98, 99, 147, 152, 190
Parkin, Arthur, pharmacist and optician, 129, 214
Parkin, Ernest, Jr., pharmacist, 214
Parkin, Ernest, Sr., pharmacist, 129, 154, 214
Parkin, Miss Gwen, Infants' School headmistress, 135, 243
Parkinson, the Rev. Mr, Wesleyan Minister, 141, 160
Parr, Ernest, builder and churchwarden, 156, 231
Parr, Herbert, builder, 231
Parr, Joseph, 159
'Parr's Yard', Bonfire Night celebrations in, 231
Parr, John and Sons, builders, 46, 155, 170, 231, 244
Parratt, Mrs Winifred, baker, 49, 52, 74
Pawn shops, visitors to Hoyland, 228-9
Pedestrian crossings, 120
Penna, the Rev. J. Edward, Wesleyan Minister, 160
'Penny-in-the-Pound' hospital insurance scheme, 202-3
Pharmacies, 213-6
Piano accordians, 'thirties craze for, 182
Pickering, John Willie, newsagent, 61
Picture palaces, 170-4

Pindar Oaks Maternity Home, Barnsley, 206
Pit buzzers used as air-raid sirens, 16, 87
Pit canteens, 92
Pit-top baths, 91
Platts Common, development of, 3, 83
Police, duties, routine, 24; houses, 23; Service, 21-5; Station, George Street, 21-2, 25; Station, Birdwell, 25, 111; Station, Hoyland Lane End, 25, 241
Polden, Councillor Richard J., 10, 243-4
Popular songs of the 'thirties, 182
Postal charges, 27; collections and deliveries, 27; Service, 25-7, 71
Postmen, 27
Post Office, moved to Ryecroft Place, 26
Powell's market sweet shop, 67-8
Pratt, Rev. Algernon Bertie, Vicar of St Peter's, 147-8
Pratt family, members of the, 147-8
Primitive Methodist chapel, original, 62, 100, 161
Primrose Hill, 88, 233
Princess Theatre, 6, 56, 72, 141, 170-1
Printing, method of, 95-6
Prospect Tavern, 75
Prudery, remnants of Victorian, 206
Public conveniences, 5
Pye, Miss Winifred, newsagency manageress, 62-3

Queen's Head, 71-2, 73, 170, 232
Quinn, Father, Roman Catholic Priest, 158

Radio, construction of early sets, 167-8; enthusiasts, competition among, 168; programmes, early, 168-70
Railways as 'common carriers', 110-11
Raley, Sidney Charles, 11
Raley, Colonel William Elmsley, 11
Ramsey, Harold, church organist, 19
Ramsey, Miss Lydia, companion to Mrs Bartlett, 155, 230
Ramsey's, drapers and outfitters, 19
Rates, objections to payment of, 14
Rating Department, Town Hall, 5, 14-15
Rawlin, Dr Brian, 197
Rawlin family, members of, 102-3
Rawlins, plumbers and decorators, 17, 102-3
Refuse disposal, 6, 13-14
Reid, Gibson, colliery manager, 220
Religious intolerance, 138, 158
Rent dinners, Wentworth, 187-8
Rented terrace houses, characteristics of, 238-9
Reynolds, Albert, Maypole Dairy Co. Manager, 37

INDEX

Reynolds, Mrs Ethel, 37
Richardson, David John, pharmacist, 215, 216
Riley, William, Co-op drapery manager, 55
Ritchie, Dr Horatio Nelson, 197
Ritchie, Misses Janey and Mary, 221
Ritchie, Dr William, 196-7, 198, 221
Riversdale, Market Street, 196-7, 220-1
Robinson, Frank, licensee, 74
Roby, William, Kirk Balk headmaster, 140
Rock Inn, 74-5, 227
Rockingham Colliery, 85, 110, 220
Rogers, Rev. Thomas Godfrey, Vicar of St Peter's, 145-6
Roller skating, organized, 179
Roman Catholic processions, 47, 74, 158-9
Roome, Rev. James Vesey, Vicar of Elsecar, 141
Royal Hallamshire Hospital, 204, 205
Royal visits to the area, 77, 86
Royal weddings in 'thirties, 188-9
Royston Hill Estate, 15, 242
Rush, 'Old Math', verger of St Helen's, 158
Rushworth, John, piano tuner, 205

St Andrew's Centre, building of, 221
St Andrew's Church, 37, 84, 103, 135, 136, 145, 150-4, 155, 156, 164, 174, 185, 196, 219, 221
St Andrew's Mission Church, 83, 154
St Andrew's Vicarage, original, 221-2
St Helen's Church, 77, 158, 235, 240
St Helen's Church, original, 137, 157
St Helen's Hospital, Barnsley, 143, 203, 204, 205, 206
St Helen's Roman Catholic School, 10, 91, 137-8, 158, 174, 235
St Peter's Church, 15, 40, 56, 136, 144, 145-50, 151, 154, 191, 193, 196, 245, 250; gift of clock to, 3-4, 151
St Peter's Churchyard, 8, 103, 148-9, 197, 213, 224, 233
St Peter's Mission Church, 15, 148, 154
St Peter's School, 85, 136-7, 138
Sale, the Rev. Henry, Vicar of St Peter's, 145
'Salmon Tin Row', 231
Salvation Army, 51, 164-5, 190; attitudes towards, 165; Citadel, Hoyland, 51, 164; Citadel, Hoyland Common, 165
Sanitary Inspectors assistant, 13
Saunders, Miss, King Street teacher, 127
Sayer's frozen meat shop, 43, 49
Scarborough, family holidays at, 183
Scarr, Leonard, newsagent and insurance agent, 62
Scarrott, Mrs, market shopkeeper, 67

School classes, size of, 129; doctor, visits of, 131-2, 210; holidays, length of, 129; milk, 131; punishments, 131; sports, 132
Searson, Mrs Mabel, licensee, 70
Seaside, bus services to, 116
Sebastopol, 49, 81, 232-233, 234, 236
Selway & Co., estate agents, 30, 42, 219
Senior, John, coal leader, 112
'Service', going into, 248
Sharpe, Rev. Charles Molesworth, Vicar of Elsecar, 158, 202
Shaw, Dr, 198
Shaw, Eric, newsagent, 15
Shaw, Peter W., building contractor, 102, 230
Sheffield Royal Hospital, 201-2, 204
Sheffield Royal Infirmary, 201-2
Shephard, John R., Council Surveyor, 15, 193
Shepherd, Walter, school caretaker, 131, 155, 230
Sherwell, Norman, bank manager, 29-30
Shevill family, members of, 40
Shoes, fashions in, 54
Shop work, girls' preference for, 248
Shortwood Sewage Works, 9
Siddall, John, licensee, 70
Silver Jubilee souvenirs, 190, 193
Silverwood, Mr, picture house proprietor, 221
Simpson, Reuben, colliery under-manager, 88, 233
Skiers Spring Bungalow, 88; Brick Works, 93; Iron-stone Pit, 80, 93; Lodge, 15
Skitt, Mr, Sanitary Inspector, 12
Skorrow, George, bank caretaker, 30
'Slosh' School, Tankersley, 181
Slowen, Mrs Elsie, baker, 49, 50, 54, 181
Smallpox vaccination, compulsory, 195
Smith, Father, Roman Catholic Priest, 158
Smith, Charles, pork butcher, 43, 52, 74, 103
Smith, Horace, Sanitary Inspector, 13
Smith, Joseph, off-licence proprietor and baker, 51-2, 74, 239
Smith, Lady Mabel, 139
Smithies, Ben, newsagent, 61-2
'Smoothing Iron', the, 108
Solomon, Laban, composer of church music, 164
Solomon, William, chapel organist, 72, 164
Sorby, Ben, fishmonger, 48
Sparling, Police Constable, 23
Speculator builders, Hoyland rise of, 244
Speed limit, introduction of, 119
Springfield Road, building of, 241
Staffordshire miners at Elsecar, 86
'Staggy's Alhambra', 9

Steele, the Rev. Charles, Vicar of St Peter's, 145, 146, 202
Stenton, Edwin, Gas Works Manager, 18, 40
Storey and Cooper, ladies' outfitters, 16, 56-7, 88, 248
Storrs, Willie, baker, 49, 125, 215
Strafford Arms, 66, 75-6, 114, 142, 164, 171, 218
Strafford Avenue, 'Model Village', 93, 241
Strafford, Thomas Wentworth, Earl of, 76
'Subsidy' houses, 243
Surtees, the Rev. Geoffrey, Vicar of St Andrews, 153
Sweet and tobacco shops, 51-3
Swift, Mr, Sanitary Inspector, 12
Swift, Mrs, licensee, 71
Sykes, Walter John, architect, 3, 151
Sylvester, Walter, licensee, 24, 71

Tankersley Church and Rector, 146, 151, 174, 197, 212
Tankersley Clyppings, 174
Tankersley Hall, 79, 109
Taylor, Andrew, school caretaker, 133
Taylor, May, ladies' and children's outfitter, 56
Taylor, W.H., watchmaker, jeweller and optician, 121
Taylors' Electrical, 7, 37, 120
Telegraph boys, 28
Telegrams, 28
Telephone and Telegraph Service, 27-8
Telephone, call-boxes, 28; exchanges, 28, 194; ownership of, 27-8; receivers, 28
Thawley, Adrian and Wendy, newsagents, 62
Thawley, Geoffrey, farmer, 62
Thawley, Horace, Sr., farmer, 64
Thick Twist, tobacco, 53
Thompson, Arthur, newsagent, 62
Thompson, Major Augustus, 92
Thompson, Edwin, grocer and general dealer, 72, 153
Thompson, Miss Florence, violinist, 72, 153
Thompson, Fred, butcher, 11, 42
Thompson, Herbert, 92
Thompson, Ralph, brick works manager and guest house keeper, 92
Thompson, Robert Humphreys, organist and music teacher, 72, 103, 153
Thompson, Wilfred, antique dealer, 26
Thorne, Willie, dental surgeon, 212
Thornley, Harry, Co-op tailoring manager, 58
Thorpe Hesley, 79, 139, 235
Threshing machines, 83, 226
'Tinglairy', visits of the, 180

Tipler, Ernest, motor coach proprietor, 22, 117-18, 184
Titcombe, Mrs Charlotte, licensee, 71, 170
Titcombe, Fred, comedian, 72, 170
Tithe barn, 223
Tithe Laithe, 198, 223, 227, 239
Tomatoes, 'Golden Sunrise', 211
Tomlinson, Sir Thomas, 10, 242
Tonsillectomies, common in 'twenties and 'thirties, 211
Totty, Mr, Bank Manager, 30
Townend family, farmers, landowners and church builders, 145, 148, 211, 237
Town Field, 71, 138, 174, 178, 190, 235
Town Hall, clock tower and 'Old Martha', 3-5, 151; history of, 3-5; horse trough, 4
Town Hall Square, traffic problems, 4
Tremayne, Rev. Charles, Vicar of St Andrew's, 151
Tuberculosis, prevalence of, 206-7
Turf Tavern, 58, 73-4, 100, 161, 227, 249
Turner, the Rev. Mr, Rector of John Knowles', 155
Turner, Percy, manager of Co-op butcher's, 43
Turner, 'Tommy', grocer's assistant, 34
Turnpike road, 79, 88, 105-6, 107, 115, 233
Typhoid fever, still prevalent in 'thirties, 209

Upper Hoyland, 2, 57, 92, 145, 225, 237
Urban District Council, chairman's chain, 7; composition of, 6; elections, 11-12, 98-9; end of, 5; formation of, 5; meetings of, 11
Utley, Harry Cecil, colliery cashier, 219
Utley, Miss Norah, King Street teacher, 128, 141
Uttley, Miss Bessie Eileen, King Street teacher, 128
Uttley, Harry, mural painter, 153

Vaines, Mr and Mrs Alfred, 225
Verminous homes, fumigation of, 13
Vernon Cottages, 12
Vizard, William, mine owner, 82-3, 220

Wage, average weekly, 32, 138-9, 204, 245
Waggonettes, 113
Waggon line, Hoyland Silkstone, 83, 122
Waggon line, Lidgett, 88-9
Wainwright, Reginald F., pharmacist, 215
Walderslade, home of the Fairclough family, 199-200, 216
Walker, Miss, Market Street infants' headmistress, 134
Walker, Miss Nora, trained midwife, 205

INDEX

Walker family, members of the, 60, 118
Walker's newsagency, 60-1, 62, 120
Water mains, burst, 20; rate, 21; supply, 19-21
Wath Wood Hospital, 208
Watkinson, Mrs Elsie, J.P., 133
Watkinson, Joseph E., Market Street headmaster, 133, 141
Watson, Rowland, greengrocer, 46, 191, 249
Watts, Mr, Co-op pharmacist, 214-15
Wedding customs, 99, 113, 245-7
Welburn, Ernest, boot and shoe repairer, 29, 251
Wellock, George A. and Sons, gentlemen's outfitters, 58
Wentworth Castle, 'folly' at, 20; Training College at, 154
Wentworth Station, 79, 80, 88, 109
Wentworth Woodhouse, 76, 85-6, 147, 184, 187
Wesleyan Chapel, Market Street, 30, 38-9, 55, 58, 159-60, 161, 219, 223, 225-6
Wesleyan Manse, 76, 141, 160, 228
Wesleyan Reform Chapel, Elsecar, 10, 163
West Street Infants' School, 21, 135-6, 243
Westwood, Mrs Florence, schoolteacher, 100, 137
White, Father, Roman Catholic Priest, 158
White, Mrs Annie, 'Supply' teacher, 128
White, Ted, newsagent, 63
Whitehead, Rev. William, Rector of John Knowles', 156
Whittaker, Police Constable, 23
Whittlestone, Alwyn, librarian, 228
Whittlestone, Reginald, gentlemen's hairdresser, 249-50

Whitworth's Brewery, 24, 76-7
Whorton, Leonard, butcher, 42, 52
Wigfield family, maltsters and nail merchants, 166, 216, 235
Wiggins, Dr Barclay, Jr., 198-9
Wiggins, Dr Barclay, Sr., 159, 198-9, 221, 251
Wilkinson, Councillor Albert Edward, 10, 242
Wilkinson, Alfred, book-keeper, 120
Wilkinson, George, tobacconist, 22, 51, 140
Willey, 'Jossy', pharmacist, 213
Wilson, Rev. Mr, curate at St Andrew's, 151
Window Tax, 112
Woffenden, John, Tankersley's sexton-poet, 107
Wood, John, farmer, 241
Woodall, Police Constable, 22, 117
Woodhouse, 211-12, 237
Woolley, Albert, baker, 35, 49, 166, 234, 250
Worthy, Bessie, child athlete, 132
Worthy, George, lamplighter, 19, 230
Wrightson, Fred, King Street schoolteacher, 129, 141, 172

Yards, Hoyland, 80, 227, 234
Yates, Albert Vernon, dental surgeon, 212
Yates, Miss Beryl, ladies' hairdresser, 212
Yates, John, Sanitary Inspector, 12
Yeast, sale of, 50-1
Yorkshire Electric Power Company, 17, 19
Yorkshire Penny Bank, 30-1, 239
Yorkshire Traction Company, 59, 91, 115-17, 139, 184, 206; parcels service, 117
Young, George, pharmacist, 141, 215
Youth Hostels Association, expansion of, 178

Note to readers

The publishers of this book hope that you have enjoyed reading it. They are always interested in considering good manuscripts, on any subject, with a view to possible publication. An approach should be made in the first instance by means of a letter addressed to: The Editor, Bridge Publications (Ref 189), 2 Bridge Street, Penistone, Sheffield S30 6AJ.

Also from Bridge Publications:

Echoing Hills

by Phyllis Crossland

A story of three generations of country folk living in the upper Don valley during the eighteenth and early nineteenth centuries.

Life on the homestead is hard, illness and death never far away, but Thomas and Ellen Brammer are strong enough to survive to old age. They end their days at Truns just as the gipsy predicted. Other prophecies relating to the family are also fulfilled, good and bad, through the next generations.

In an age of violence and brutality, the rural scene is not always peaceful. The Land Enclosure Act makes life difficult for Thomas's family, who turn to butchering as a means of augmenting their income. Their cottage neighbours are in worse straits. When a child is caught in a man-trap, murder ensues.

Railway builders, wire drawers and quarry workers influence the lives of the third generation at Truns. Friction and jealousy within the family lead to more unlawful killings.

The homestead at Truns passes out of the family when, much against his will, James is forced to leave by circumstances he cannot control. Yet, as the gipsy foretold to Ellen, their descendants do return to the place more than a century later. Thomas's footsteps are then retraced and the hills echo again with voices from the past.

Echoing Hills (ISBN 0 947934 20 0); hbk £12.95

From any bookseller or, in case of difficulty, by post (add £1.00) from the publishers.

Also from Bridge Publications:

Thinking It Out
Christianity in Thin Slices

by Ian Dunlop

Foreword by the Archbishop of York

Probably the most concisely logical book available for directing the purposeful enquirer towards an understanding of Christian belief.

For almost twenty years the author, a Canon and the Chancellor of Salisbury Cathedral, has been answering readers' questions in the *Church Times*. This book comprises a selection of his answers on subjects as wide—ranging as 'How to Start Praying', 'Faith and Reason', 'Hymns with Everything?', 'True Penitence' and 'The Authority of the Bible'.

There are plenty of books on the market which offer Christianity in large chunks. Canon Dunlop has successfully resisted pressures on him to add to them. Instead he offers what he describes as 'Christianity in thin slices - a bedtime book for those who prefer their reading to be little and often'.

Its author shows himself a sincere churchman, tolerant of most tenable shades of Christian belief, who maintains a balance between Church tradition and scripture, and the spiritual and secular facets of his faith, and is never at a loss to find an apt quotation in the great works of English literature.

* * *

There is nothing superficial about these brief essays.
Apt quotation, good illustration, and a simple directness of style make them easy to read, and well worth pondering at greater length.

The Archbishop of York

A brilliant selection

The Bridge

Thinking It Out (ISBN 0 947934 06 5) pbk, £3.50;
(ISBN 0 947934 07 3) hbk, £6.50;

From any bookseller or, in case of difficulty, by post (add 50p) from the publishers.

Also from Bridge Publications:

A House Divided
The Life and Death of John Billam of Thorpe Hesley

by Stephen Cooper

This is more than just a gripping tale of madness, avarice and family feuding. The author presents us with a cameo of life in an eighteenth century South Yorkshire village whose characters (blacksmith, cordwainer, maltster, farmer, gardener, labourer and domestic servant) each have a part to play in Billam's life and comment with homely wisdom on his story like the rustics in Thomas Hardy's Wessex novels.

In addition, *A House Divided* helps to place textbook history in perspective. During the years when these events occurred, Britain lost her American colonies, the French Revolution took place and Napoleon beat his ignominious retreat from Moscow. Yet, just as today some minor crisis nearer home looms larger than cataclysmic events abroad, so two hundred years since in this corner of England, Billam commanded more attention than Bonaparte.

All the facts recorded in this book are true, unearthed in the course of meticulous research.

They serve, moreover, to prove the old adage that truth is frequently stranger than fiction.

They also have literary overtones. Deranged, and callously treated by his wife and daughters, John Billam, at the centre of events, is a village King Lear. Furthermore, the misfortunes which dog his self-seeking heirs after his death seem to possess the inevitability of nemesis in Greek tragedy.

* * *

'... *an important milestone in local history writing in the South Yorkshire area* ...'
The Hallamshire Historian

A House Divided (ISBN 0 947934 11 1); pbk £4.50
(ISBN 0 947934 12 X); hbk £8.95

From any bookseller or, in case of difficulty, by post (add 60p) from the publisher.

Also from Bridge Publications:

The Penistone Scene
Captured in photographs over the years

by R.N. Brownhill, assisted by J. Smethurst

In recent years many large cities have had books of photographs published tracing their history. The same cannot be said for many small Pennine market towns.

The Penistone Scene is a new book covering the changing face of the ancient market town of Penistone from the earliest days of photography to the present day. The authors, who both have a long association with the town, have spent countless hours compiling a unique collection of almost 200 prints of Penistone's places, people and events.

The result is a book which captures the personality of this small bustling community through the years.

The Penistone Scene will be of interest to anyone who has an association with the town or an interest in the area. It will be enjoyed by residents and visitors alike and will make an ideal gift or souvenir.

* * *

'To anyone interested in their heritage, the book will be priceless.'
Barnsley Chronicle

'... a well-annotated selection, presenting a record of buildings and social life mainly in the earlier 20th century.'
Yorkshire Post

The Penistone Scene (ISBN 0 947934 15 4); pbk £5.95

From any bookseller or, in case of difficulty, by post (add 60p) from the publishers.

Also from Bridge Publications:

Frontier Challenge

The story of the Revd W.J. Ringer and the Afghan Border Crusade, 1904-1985

by L.T. Daniels

At the age of sixteen Jack Ringer succeeded in joining the Coldstream Guards by claiming to be eighteen. Settling into a selfish routine of drinking, smoking and gambling, he soon became the battalion book-maker!

But the death of a colleague led to Jack's conversion to Christ and eventual work as a missionary (ably supported by his wife Elma) amongst the staunchly Muslim Pathan tribes of the North West Frontier Province of Pakistan.

This book recounts the challenges faced, and adventures experienced, in a lifetime of service to his fellow humans in what could on occasions be a distinctly inhospitable environment.

* * *

... a real-life ripping yarn about missionaries in war-torn Pakistan.
Wiltshire Gazette

... read this book, see what life there is like and be challenged indeed!
Evangelical Times

Buy it and read it; it will do you good!
Tony Wood

Frontier Challenge (ISBN 0 947934 13 8); pbk £4.95
(ISBN 0 947934 14 6); hbk £9.95

From any bookseller or, in case of difficulty, by post (add 60p) from the publishers.